Networking of Elected Women Representatives at Grassroots

About the Authors

Prof. Ganapathi Palanithurai, Coordinator in Rajiv Gandhi Chair, Gandhigram Rural Institute, presently heads the Department of Political Science and Development Administration in Gandhigram Rural University, Tamil Nadu. He is also Associated with Centre Planning Commission, State Planning Commission of Tamil Nadu, Population Foundation of India, Ford Foundation, UNICEF, Rajiv Gandhi Foundation, CAPART, Ministry of Rural Areas and Employment and DANIDA (Danish-Indo Development Agency) in specific areas of activities in connection with empowerment of people.

Prof. Palanithurai has to his credit twenty-nine books and seventy-five articles on three major areas, namely, legislative behaviour, ethnicity and Panchayati Raj System. He was recipient of Fellowship from Sastri Indo-Canadian Institute, New Delhi and World Academy of Art and Science, USA. He is the Chairman of the Tamil Nadu Council for Sustainable Livelihoods. He was a visiting fellow in the MiGill University, Canada in 1989. He is a member of the expert committee constituted by the Government of Tamil Nadu to monitor the training programme for local body leaders.

G. Uma, is a research coordinator in Rajiv Gandhi Chair for Panchayati Raj Studies, Gandhigram Rural University. Her research interests include local governance, Panchayati Raj Systems, disaster management and networking for elected women leaders of local bodies. She did her Ph.D. on "Networking the Women Panchayat leader in Tamil Nadu". An effective gender trainer and facilitator in networking and associating women Panchayat leaders, she is sensitizing media to cover the issues of elected women representatives. She has to her credit three books and two monographs, besides a good number of articles published in journals of repute.

Vanishree Joseph is a Lecturer in Political Science in Gandhigram Rural University. Her doctoral thesis was on "Gender and Governance". She has published a number of articles on Gender and Governance based on her field activities. She has co-authored two books. She is in a network of scholars working in the field of 'Capability Approach'.

Networking of Elected Women Representatives at Grassroots

G. Palanithurai
G. Uma
J. Vanishree

CONCEPT PUBLISHING COMPANY, NEW DELHI-110059

ISBN-13: 978-81-8069-618-3 ISBN-10: 81-8069-618-9

First Published 2009

Published and Printed by

Concept Since 1974

Concept Publishing Company

Regd. Office:

A/15-16, Commercial Block, Mohan Garden

New Delhi-110059 (India)

Phones : 25351460, 25351794, *Fax* : 091-11-25357109

Email : publishing@conceptpub.com,

website: www.conceptpub.com

Editorial Office:

H-13, Bali Nagar, New Delhi-110 015, India.

Cataloging in Publication Data--*Courtesy:* D.K. Agencies (P) Ltd. <docinfo@dkagencies.com>

Palanithurai, G. (Ganapathy), 1953-

Networking of elected women representatives at grassroots / G. Palanithurai, G. Uma, J. Vanishree.

p. cm.

Study conducted in Tamil Nadu, India.

Includes bibliographical references (p.).

Includes index.

ISBN 13: 9788180696183 ISBN 10: 8180696189

1. Women in politics--India--Tamil Nadu. 2. Panchayat--India--Tamil Nadu. 3. Women--Social networks--India--Tamil Nadu. 4. Women local officials and employees--Training of--India--Tamil Nadu. 5. Elected Women Representatives' Federation. I. Uma, G., joint autho.. II. Vanishree, J. (Joseph), joint author. III. Title.

DDC 305.433 208 409 548 2 22

TO

THE DIVINE MOTHER

Preface

Exactly ten years ago, a Woman Gram Panchayat President from a remote village asked me a question on the last day of the training programme which we organised in Gandhigram Rural University under the auspices of the Rajiv Gandhi Chair for Panchayati Raj Studies with the support of CAPART: "Who is there in the village to support me when I, as a woman, hold power as President and face problems, barriers and obstacles to carry out the duties and responsibilities? In the training programme everything is fine. Good food, fine reading materials, excellent expert—delivered lectures, visits to the field where schemes have been excellently carried out. But, when I go to my village, I have to face a volley of problems from my husband, family, mother-in-law, son, political party, community, the clerk, and higher officials. How can I manage? When I turn to anybody for help, every one is willing to help with the proviso that I have to accept what they say. Otherwise nobody will come to help to carry out my responsibilities. What I need is a handhold support when I am in the field facing problems". Till then I was of the view that, after the training, the elected women representatives (hereafter referred to as EWRs) will perform their duties and responsibilities to the satisfaction of the community. The Woman Gram Panchayat President made me realize that we have to go beyond training, to support EWRs for their effective functioning. Otherwise the EWRs will remain as tokens.

Subsequently I attended a meeting at Chennai, organised by an NGO where I was asked to speak to a group of EWRs. As a preliminary, I asked a few EWRs to share their experience in Panchayat governance. One EWR made a statement: "Women are elected without their consent and, after that they are asked to remain silent in their houses and asked to do the family chore while the activities are carried out by their husbands, brothers, fathers-in-law or any male member of the family. On many occasions even the

President's signature is affixed by their male family members and it is being accepted by the officials. Unless these things are exposed, the women will remain tokens". This strengthened my belief that a different strategy is needed to empower the elected women representatives beyond the training.

Later I was asked to address a Gram Panchayat Presidents' meeting at Virudhunagar by the Virudhunagar District Administration. I attended the meeting along with the District Collector. Both the District Collector and I addressed the meeting. After our speeches, the Collector asked the participants to interact. One lady President immediately raised her hand. In the meanwhile a lot of hands from the men section were also raised. The sensitive Collector asked the woman leader to speak first. She made a plea to the Collector to pass an order that in all official meetings only the elected women representatives should attend and others should not attend on behalf of the elected women representatives. Further, she urged that the officials should be given necessary instructions that they should not allow proxies to attend official meetings on behalf of the elected women representatives. There was a hue and cry after her representation. The District Collector immediately responded by asking the officials to check, if there was any proxy in the meetings. Many hands raised in the male section of the audience slowly moved out of the hall. After the meeting was over I had an interaction with the woman President for a while. She said that she had formed a small forum for women Presidents to raise their issues collectively. Whenever the women Presidents go in a delegation along with men, they are marginalized by the males. Hence, she said, she had formed a Federation. Whenever they wanted to meet the Collector, all the women EWRs hire a vehicle and go to the Collectorate and discuss with the Collector and sort out their problems. She underscored the success achieved by their Federation.

I got the idea of networking women leaders only from that leader from Virudhunagar District. Based on this idea we developed a proposal and had a discussion with Devaki Jain. Subsequently along with other partners from Lok Satta, Hyderabad, and Sakhi, Thiruvananthapuram, we presented a proposal to the Ford Foundation. With the support of the Ford Foundation, we formed a Federation, strengthened the Federation, enabled the Federation to organise meetings, have interface with officials, political party leaders and Ministers to sort out their problems. For about four years we have done this exercise in Tamil Nadu. Now it has become a buzz word everywhere and in every organisation.

Several success stories, struggles, problems have surfaced in the whole process. Now the women leaders have different organisations at different levels. This has paved way for the formation of such a Federation for men also. This book is a sharing of the experiences of the networking of elected women representatives in Tamil Nadu. I consider it a source book and the data provided in this book can be analyzed as such. I am presenting here the narratives of the activities carried out over a period of four years.

Acknowledgements

This book is the result of a project on "Networking of Elected Women Representatives of Tamil Nadu" supported by the Ford Foundation, New Delhi. The activities of the project were carried out in partnership with the Singamma Sreenivasan Foundation of Bangalore, Lok Satta of Hyderabad and Sakhi of Thiruvananthapuram. The above organisations lent valuable support to our activities by providing needed concept and activities and impacted continuously from their own experience in the respective States. Likewise, a large number of Non-Governmental Organisations, women activists, feminists, Women Elected Representatives, media representatives, academics, political party leaders, researchers, officials at different levels actively involved themselves in the activities of this project in strengthening the Federation of Elected Women Representatives of Tamil Nadu. In our patriarchal society all those who extended support to the project activities were gender sensitive and positive. Many officials, at both the higher level and the lower level, appreciated the initiatives and they participated in the process throughout and hence it is necessary to record my sincere thanks to them. The staff members who worked in this project worked with a sense of dedication. Our project staff never considered themselves staff. They were involved totally in the project and, with a sense of joy and commitment, they worked to transform this Federation into a movement. They were ever at the service of the Elected Women Representatives. By seeing the commitment of our project staff many higher level officials voluntarily extended support to our activities beyond the official framework. Our project staff worked in such a way that they rendered their services in the four years, they have emerged as expects and enhanced their capacity and capability. I owe a great deal to them. I only facilitated activities which were owned by them. Equally my colleagues in the Department also extended all possible help to me to carry out the project activities. Our teaching staff in the Department shared my work load and joined me in carrying out all the activities without expecting anything from me. They felt that it was their responsibility to extend support to me. I always value and cherish their fine sentiments. Moreover, they provided a harmonious and congenial atmosphere in the Department to initiate any challenging activity. My special thanks are due to them. My family members were also very supportive in all my academic, research and extension activities. I never give my time to my family. Yet they tolerate me and love me. My wife and children are always affectionate towards me despite my negligence in attending to their concerns. I have not mentioned the names of the individuals, organisations, institutions who have extended support because their names are in the text. I place on record my sincere gratitude to all of them.

G. Palanithurai

Contents

1

Introduction

Reservation of seats for women in Local Governance has triggered a series of questions among researchers and activists[1] of many countries in the world. Primarily the questions are on skills, capacity, perspectives, capability of the elected women representatives in governance, management and administration of Local Bodies in South Asia more specifically as the problems of the South Asian women which are different from those of the women in the West. When they ask such questions, they assume that women do not have such skill, capacity and capability needed to manage and govern these institutions. The second set of questions are on the impact and implications of their presence in the institutions in the process of development and governance of the society. It has been demonstrated in the West that the elected women representatives made a difference in perception, perspectives and performance which made scholars to raise certain questions. Whether they make any difference in governance and delivery of services is the concern of everyone. While raising such questions based on the Western experience, one has to understand the conditions in which the women emerge as leaders to perform certain critical functions which are not critical for women in the West.

For the activists, the conditions in which the Elected Women Representatives live, the conditions through which they are recruited and the environment in which they perform their roles and responsibilities are more important than looking at the performance of the elected women representatives. The process by which they are drawn towards the public space itself is a painful struggle. Coming to that space itself is a problem. No doubt it is necessary and imperative to assess and evaluate the performance of the elected women representatives as they are holding offices, powers and authority. But, while doing so, it is equally important and imperative to consider the conditions in which they perform their roles and responsibilities. It is obvious that, in India, the elected women representatives however skillful, capable, sensitive, visionary they are, they have to face a volley of problems as they are in a feudal, hierarchical and patriarchal society.

All the elected women representatives do not have the required skills, ability, capacity and capability as their social, economic and political conditions had not enabled them to acquire such skills and capabilities. The elected women representatives are not functioning in a vacuum. They have to be in a society with given socio, political cultural conditions and they have to interact with the society. Thus the interaction is between the perspectives of the new leaders and the conditions of the society. The tasks which are assigned to women leaders are no so simple. First the elected women representatives have to transform themselves as leaders with needed skill to transform the community to become more gender-sensitive, inclusive and development-oriented. Secondly, they have to attend to the works left unattended by men at the community level for the past several decades as our men leaders were not so sensitive to the problems of women, children, *Dalits* and other marginalized segments. How the elected women leaders are able to transform the society with their perspective is a major concern of every one. They are brought to the offices with several disabilities and constraints.

While assessing the performance of the Elected Women Representatives, it is to be noted that the difficulties and the barriers confronted by them in the community, offices, family and political parties have to be taken into account. Sen has said that the society expects the elected women representatives to perform an agency function. He says "The role of a person as an 'agent' is fundamentally distinct from (though not independent of) the role of the same person as a 'patient'. The fact that the agent may have to see herself as a patient as well does not alter the additional modalities and responsibilities that are inescapably associated with the agency of a person... not only are we well oriented, but we also act or refuse to act, and can choose to act one way rather than another. And thus we—women and men—must take responsibility for doing things or not doing them. It makes a difference...." In most countries the women are not enjoying equal status and women are in a position to advance their conditions through the welfare approach of the governments, civil society organisations, bilateral and multilateral development agencies[2].

Enacting legislation for quota of seats for women in authoritative bodies is the first step. To realize the basic objectives of legislation, the elected women representatives have to be enabled to perform their roles and responsibilities for which an array of activities has to be initiated. The elected women representatives establish themselves by crossing over all the barriers as leaders and set an agenda to transform the communities, more specifically the women and other marginalized segments. There are two issues involved in it. Primarily they are all elected representatives and hence they have legitimate roles and responsibilities as representatives for the whole constituency. Secondly, they are to attack the critical issues which had not been tackled, so far in the society because of the patriarchal nature of the society.

To perform the above tasks the elected women leaders have to be empowered through a variety of activities. Initiatives have to be taken at different levels and by different stakeholders. From the central government to civil society organisations working at grassroots level, all have to involve themselves in empowering the women and *Dalit* leaders. In India, there is no dearth of good legislation. But all good legislations remain good legislation without proper implementation. They are considered tokens. People who are going to get benefits out of such good legislations are not adequately aware of such legislations and they are not allowed to claim those benefits. To address the basic issues which are being confronted by the marginalized, there are very fine legislations enacted through our legislative institutions. Yet, these legislations are not translated into action. Neither the stakeholders nor the responsible officials have taken steps to translate all those legislations into action. If India exhibits its professionalism in enacting legislations and not in implementing them, India fails miserably. The constitutional amendments for decentralisation of powers are historic and path-breaking and they have rich potential to alter the paradigm of governance, administration and development. But the question lies in translating the legislation into action[3].

It is to be noted here that before evaluating the performance of women and *Dalit* leaders one should understand why reservations are made for women and *Dalits*. Many argue that it is with a view to bringing out the problems which are never discussed in any public fora at a micro level, namely the issues of women and *Dalits* by women and *Dalits* as representatives. It is also argued that the services designed to meet the needs of women and *Dalits* have to reach the destination more effectively and efficiently. There is yet another argument being posited for this reservation. Even in training, women and *Dalit* leaders are oriented to look at the issues of women and *Dalits* without knowing the basic principle for this reservation. Marginalized segments, over centuries, have not been given an opportunity to become part of the mainstream in governance[4]. They may have their own perspectives and understanding. The *Dalits* and women have so far not been given legitimate space in the governance structure. They should also be part of governance. Hence they have to act as representatives, not of women and *Dalits* alone. They have to act for the whole of the constituency. To become part of governance they have been provided with reservation of seats. To claim the rights provided by the Constitution the marginalized groups need a support structure. With an array of impediments and barriers they come to the positions. But it is not so easy to be in those positions and discharge their duties and responsibilities.

In a democracy, it is natural that those who are in power should try to be in power continuously, for which all kinds of strategies will be evolved when they are barred by fixing a quota for the marginalized and underprivileged. One cannot assume that those who are in power will smoothly allow the marginalized to make use of the opportunity to take on power. Transfer of power from one level to another and from one group to another will not happen without a prolonged struggle and one should not assume that it will happen smoothly. A multi-pronged effort is needed for which an array of steps are needed from different stakeholders. It is the responsibility of the government which shows its commitment by bringing in the legislation to exhibit equal concern to see that the marginalized occupy these positions and perform their duties without much difficulty.

It has been noticed that, when a general constituency is reserved for women, the man who has so far occupied the position asks his wife to file her nomination by which he wants to continue his sway over the society. By keeping his wife in position and not in office he will see that she remains in his house itself. In such a way, devices have been evolved to keep the power in the hands of the privileged. India is known for its rituals and tokens. Women are brought to the offices through elections but men are in action on behalf of the women. Women are allowed to contest in the elections but they are not allowed to go to offices and occupy their positions. Positions are with women, powers and offices are with men. When power moves from dominant groups to marginalized ones in an unequal society, it will flow only after a prolonged struggle waged by the stakeholders. In a caste ridden and patriarchal society, one cannot expect power to flow automatically from the dominant to the weak. It has to cross various stages by crossing a variety of barriers.

To change the conditions, the elected women representatives have to be empowered, capacitated and supported while they take power into their hands. Unless the marginalized realize the importance of the reservation of seats for them and act vibrantly and vigorously, the reservation will not help the marginalized. To change this culture of proxy, an array of initiatives has to be taken. First women have to be allowed to decide to contest. Women should not be compelled or driven to contest. Generally men take the decision about the contest being the contestants. Whether they like it or not women are asked to file nominations. They do not know anything about the role to be performed. When they are in the houses, they are not part of democracy, governance and development even though they contribute to them. But now, because of reservation of seats, they have to come out. If they come on their own, it is fine. But in our society women are driven to come out. Even after filing the nomination, men work for the victory of the women candidates. By doing so men give the impression to the women that electioneering is tough, difficult and troublesome. Further, they are giving another impression that men work for women and therefore the women are coming to power only because of the men. This kind of perception is being given to women. Thus, though it is a women's space, women are not allowed to move into the space.

Women have to be oriented before they file nominations. Women have to take decisions about the contest. They should be enabled to contest. They should be motivated to contest. The fear of contesting in elections has to be removed. Women have to be allowed to mobilize the people for their own contest. Let them be in the forefront. In such a way a conducive and women-friendly environment has to be created. They should be allowed to be with the crowd and especially with women. Men who want to empower them should stand behind the women as enablers and facilitators. Once they are elected they are to be allowed to sit in their offices and discharge their roles and responsibilities on their own for which an enabling environment has to be created. It is the practice we witness in India that the men who fielded women argue that they do not know anything in governance and hence their roles are to be performed by their male family members. Women are oriented to concede the argument that they are not strong in governance and in this way the women have internalized the dominance of men. Such is the mindset of men. Communities do not bother when men take this kind of decisions as they are patriarchal. It is interesting and paradoxical in India that a large number of women groups are formed and they are mobilized for economic activities and yet they do not evince keen interest in Panchayat positions. There are other women movements belonging to various political parties and yet candidates are not drawn from those organisations. Women are drawn from the movements for positions in the legislature and national political parties.

Women are allowed to become MLAs, MPs, Ministers, District Collectors, Judges and to occupy many other positions at a higher level away from the community. There will not be any objection and opposition from any section to elect a woman or a *Dalit* to the position of President of India. But much resistance is witnessed at the community level when women are elected or *Dalits* are elected to Panchayats. The constitutional provisions are operational above the communities and community laws are operational at community level[5]. Indian community laws and social laws are more powerful than the constitutional laws at the community level wherever society is not democratized. This position and practices are not contested and challenged either at the grassroots level or at the higher level. In this regard our state is so soft and weak. The government is not able to make the constitutional laws operational.

It has been noticed that many of the *Dalit* Presidents, women Presidents of the Panchayat system are not allowed to discharge their roles and responsibilities as community laws are in force. Though women and *Dalits* are elected, they are not allowed to be the leaders to mange the institutions independently[6]. They are being handled by the community leaders. On many occasions they are ill-treated. Community laws disempower them through the traditional Panchayats. Our political parties are vibrant about the areas of community operation. All representatives of Legislative Assemblies and Parliament, excepting those of the left political parties, do not want to antagonize the community leaders and the community structures as they are relying on the community leaders for votes during the time of elections. When community laws are strong at the grassroots, one can imagine the role of patriarchy in the process of empowerment of women[7]. This is not the practice all over Tamil Nadu. There are women leaders and *Dalit* leaders from Local Bodies who have emerged as models and they break new grounds. How did these leaders emerge victorious and how were they able to excel in performing their roles and responsibilities. Many of the success stories were analysed thoroughly. In all the cases there are certain key principles operating for which various players have to involve themselves. Hence the role of the Central Government should not end with the enactment of legislation and reserving 33.3 per cent of seats for women. It goes beyond this. The Central Government has to take a series of steps. In the same way the State Government has to initiate several measures to empower the elected women representatives. There are other players like civil society organizations which have to take steps to extend their support to such leaders to ensure their proper functioning. Political parties which are committed to women empowerment have to be part of the activities of the elected women representatives. They have to extend support to the cause of elected women representatives. Training institutions have to build the capacity of the elected women representatives to perform the role and responsibilities conferred on them. The whole exercise will take a long time. Though a critical mass has been formed as one-third seats are reserved for women in local governance institutions, the question remains whether the women leaders who are elected are really a critical mass capable of performing critical functions[8]. The issues and problems of women, the marginalized, the poor, and the *Dalits* are to be tackled by them. These issues have not been so far effectively tackled through the policy and programme initiative of the Central and State Governments in India. To address all those issues the representatives need more skills, capacity and capability. One cannot expect that the elected women representatives, after building up their capacity and capability, will perform their roles and responsibilities smoothly and that the communities in which they are going to perform their roles offer a level playing field and hence it is necessary to extend handhold support to all the leaders who are facing problems in discharging their duties and responsibilities. In fact in India women are driven towards electoral contest. They are elected to various positions in local bodies. Are they facilitated to discharge their expected duties? It is a moot question.

It is obvious from research studies from the West that the critical mass formed in the Western legislatures faced a volley of problems and performed their roles and responsibilities not to the extent of the expectation of the people. Yet the number of women in politics and decision-making bodies has a positive impact on policies, decisions, resource allocation for development works[9]. It is unequivocal that South Asian women and leaders are having a different set of problems which need a different kind of approach.

When we witness a large number of women representatives returned to Local Governance, curiosity arises as to how women are performing. Having identified the disabilities and problems for women representatives a concerted action was initiated to build their capacity and capability and a support structure for the women leaders. The initiatives are taken by different agencies at different levels. Some of the agencies have conducted capacity-building exercises. Many institutions periodically organize programmes to educate them on key issues faced by women. A few organisations have been extending support to the affected leaders. There are a few institutions which conduct programmes to raise their problems for policy advocacy. The Rajiv Gandhi Chair has taken serious note of their conditions and started capacity-building as a major programme for the elected women representatives, for which, the Hunger Project, New Delhi, has extended support. When the leaders went with the needed information and capacity, in their office and the field, they met with several obstacles and problems. To overcome the problems they were in need of a support structure. So a support structure was thought of and for this support structure, the Ford Foundation extended its support. Support structures are of two kinds. One is external and the other is internal. Agencies working with elected women representatives are continuously helping the leaders in getting things done. They act in support of the women leaders[10]. There is yet another device and mechanism by which the elected women leaders are enabled to act on their own. They form their own organisation and support each other collectively.

How to form an organisation is a major question. When the elected women leaders came to Gandhigram for the capacity-building exercise, they were briefed about the new proposal of creating a support structure which will be facilitated by the Rajiv Gandhi Chair for Panchayati Raj Studies. Batch after batch were briefed and enrolled as members of the Federation. Once, they are enrolled members of the Federation, it is necessary to develop a perspective for their functioning and the leaders of the Federation have to be trained in organizational management. They said Federation must have regional level, district level and even block level coordinating units and they require handhold support and the handhold support has to be obtained from the civil society organizations. In order to enable the Federation to have tie up with local level Non-Governmental Organizations, regional level meetings are arranged as interface between the NGOs and the elected women representatives Federation. Organizations which are down below the district level have to have interaction with officials, retired officials and local NGOs for their association activities[11]. They need to have media interaction periodically to expose the issues and problems they face in local governance. They should have proper orientation for media interaction. Hence they need to have a media strategy. After the regional activities for the whole year, to draw the attention of the political parties, policy-makers and the government, an annual convention is arranged and consolidated issues are discussed and resolutions adopted.[12] They will be presented to the policy-makers and political parties. Periodical interactions with higher level officials and political parties' representatives are necessary to address their issues. Interface with other State representatives, officials and political parties will strengthen the base of the association. It is also a strategy that the association takes the support of the government for many of its activities. Many issues are being discussed in the presence of the concerned ministers or the officials by which the association makes the government a partner in the process. The continuous activities of the association bring results in varied dimensions. The association itself develops politics. Many landmark decisions have been taken by the government. The attitude of the officials has been changed. The critical mass which has been formed because of the quota for women in governance at the grassroots has really equipped them to perform the critical functions.[13] The moot question here is how this happens. To answer this question, an attempt is made to analyse the implications of a project conducted in Tamil Nadu with the support of the Ford Foundation.

It is necessary to understand the background of the efforts before analyzing the whole process of networking the elected women leaders to address their issues in the process of discharging their role and responsibilities. After the 1996 elections to the Local Bodies, every one talked about the absence of women in the offices though they are elected. There were incidents of intimidation, ill treatment and expulsion which dominated the newspapers, which prompted the Rajiv Gandhi Chair for Panchayati Raj Studies to take up this issue. By following a framework, all the activities will be explained schematically in the following chapters. Before going into the analysis one has to understand and appreciate the framework of the study of the critical action of the critical mass.

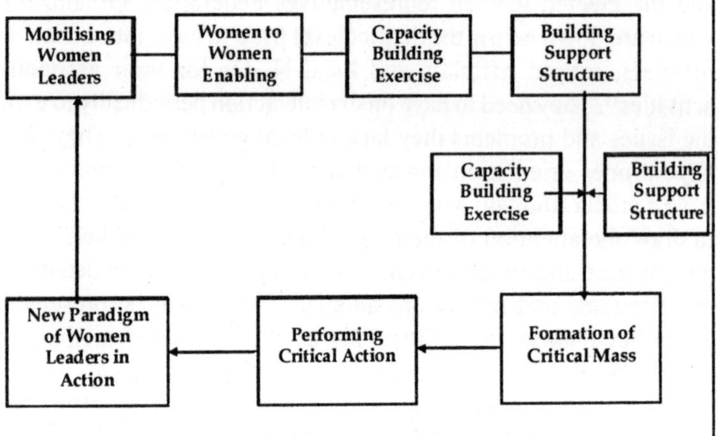

Framework to Study Critical Action by the Critical Mass

It is natural that women are driven to the space by many forces with both optimistic and pessimistic assumptions. The whole process of transformation starts only after the elections. There are certain organisations which will voluntarily go with the women even before the elections with the aim of mobilizing a large number of women in support of women candidates. The ultimate objective is to fill the space fully with women for electioneering. Whether filing nomination, canvassing for votes, nominating booth agents, in all the places women from civil society organisations were appointed. Tokenism will disappear only when these activities are carried out by women. One should not forget that the women who are working with women candidates are not working against men or the community. The women have to give a categorical message that they are not for removing men form the space. But they intend to add strength. Even after the elections, the elected women leaders have to be engaged politically and administratively for which they need leadership, orientation, political orientation and administrative orientation. This orientation has to be arranged for the elected women representatives for which capacity-building exercise has to be arranged.

It is a normal tendency that the dominant males who have fielded the women for electoral contest want to retain them in their houses and that the roles to be performed by the elected women representatives will be attended to by men. This is the underlying assumption prevailing among men. Men who are elected to positions at grassroots, whether they are trained or not, will perform their roles. Hence the easiest way to keep the elected women representatives in the house is to keep the leaders away from attending the capacity building programmes. To break this syndrome, the women leaders have to be brought to training programmes and made to equip themselves to handle offices. The next step is to take the elected women representatives out of their houses for training and make them get into large collectivities of women leaders. The moment they complete their training, they come into contact with the community for developmental action for which a support structure is needed. They are of two types. One is external. They are civil society organizations, Non-Governmental Organizations and so on. The other is the elected women representatives themselves forming organizations or networks very loosely at block level, district level and State or provincial level. The support structure constantly motivates the women leaders to work on critical issues. The numerical strength will bring about a change quantitatively and the representatives will involve themselves in attacking critical issues which are affecting the life of the poor, the marginalized, women, *Dalits* and children. The elected women leaders are bound to face barriers and obstacles. They have to struggle in the process of governing the institutions and achieving development. All development stories of success and struggles have to be documented and disseminated for dual purposes. One is to sensitize the government to look at the barriers and obstacles faced by the elected women representatives; the other is that leaders learn from these experiences and for this the media's role is imperative. The media tie-up plays a significant role. It is a source of support to the elected women representatives.

The elected women representatives periodically meet at block level, district level and State level officials and sort out their problems and issues by pursuing a policy advocacy work. At the block level, the elected women representatives have to meet the officials and get their work done at the block level. They move with officials with authentic facts and get things done. In the same way district level officials are to be met to get things done. Finally, they have to work with State level officials and leaders of all political parties. Periodically they meet the political party leaders and discuss their problems. Continuously they do policy advocacy. In the whole process of interface with officials at different levels and policy advocacy with the policy-makers the usual fear syndrome among the women leaders will go away. Really they will bring the officials under their fold. Then numbers will ensure the building of confidence so that the women leaders will perform their duties and responsibilities. They specifically attack the issues of gender, children, marginalized, environment, inequity and inequality. Their achievements draw the attention of the outside world. They start moving towards other States and other countries for sharing the experiences and thus they demonstrate the power of numbers. The activities explained so far need not happen in the sequence explained above. The expected number has come to public institutions but they have to perform in their own orbit of governance and administration.

The whole range of activities of the project are explained in fifteen chapters. The Second Chapter gives the readers the reality of the devolution process in Tamil Nadu. The Third Chapter explains the actual problems faced by the women leaders in Local Bodies. The Fourth Chapter deals with the capacity-building exercises conducted for elected women representatives. The Fifth Chapter narrates the views expressed by feminists and supporters of EWRs to build a perspective when they create a support structure in the name of networking. Chapter Six explains the role of partners, preferably Non-Governmental Organisations in building the support structure and helping the support structure. Chapter Seven gives an account of the regional meet of the EWRs Federation. Chapter Eight presents the proceedings of the Annual Convention of the Federation of Women Leaders. Chapter Nine elaborates the experience of the elected women representatives when they have interface with institutions. Chapter Ten gives the account of interface with officials. There is yet another interface with media by the elected women representatives which is captured in Chapter Eleven. Chapter Twelve assesses the mood of the elected women representatives when they complete a period of five years in office. The Thirteenth Chapter makes an integrated analysis and the Fourteenth Chapter sums up the study.

NOTES

1. Jean Dreze, *Women in Local Government in Asia and the Pacific* (Unpublished Report) New Zealand: Victoria University of Wellington, 2001; UNDP, *Women's Political Participation and Good Governance 21st Century Challenges*, United Nations Development Programme, 2000; Ishrat Shamim and Ranjana Kumari *Gender and Local Governance: A New Discourse in Development*, New Delhi: Centre for Social Research, 2002; Shantha Mohan and *et al.*, *Women and Political Participation in India*, Kuala Lumpur : International Women's Rights Action Watch Asia Pacific, 2001 and Asian Development Bank, *Gender and Governance Issues in Local Government*, Manila: South Asia Regional Department 2004.
2. Lina Hamadeh Banerjee "Women's Agency in Governance" UNDP, *Women's Political Participation and Good Governance 21st Century Challenges*, UNDP, 2000, p. 7.
3. G. Palanithurai "Panchayats: Relevance and Potentials" in T.M. Joseph (ed), *Local Governance in India*, New Delhi : Concept Publishing Company, 2007.

4. Martha, Nusssback, Amirta Basu, Yasmin Tambiah and Niraja Gopal Jayal, *Essays on Gender and Governance*, New Delhi: UNDP Human Development Resource Centre, 2003.
5. G. Palanithurai, *Constitutional Laws* vs. *Community Laws*, (Endowment Lecture delivered in Madurai Kamaraj University) Gandhigram: Rajiv Gandhi Chair for Panchayati Raj Studies, 2007 (Monograph).
6. Tamil Nadu Federation of Women Presidents of Panchayat Government, *Voices of Women Presidents of Panchayat Government in Tamil Nadu*, Chennai: TNFWPPG, 2002.
7. G. Palanithurai, *Empowerment of Women: Experience of the Elected Women Representatives in Grassroots Institution*, Gandhigram: Rajiv Gandhi Chair for Panchayati Raj Studies, 2007.
8. The critical mass theory argues that the required number will make significant impact in their actions from policy domain to policy implementation. It can work very well in western society but in South Asia conditions are different. More number cannot do anything. Number has to be changed into member. For more details, D. Dahlerup, "From a Small to a Large Minority: Women in Scandinavian Politics" *Scandinavian Political Studies* 11:4 (1998); Pippa Norris and Lovenduski Joni, "Blair's Babes: Critical Mass Theory, Gender on Legislative Life" Paper presented in the seminar on Women and Public Policy Programme on 28th Sept., 2001 in Kennedy School of Government, US.
9. Pippa Norris, "Women Politicians: Transforming West Minister" *Parliamentary Affairs* 49:1 (1996) pp. 93-101; J. Jackquette "Women in Power: From Tokenism to Critical Mass" *Foreign Policy Fall*, 1997.
10. Amitabh Behar and Yamini Aiyar "Networks of Panchayat Women" *Economic and Political Weekly* (November 22, 2003)
11. Rajiv Gandhi Chair, *Report of Regional Workshop of Elected Women Representatives of Local Bodies*, Gandhigram: Rajiv Gandhi Chair for Panchayati Raj Studies, 2004.
12. Rajiv Gandhi Chair, *Report of the Second Annual Meet of the Elected Women Representatives*, Gandhigram: Rajiv Gandhi Chair for Panchayati Raj Studies, 2002.
13. G. Palanithurai, "The Genre of Women Leaders in Local Bodies : Experience from Tamil Nadu" *The Indian Journal of Public Administration*, Vol. XLVII: No. 1 (Jan-Mar, 2001).

2

New Panchayati Raj System in Tamil Nadu

Introduction

Tamil Nadu had an experience of a century in local governance in the pre-independence period which, in fact, forms the basis of the new local governance in the post-independence era. Though it was intended to create Panchayats as institutions of self-governance, in practice, they were made institutions to implement the schemes and programmes of the Centre and State Governments. Till the enactment of the 73rd Amendment, the structure of the Panchayat system in Tamil Nadu was of three tiers and two tiers in two different periods. In the three tier Panchayat system, District Boards, Taluk Boards and Village Panchayats constituted the structural arrangement in the pre-independence period. Even after the enactment of the 73rd Amendment to the Constitution of India, discussion was on about the two tier system. But to confirm the 73rd Amendment in 1994, the Tamil Nadu Government enacted a conformity legislation in which the three tier Panchayat system was created. Originally, in the pre-independence period, from 1884 to 1934, it was a three tier structure and, when the Taluk Boards were abolished by the Government, the two tier system came into vogue. In post-independence India, as per the 1950, decision there were two tiers, namely District Board and Village Panchayat, through two different Acts. With regard to powers, service functions were entrusted to local bodies during the pre-independence period and development functions were entrusted to local bodies along with service functions in the post-independence period. The Tamil Nadu Panchayat Act of 1994 has evaded assigning a precise role to Panchayats.

When the political climate prepared for the general elections in 1996, Panchayati Raj drew the attention of the political parties and it was incorporated in the manifesto of the political parties. The Dravida Munnetra Kazhagam (DMK) gave prominence to it in its manifesto. The DMK gave promises also during the elections that the DMK would conduct the elections to Panchayats and accused the All India Anna Dravida Munnetra Kazhagam (AIADMK) of not conducting the Panchayat elections. Thus it was the expectation at every level that 1996 would be a turning point for the Panchayats. In the general elections the AIADMK was defeated and the DMK won the elections and, to fulfil the poll promise, it conducted the Panchayat elections at one stroke.

Even before the conduct of the Panchayat elections, the Government of Tamil Nadu constituted the First State Finance Commission. After the elections a high level committee was constituted in the State Planning Commission under the leadership of L.C. Jain. In the meanwhile steps were taken to give assignments to all the three tiers. As a result the rural development schemes were distributed among the three tiers. In the meanwhile, the First State Finance Commission submitted its report. Before finalizing the decision on functions and responsibilities among the three tiers, the State Finance Commission had made recommendations. Subsequently L.C. Jain submitted his Committee's report. Based on the recommendations, orders were issued with regard to entrustment of responsibilities to the three tier Panchayats. Arguments and criticism were levelled against the Government for poor devolution of powers. As a result, under the Chairmanship of the Local Administration Minister, a high power committee was constituted with representatives of the political parties. This committee also submitted its report. Following the submission, orders were issued. From the above steps the following are the powers and responsibilities of the three tier Panchayats in Tamil Nadu.

Panchayats Structure

The New Panchayati Raj System came into being in Tamil Nadu after enacting a new law for local body institutions in the year 1994.

The salient features of the new Act are as follows:

(a) A three tier system;
(b) Gram Sabha;
(c) Establishment of Election Commission;
(d) Constitution of Finance Commission;
(e) Reservation of seats for SC/ST proportionate to their population;
(f) One-third reservation of seats for women; and
(g) Constitution of District Planning Committee.

Some Vital Statistics on Panchayats in Tamil Nadu

Table 2.1: Details of Seats and Offices

1. Village Panchayat Wards	40,879
2. Village Panchayat Ward Members	97,458
3. Panchayat Union Wards	6,570
4. District Panchayat Presidents	656
5. Village Panchayat Presidents	12,618
6. Panchayat Union Chairpersons	385
7. District Panchayat Chairpersons	29

The Table 2.5 sums up the number of position of Elected Panchayat Representatives in Tamil Nadu as per the provisions in the Tamil Nadu Panchayats Act 1994 and the Tamil Nadu Panchayats (Reservation of seats and Rotation of Reserved seats) Rules 1995.

Table 2.2: Panchayats in Tamil Nadu

1. Total Village Panchayats	12,618
2. Total Panchayat Unions	385
3. Total District Panchayats	29

Table 2.3: 2001 Rural Population in Tamil Nadu

1. Total Population	3,49,21,681
2. Male Population	1,75,31,494
3. Female Population	1,73,90,187

Table 2.4: Village Panchayats Based on Population in Tamil Nadu

1. Less than 3,000 population	8,945
2 Above 3,000 population	3,673

Table 2.5: Elected Panchayat Representatives in Tamil Nadu

1. Village Panchayat Members	97,195
2. Village Panchayat Women Members	32,485
3. Village Panchayat Presidents	12,618
4. Village Panchayat Women Presidents	4,329
5. Panchayat Union Members	6,568
6. Presidents of Panchayat Union	385
7. District Panchayat Members	656
8. District Panchayat Presidents	29

Table 2.6: Reservation in Panchayats

Category	*Unit of Population Used for Determining the Proportion of Seats to be Reserved*	*Authority Competent to Notify the Reservations*
Village Panchayats Ward Member	Village Panchayat Population	Inspector of Panchayats (Collector)
Village Panchayat President	Panchayat Union Population	Government
Panchayat Union Ward Member	Panchayat Union Population	Government
Panchayat Union Chairperson	District Rural Population	Government
District Panchayat Ward Member	District Rural Population	Government
District Chairperson	State Rural Population	Government

Gram Sabha

Gram Sabha by introducing sub-quorums for the participation of women and SCs/STs, conduct of Gram Sabha meeting in each of the wards by rotation and for keeping photographic record of the proceedings.

Village Panchayat

There are 12,618 Village Panchayats in the State spread across the 29 Districts and the 385 Blocks. The average number of Village Panchayats per district is 435 and per Block is 32. The Nilgris District (35), Kannyakumari (99), Theni (130) and Karur (158) are some of the districts with fewer Village Panchayats while Villupuram (1104),

Tiruvannamalai (860), Vellore (753), Cuddalore (681) and Kancheepuram (648) are some of the districts with a large number of Village Panchayats. As can be seen from Table 2.7, the number of Village Panchayat having populations even below 500 while others have populations exceeding 25,000.

Table 2.7: Classification of Village Panchayats on the basis of Population (2001 census)

Sl. No.	*Population*	*Number of Village Panchayats*
1.	Below 500	66
2.	501-3,000	8,418
3.	3,001-10,000	3,948
4.	10,001-25,000	174
5.	Above 25,000	12
	Total	**12,618**

Similarly, wide variations are also noticed in the income levels of the various Village Panchayats as can be seen from Table 2.8 given below.

Table 2.8: 2005-06 Income-wise Classification of Village Panchayats

Sl. No.	*Income Range*	*Number of Village Panchayats*
1.	Upto Rs. 50,000	16
2.	Rs. 50,000 to Rs. 1 lakh	142
3.	Rs. 1 lakh to Rs. 5 lakhs	7,028
4.	Rs. 5 lakhs to Rs. 10 lakhs	3,718
5.	Rs. 10 lakhs to Rs. 25 lakhs	1,444
6.	Rs. 25 lakhs to Rs. 50 lakhs	195
7.	Rs. 50 lakhs to Rs. 1 crore	45
8.	Rs. 1 crore to Rs. 3 crores	29
9.	Above Rs. 3 crore	1
	Total	**12,618**

Gram Sabha

The Gram Sabha is the nucleus of the New Panchayati Raj System. All the registered voters are members of the Gram Sabha of that Village Panchayat. As per the Act, it has to meet thrice a year and at least once in six months. The President of Gram Panchayat is the presiding officer of the meetings of the Gram Sabha. The Gram Sabha has to give approval to the budget proposal and annual plan of the Village Panchayat. Further, it has to give approval to the annual audited statement of the expenditure of the Village Panchayat. One third forms the quorum to transact the business of the Gram Sabha as per the Act. In Tamil Nadu the Gram Sabha is a neglected subject and unit in the local body arrangement as both elected leaders and officials have not shown any interest in it due to many reasons. As per the Government orders, even beneficiaries for many government schemes are to be selected only in the Gram Sabha. But in reality it does not happen. Beneficiaries are selected not in the Gram Sabha but in the Panchayat Council, which is violative of the provisions of the Local Body Act of Tamil Nadu. It is a government approved unconstitutional activity. The Government of Tamil Nadu emphasizes transparent activities in all government programmes and schemes but there is no way to execute it as the Gram Sabha is made defunct. It is a nightmare to many who have been enjoying power and resources all along. In order to strengthen the Gram Sabha, recently, the government passed an order that all Gram Panchayats have to convene the Gram Sabha meeting four times in a year on 15th August, 2nd October, 26th January and 1st May and transact the activities as per the provisions available in the Act. Further the quorum for the Gram Sabha has been reduced from one-third to one-tenth. Officials from all the Government offices related to development will also participate in the Gram Sabha meeting as observers of the meeting and will report the proceedings to the Inspector of Panchayats. The responsibility of the observer is to provide the details of the government schemes and programmes to the people in the Gram Sabha. Recently in the State Legislative Assembly, a policy note was placed and the same was approved and in the policy note it is mentioned that participation of women and *Dalit* Gram Sabha members is a must and for which a quorum has to be fixed.

Village Panchayat

A Village Panchayat or Gram Panchayat is constituted for a minimum of five hundred population. The Village Panchayat has got members ranging from a minimum of five to maximum of a fifteen. In the Village Panchayat the Ward Members and the President, are to be elected directly by the voters. The Vice-President of the Village Panchayat is elected indirectly from among the elected Ward Members of the Village Panchayat. The Village Panchayat has to look after the following subjects:

(a) Construction, repair and maintenance of Village Panchayat roads;
(b) Lighting of public roads and public places;
(c) Providing drainage facilities;
(d) Cleaning of streets;
(e) Providing public latrines;
(f) Providing burial and burning grounds;
(g) Providing water for washing and bathing purposes; and
(h) Such other duties notified by the Government then and there.

To enable the Village Panchayat to perform its functions the following decisions have been taken and notified through Government orders:

(a) All Village Panchayats will get financial resources from the Government directly without any intermediary. Panchayati Union or Block Panchayat will not interfere in the process;
(b) Gram Panchayat Presidents have been designated as Executive.Heads and they have been entrusted with powers and responsibilities;
(c) Village Panchayat roads can be taken up for works with the resolution of the Panchayats;
(d) Facilities like street light, water supply can be maintained and attended to if there is any disrepair;
(e) Part time clerks can be appointed by the Panchayat President;
(f) House construction plan approval has to be given by the Village Panchayats;
(g) Beneficiaries for the Central Government schemes and programmes have to be selected by the Gram Panchayat in the Gram Sabha;
(h) New Library and information centre in the villages has to be established by the Village Panchayat.

Panchayati Union

For each development block a Panchayat Union is formed. Each Panchayati Union has a Chairperson and a Vice-Chairperson elected indirectly by the members of the Panchayat Council. Union Council Members are elected directly by the people. For every 5,000 population, one Union Council Member will be elected by the people. Members of Parliament and Legislative Assembly elected from that area are *ex-officio* members of the Panchayat Union Council.

The Panchayati Union has the following duties and responsibilities:

- (a) Construction, repair and maintenance of Public roads;
- (b) Establishment and maintenance of dispensaries;
- (c) Construction and maintenance of elementary schools;
- (d) Preventive and remedial measures connected with any epidemic;
- (e) Conduct of fairs and festivals;
- (f) Vetenary relief;
- (g) Opening and maintenance of Panchayat Union markets;
- (h) Extension of village sites and regulation of buildings;
- (i) Maintenance of statistics related to births and deaths;
- (j) Improvement of agriculture and agricultural stock;
- (k) Promotion and encouragement of cottage industries;
- (l) Other duties and responsibilities entrusted to Panchayati Union by the Government through Government notification.

To enable the Panchayati Union to perform its duties the Government of Tamil Nadu has issued a notification to take up the following activities:

- (a) Construction and maintaining Panchayati Union roads, irrigation tanks, and lakes, initiating family welfare activities, executing noon meal schemes and implementing schemes for Adi Dravidas;
- (b) Works have to be identified from Employment Assurance schemes and they are to be executed;
- (c) Draught relief works have to be identified and executed;

(d) M.P. and M.L.A. area development schemes akin to union schemes have to be executed;
(e) Panchayati Union buildings have to be maintained by the union itself;
(f) Panchayati Union can supervise the activities in the domain of public health, primary education, drinking water supply, roads, small culverts, khadi and village industries works, technical training education, libraries, rural electricity and non-conventional energy.

The Panchayati Union administrative arrangement has been modified by which works have been classified into two divisions and entrusted to Block Development Officer and Assistant Block Development Officer. The two sections work independently with their supporting staff. Infrastructural facilities have also been divided and attached to the two divisions.

District Panchayat

The District Panchayat is constituted with directly elected members for every 50,000 population and indirectly elected Chairperson and Vice-Chairperson from among the Council Members. Members of Parliament and State Legislative Assembly of that area are the *ex-officio* members of the District Panchayat Council. The District Panchayat will have to perform the following functions:

(a) Advise the Government in all matters concerning Panchayati Raj Institutions particularly on services and development programmes;
(b) Watching the progress of the measures undertaken by the Government, Village Panchayats and Panchayati Union Councils in the districts as under the administrative control of the districts;
(c) Classification of markets, fairs and public roads in Panchayati Raj Institutions; and
(d) Collection of data, publication of statistics, demanding any information from Village Panchayats and Panchayati Union Councils.

To enable the District Panchayat to perform the earmarked functions, an administrative change has been effected by which the Divisional Development Office which is nearer to the district headquarters will supervise the District Panchayat activities. Yet another office which is away from the headquarters will look after the auditing of the District Panchayat activities and the third one will be attached to the District Panchayat.

Resources

Gram Panchayat

The important sources of revenue for the Village Panchayat are:

(a) Tax Revenue

Among the three tiers, the Village Panchayat alone has the power to levy taxes, House Tax, Profession Tax, Advertisement Tax are the commonly levied taxes.

(b) Non-Tax Revenue

Licensing fees for building plan and lay out approval, fees and charges on dangerous and offensive trades, water charges, fees on cart-stand, social forestry auctions, fishery rentals, 2C patta fees, income from markets and fairs, ferries, fines and penalties and so on.

(c) Assigned and Shared Revenues

Local cess, surcharge on stamp duty, entertainment tax (70% share), seignorage charges on mines and minerals.

(d) Grants

Central Finance Commission Grant, State Finance Commission Grant, development grants under Centrally-sponsored and State Sponsored Schemes.

Block Panchayat

Panchayati Union can not levy any tax. The revenues of a Panchayati Union consist of the following:

(a) Non-Tax Revenues

License fees, market fees, receipt from rentals and properties, fines and penalties.

(b) Assigned and Shared Revenues

Local cess surcharge and entertainment tax (30% share).

(c) Grants

Central Finance Commission Grants, State Finance Commission Grants, development grants under Centrally sponsored schemes and State schemes, grants for maternity centres, rural dispensaries. The Panchayati Union Councils can sanction and execute works up to Rs. 5 lakhs from their general funds without any external approvals. However for Centrally sponsored and State schemes, prior administrative sanction of the District Collector is necessary.

District Panchayat

The District Panchayat has not taxation powers. Its only source of revenue is from statutory grants like State Finance Commission Grants and development grants under Centrally sponsored schemes. District Panchayats can sanction and execute works up to Rs. 10 lakhs from their general funds without any external approvals. However in the case of Centrally sponsored schemes, prior administrative sanction of the District Collector is necessary.

State Finance Commission Grant

To augment the resources of the local bodies, financial devolution to the local bodies is made on the basis of recommendations of the State Finance Commission (SFC). Currently 8 per cent of the State's total own net tax revenues (other than entertainment tax) is devolved to the rural and urban local bodies in the ratio of 58:42 respectively.

87 per cent of the allocation for rural local bodies is being shared among the three tiers in the ratio of 47:45:8 among Village Panchayats, Panchayati Union Councils and District Panchayats respectively. This grant is being released every month to the local bodies. The balance 13 per cent consists of Equalization Fund (6%), Incentive Fund (5%), and Reserve Fund (2%).

The SFC grant is generally utilized for the following:

(a) Salaries, pensions, office maintenance, etc.
(b) Maintenance of drinking water facilities.
(c) Maintenance of street lights, payment of electricity charges.
(d) Maintenance of Village Panchayat and Panchayati Union roads.
(e) Maintenance of minor irrigation tanks.
(f) Public health, sanitation, sewerage, etc.

In 2006-07, Government has allocated Rs. 1,224.76 crores at the State Finance Commission grant for the rural local bodies.

Central Finance Commission Grant

On the basis of the recommendations of the Twelfth Finance Commission (TFC), the Government of India has allotted a sum of Rs. 870 crores for the period from 2005-06 to 2009-10. The guidelines issued by the Government of India stipulate that the TFC Grant should be used for improving the service delivery in respect of water supply and sanitation. The grant can also be utilized for repairs, rejuvenation and also operation and maintenance costs incurred for water supply and sanitation. The grant is shared between the Village Panchayats and Panchayati Unions in the ratio of 80:20. A sum of Rs. 174 crores is provided for the year 2006-07.

District Planning Committee

The Government of Tamil Nadu shall constitute in every district a District Planning Committee to consolidate the plans prepared by the District Panchayat, Panchayati Union Councils, Village Panchayats, Municipal Councils, and Municipal Corporations in the district and to prepare a draft development plan for the district as a whole. The Committee shall consist of the Collector of the district, members of the House of People who represent whole or part of the district, members of the Council of States, Members of Legislative Assembly whose constituencies lie within the district, the Mayor of the City Municipal Corporation and all Chairpersons of the Municipalities of the district, Chairpersons of the District Panchayats, one-fifth of the total number of chairpersons of the Town Panchayats and Panchayati Union notified by the Government every year by rotation, and such number of persons not less than four-fifth of the total number of the committee as specified by the Government elected from among the members of the District Panchayat, Town Panchayats, Municipal Councils and Corporations in the district in proportion to the ratio between the population of the rural areas and the urban areas. The District Collector is the Chairperson, the District Panchayat President is the Vice-Chairperson and Chief Executive Officer of the District Panchayat is the Secretary of the District Planning Committee. The Committee shall allocate funds to various schemes in the Panchayats and Panchayati Unions and shall monitor the implementation of the schemes. Now the Government has changed the chairmanship of the District Planning Committee from the Collector to the President of the District Panchayat. It is an irony that the District Planning Committees of the districts have convened their meetings and reviewed the activities of the sectoral departments but never took any step to prepare the District Plan. Further it is to be noted that even in the review meeting, district level officials do not participate. They send their officials to these meetings. It is a routine meeting without much of importance. But efforts are on in preparing Gram Panchayat level plans in four districts at the initiative of civil society organizations. Based on these activities a new scheme 'Namathu Gramam' was evolved by which each and every Gram Panchayat has to plan for social development.

Reservation

One-third of positions at all levels of the bodies are reserved for women. SC and ST get reservation of positions at all levels of the bodies in proportion to their population. In Tamil Nadu the rotation of positions, especially for women and *Dalits,* is for once in ten years. It is unique in the whole of the country. This change was due to the pressure given by the women Panchayat leaders through their Federation.

Election and Finance Commissions

An Election Commission headed by the State Election Commissioner appointed by the Governor to conduct the local body elections is mandatory. The Election Commissioner enjoys the powers and privileges and status of a judge of the High Court. The tenure of office of the Election Commissioner is two years. However, the Commissioner can be given extension for four more years. In Tamil Nadu elections are conducted on party lines for District Panchayats and Panchayati Unions. Elections to Village Panchayats are not on party lines. In Tamil Nadu elections to Local Bodies, both urban and rural, will be conducted at one stroke. When the election was conducted in few places auctions were conducted, bidding was made, nominations were made by the traditional Panchayat leaders for Gram Panchayat Presidents' posts.

There will be a Finance Commission constituted every five years to review the financial position of the Panchayats and to make recommendations to the Governor to fix the principles to govern the distribution between the State and Panchayats of the net proceeds of the taxes, duties, tolls and fees leviable by the Government and to identify the logistics for making grants in aid to the Panchayats from the Consolidated fund of the State and the measures needed to improve the financial position of the Panchayats. The Finance Commission shall consist of a chairman and four other members. In Tamil Nadu the First Finance Commission has recommended only 8 per cent of the total revenue to the Panchayats with an increase of 1 per cent every year. The Government have given already 8 per cent of the total revenue to local bodies. The State Government has not increased the amount of share to the Panchayats as per its commitment of 1 per cent more every year. It became stagnant at 8 per cent. The Government of Tamil Nadu have constituted the Second Finance Commission. The Second Finance Commission has also recommended the same 8 per cent of the total revenue to the Panchayats without any increase.

Critical Evaluation of Decentralization

The present Act does not provide much scope for giving life to the spirit of the 73rd Constitutional Amendment Act in Tamil Nadu. Subjects in the 11th Schedule do not find a place in the body of the

Act, especially in the chapter on "Functions of Panchayat Bodies." Development officials who work in the Panchayat bodies are declared Government officials and they do not come under the perview of local bodies. As a result, the local bodies can not supervise the activities of the officials of local bodies. While comparing the old Act of Panchayati Raj of 1958 with the new one, one finds adequate powers to local bodies in the old act to supervise, regulate and control the officials working in the local bodies. In the new Act the District Collector is vested with the power of controlling the functioning of Village Panchayats. The District Collector's power to suspend and dissolve the Gram Panchayats is against the spirit of decentralization of powers. The DRDA (District Rural Development Agency) is a registered society, which is under the control of the Project Officer and the District Collector.

The Gram Sabha has not been activated to develop democratic culture in decision-making, to bring about transparency in the activities of the Government and to involve the people in the development process of the community. Enactment of legislation and conduct of elections alone will not bring about any change in the functioning of the local bodies. Proper enhancement of the capacity of the leaders, enabling suitable Government orders and provision of adequate resources can alone bring about needed change in the functioning of the local bodies.

Steps have been taken to train the Panchayat leaders for which training modules have been prepared. In the meanwhile training programmes have been conducted by a few institutions. Panchayat leaders have formed their associations to exert pressure on the Government for more devolution of powers. Gram Panchayat Presidents have formed an association. Likewise the elected women representatives of Gram Panchayats have formed their own association. *Dalit* men and women elected to Gram Panchayats have formed their association. District Panchayat Presidents have formed their forum. Likewise the Block Panchayat Presidents have formed their association. Even among the Block Panchayat Presidents *Dalit* women Presidents have formed their association. All these above associations prepare a charter of demands and sent it to the Government periodically. Of the associations the Gram Panchayat Women Presidents Association is vibrant and active. It is always visible and highly articulate. As a result of the elected women representatives' continuous demand, the Government of Tamil Nadu has made an amendment in the existing arrangements for reservation in Tamil Nadu to reserve the constituencies in all the three tiers for two continuous terms to the women and *Dalits* by which whether it be a Ward of the Gram Panchayat or Gram Panchayat or a Ward of the Block Panchayat or Ward of the District Panchayat once reserved for women and *Dalits* will be reserved for two terms. The concept of rotation of reservation of position in Tamil Nadu is for ten years not for every five year term. The Government issued a directive to all the District Collectors that whenever the elected women representatives organization demanded a meeting with officials to sort out their problems, the District Collector has to organize such interface and sort out the problems faced by the women leaders. It is for women leaders alone.

In terms of resources, the Panchayat has to face a financial crisis due to the changes made in the formula for matching grant. Panchayats got matching grant from the State Government on a regular basis. If the Panchayat collects 100 per cent house tax it will get three times the amount from the State Government. Now it has been reduced to 125 per cent and that too only if the Panchayat has revised the house tax. Sizeable reduction of resources from the State Government has reduced the activities of the Panchayats. Further revenue from minor minerals and sand quarrying from the Panchayat area has been totally stopped as the activity of sand quarrying has been taken over by the State Government. Dues from Social Forestry is not being given as the money has yet to come from the Social Forestry Department.

The next important issue is that the tariff of the Electricity Board for the electricity consumption of Panchayats. Panchayats have to pay commercial rates for the consumption of electricity. It has been raised from Rs. 1.20 to Rs. 3.40 per unit for public consumption by the Panchayats. This has increased the expenditure of the Panchayats. The entire electricity charge has been excluded from the State Finance Commission grant which is due to the Panchayats. The Block Panchayat Councillor is operating schemes which are meant for the village independently without consulting the Gram Panchayats. District Panchayat Councillors are also operating their schemes without consulting the Gram Panchayats. MLAs are operating their constituency development fund without consulting the Gram

Panchayats. In the same way MPs are also spending their money without consulting the Gram Panchayats. Apart from the above, the sectoral departments have their own funds. They carry out their activities without consulting the Gram Panchayats. Money is being spent in a huge quantities but not on the demands of the people. They spend the money as they prioritize the works. In all the four Gram Sabha meetings people project their felt needs but to meet the felt needs of the people there is no untied fund available at the disposal of the Gram Panchayat. Even the small quantum they get from the State Finance Commission is deducted at source for electricity charge remittance. Virtually funds are operated by different agencies on their own priorities and not on the priorities of the people finalized in the Gram Sabha. As a result the Gram Sabha has been weakened. It is being made a ritual. The District Planning Committee has been constituted and they meet periodically and review the works of the departments. There is no concerted effort on the part of the District Planning Committee to prepare a plan. Neither the District Planning Committee nor the officials show any interest in planning exercise at the grassroots level. The State Planning Commission has developed a module for training in multi-level planning and conducted a training programme also. They have prepared guidelines for the preparation of perspective development plan for the whole of a district. Nothing moves in the absence of political will. Finally the State Planning Commission has given instructions to all District Planning Cells to prepare Village Development Reports (VDR) in select Panchayats. It is a mere compilation of data. In select districts, the Village Development Plan was prepared in select Panchayats with the assistance of the development organizations for which the respective Collectors helped and in turn the District Collectors passed orders to all the sectoral departments to work on the prioritized activities of the plan prepared by the people. This new voluntary initiative of the Gram Panchayats drew the attention of the State Government and the State Government passed a Government Order to initiate such a planning exercise at the Gram Panchayat level which is called "Namathu Gramam"—Our Village. This initiative is to encourage the Village Panchayats to work on social development issues.

In the context of the non-functioning of the District Planning Committee, the recent notification of the Government Order, G.O. (Ms.) No. 140 dated 10.09.2004, is a path breaking event as it envisages a holistic development plan for each and every Gram Panchayat with the participation of the people. The new proposal envisions the participation of the people in the sustainable development of villages and the improvement of the quality of life through good governance and convergence of schemes and programmes. It focuses on resource mapping and community mobilization for village development, micro-planning and prioritization of needs among village communities, convergence of funds and functionaries of all schemes at the village level, and community led improvement in the overall quality of life.

It is a path breaking exercise in decentralized governance in Tamil Nadu, which is known for its centralized culture in carrying out development activities. It is a demand driven exercise and not a supply driven one. It envisages the participation of the people. It aims at improvement of the quality of life. It strengthens the physical resources for the improvement of the quality of life. It works for the convergence of the schemes and programmes of the Government towards the needs of the community as identified by the people. It ensures the participation of sectoral departments in the implementation of the plan prepared by the Gram Panchayats with the participation of the people. It creates a synergy between the schemes and programmes of the Governments (both the Centre and the State) and the needs prioritized by the people. It specifically focuses on such sectors as water, sanitation, environment, ecology, education, health, social security and on social issues (elimination of sex selective abortions, prevention of child abuse, age at marriage of women to be not less than 21, prevention of crimes against woman and immoral trafficking, prevention of untouchability and promotion of communal harmony).

The whole exercise is expected to be in a movement mode by carrying out specific campaigns by involving all the stakeholders in the field of rural development. Awareness creation, building and enhancing the skills and capacity of all stakeholders are continuous activities. Each and every Gram Panchayat will have a legal plan document ready for implementation in the next six months. Untied funds will be given to fill the gaps. To encourage the Panchayats to carry out the plan activities incentives will be given after assessing their performance. Each Panchayat will be given three lakh rupees as incentive money, based on its performance. Indicators have been evolved to evaluate the performance of the Panchayats. Most of the indicators are social development indicators which can be achieved without investment of much money. But it requires constant mobilization of the community. If the Panchayats are able to perform such functions, Tamil Nadu will become number one State in social development.

Panchayati institutions have brought people's representatives closer to the people. For the past several years below the State Government there was no representative democratic institution close to the people. Below the State Government level it was the rule of the bureaucracy. It is a well known fact that the expansion of the bureaucracy will alienate the people. Middlemen establish links between the people and the bureaucracy and thereby brokerage becomes the accepted formula for all development activities. Now elected representatives are placed in all the areas and people can approach them easily. People will raise questions in the Gram Sabha. If water is not sufficiently available, people can raise the question face to face in the Gram Sabha. If the medical staff from the Primary Health Centre are not visiting villages periodically people will question the Panchayati leader. Likewise if the primary school teacher is not regular in reaching the school, it can be raised in the Panchayat. When they raise questions, the leaders cannot shirk the responsibility by saying that they have no power or resources. They have to seek power and finance for which they have to work hard and purposefully.

In the whole process, people have developed the attitude that these are the works to be attended to by the Panchayats for which the elected Panchayat leaders have to work. Panchayat leaders have developed the attitude that in the absence of required power and finance to fulfil the needs and demands of the people, people have to be mobilized to exert pressure on the Government to get things done for the people. In the whole process, people are being mobilized by the Panchayats. Mobilization is being done in many ways of which the Gram Sabha is an important one. No doubt in India people are mobilized for cultural activities, religious activities and political activities periodically by various groups and the political parties. But they are not mobilized for development work. But now Panchayats are mobilizing the people for development activities. It is true that the Panchayat leaders are drawn from the place wherefrom MLAs and MPs are drawn. But MLAs and MPS can keep themselves aloof from the community. Panchayat leaders have to live with the people and in the community and hence they have to be responsible and responsive to the communities. Provision has been made in the structure so that the marginalised and women can find a place legitimately in the institution for governance. Women and *Dalits*, who never had any experience in governance, have come to power. A large number of them want to be transparent because the community has a hold over them. In many places a conducive atmosphere for transparent governance by women and *Dalits* which can serve as a model for others. Women have started attending the Gram Sabha meeting. A large number of SHG members attend the Gram Sabha meetings and they raise a lot of developmental issues in the meeting as they are oriented in social development activities by the NGOs. As a result, even the process of governance at the grassroots will be changed.

Electing a good leader is in the hands of the electorate. Shaping a leader and making him good lies in the hands of everyone. The leaders at the grassroots have to be conscientised on development and their skill and capacity have to be enhanced for proper management of institutions to achieve development and social justice. Once the leaders are properly trained, they will deliver the goods to the level of the expectations of the masses.

Conclusion

It is true that there are very many weaknesses in the Act itself and a variety of existing Acts do not permit the State to devolve powers. The capacity of the leaders is not so high as to handle all the subjects earmarked for Panchayati Raj and yet leaders are alert and optimistic at present that the Panchayati Raj System is the only solution to solve most of the problems in the rural areas. Steps are on to rectify the defects. Local body leaders are putting out a one point demand to the State Government to devolve adequate powers and resources to the local bodies. Expected pressure has come from the people for devolution of powers and the leaders of local bodies have come to a stage to take powers from the State Government on their own in the event of denial of powers to the local bodies.

Thus the Panchayati Raj System in Tamil Nadu is being kept in operation not because of the devolved powers and resources but because of the leadership at the Village Panchayat level. No doubt Panchayats are fulfilling the obligatory functions. A lot of innovations have happened in Panchayats due to the exceptional leadership qualities of the Panchayat leaders. Wherever Panchayat leaders are strong, vibrant, capacitated, and committed they perform very well. Whenever the District Collector and Project Officer, DRDA, is pro-Panchayat, the Panchayats perform very well despite several problems and constraints. District Collectors and Project Officers see this dispensation as very positive as they can achieve the targets in carrying out rural development schemes through the Panchayats. Thus it becomes a partnership between the district administration and the Panchayats. In Tamil Nadu Panchayats are evolving on their own. Devolution becomes evolution in Tamil Nadu.

Panchayats are instruments of the people created for governance with the participation of the people to achieve development. Though Panchayat leaders are drawn from the place wherefrom MLAs and MPs are drawn they cannot adopt the attitude and behaviour of the MPs and MLAs as they have to work with the community closely. By increasing their capacity and sensitizing them on developmental issues, Panchayats can be prepared to achieve development and social justice. Capacity-building, continuous support extended by the support structure, forming network with the media and NGOs and providing needed information could make them achievers and path finders. If State Governments really want to achieve social development, it can be achieved through the Panchayats. People should be mobilized to participate in the development process. In the long run people will assert and claim their rights and entitlements through the Panchayats.

REFERENCES

Athreya V.B. and Rajeswari K.S., *Women's Participation in Panchayati Raj: A Case Study from Tamil Nadu,* Chennai: M.S. Swaminathan Research Foundation, 1999

Dharampal, *The Madras Panchayat System Vol-II A General Assessment,* New Delhi: Impex India, 1972.

Government of India, *Powers and Functions of Panchayati Raj Institutions: A Framework,* New Delhi: Ministry of Rural Development, 1994.

Government of India, *Renewing Local Self Government in Rural India*, New Delhi: Ministry of Rural Development, 1994.

Government of Tamil Nadu, *Democratic Decentralization: Powers Entrusted to Panchayati Raj Institutions*, Chennai: Rural Development Department, 1999.

Government of Tamil Nadu, *High Power Committee Report on Entrustment of Powers to Three Tier Local Bodies in Tamil Nadu*, Chennai: State Planning Commission, 1998.

Jennie Litvack, Junaid Ahmed, *Rethinking Decentralization in Developing and Richard Bird Countries*, Washington D.C.: The World Bank, 1998.

Palanithurai G., "Building Alliances and Capabilities among the elected women representatives of Grassroots Institutions", *Women's Link*, Vol. 10, No. 1 (Jan-Mar 2004) pp. 18-25.

Palanithurai G., "Towards Participatory Governance at Grassroots: Synergisation of Rural Communities and Institutions" *South Asian Journal of Socio Political Studies*, Vol. 4, No. 1 (Dec, 2003).

Palanithurai G., *Capacity-Building for Local Body Leaders*, New Delhi: Concept Publishing Company, 2001.

Palanithurai G., *Development Role Reversed: From Government to People*, Gandhigram: Rajiv Gandhi Chair for Panchayati Raj Studies, 2003.

Palanithurai G., Dwaraki B.R. and Narayanasamy S. (eds.), *Major Issues in New Panchayati Raj System* (eds.) New Delhi: Kanishka Publications, 1997.

Palanithurai G., *Empowering People for Prosperity: A Study in New Panchayati Raj System*, New Delhi: Kanishka Publications, 1994.

Palanithurai G., *Evaluation of Process and Performance of Gram Panchayat Women and Dalit Presidents in Tamil Nadu*, Gandhigram: Rajiv Gandhi Chair, 2003.

Palanithurai G., *Grassroots Democracy in Indian Society*, New Delhi: Concept Publications, 1997.

Palanithurai G., *New Panchayati Raj System at Work: An Evaluation*, New Delhi: Concept Publishing Company, 2000.

Palanithurai G., *New Panchayati Raj System at Work: An Evaluation*, New Delhi: Concept Publications, 1999.

Palanithurai G., *New Panchayati Raj System: Status and Prospects*, New Delhi: Kaniska Publications, 1996, pp. 57-64.

Palanithurai G., *Panchayats, Communities and Social Development*, Gandhigram: Rajiv Gandhi Chair for Panchayati Raj Studies, 2003.

Palanithurai G. (ed.), *Empowering People: Issues and Solutions*, New Delhi: Kanishka Publications, 1996.

Palanithurai G. (ed.), *New Panchayati Raj System Status and Prospects*, New Delhi: Kanishka Publications, 1996.

Population Foundation of India, *Empowerment of Panchayati Raj Institutions on Issues Related to Population, Health and Social Development, A Final Report*, New Delhi: Population Foundation of India, 2001.

Rajiv Gandhi Chair, *Functional Efficiency of Gram Sabha: A Report Submitted to II State Finance Commission*, Gandhigram: Rajiv Gandhi Chair for Panchayati Raj Studies, 2000.

Rajiv Gandhi Chair, *Problems Faced by the Gram Panchayat Leaders*, Gandhigram: Rajiv Gandhi Chair for Panchayati Raj Studies, 2000.

Rajiv Gandhi Foundation, *Dialogue on Panchayat: Summary Proceedings of four Regional Tripartite Interface Interactive Workshops*, New Delhi: Rajiv Gandhi Foundation, 1999.

Rajiv Gandhi Foundation, *Panchayati Raj in India: Status Report*, New Delhi: Rajiv Gandhi Foundation, 2000.

Rajiv Gandhi Foundation, *Proceedings of the National Seminar on Panchayats*, New Delhi: Rajiv Gandhi Foundation, 1997.

Rajiv Gandhi Foundation, *Proceedings of the National Seminar on Panchayats*, New Delhi: Rajiv Gandhi Foundation, 1993.

Rajiv Gandhi Foundation, *Revitalization of Panchayati Raj in India*, New Delhi: Rajiv Gandhi Foundation, 1999.

Rajiv Gandhi Foundation, *Voices from Below: Summary Proceedings of Sub-Regional Workshops on Panchayats: Issues and Recommendations*, New Delhi: Rajiv Gandhi Foundation, 2001.

Rukmani R., *Panchayati Raj Institutions in Tamil Nadu: A Historical Review*, Chennai: Madras Institute of Development Studies, 1996.

Rural Development Department, *Democratic Decentralization: Panchayati Raj System in Tamil Nadu*, Chennai: Rural Development Department, 1999.

Sarasvathi, *The Madras Panchayat System Vol-I A Historical Survey*, Delhi: Impex India, 1973.

Siddartha, Sivaramakrishnan, *Panchayati Raj Institutions in India—A Society Study for the World Bank*, Washington DC: World Bank, 1999.

Siddartha, Sivaramakrishnan, *Discussion: Challenges and Opportunities for Panchayati Raj*, New Delhi: World Bank, 1999.

State Finance Commission, *Summary of Recommendations of the State Finance Commission for Local Bodies*, Chennai: State Finance Commission, 1966.

State Planning Commission, *Report of the Working Group on Decentralized Planning and Panchayati Raj*, Chennai: State Planning Commission, 1997.

State Planning Commission, *Report on the Entrustment of Powers to Panchayats*, Chennai: State Planning Commission, 1997.

The Hunger Project, *Report on the Workshop on Panchayati Raj: Trials and Triumphs*, Gandhigram: Rajiv Gandhi Chair for Panchayati Raj Studies, 2003.

The Hunger Project, *Women and Panchayati Raj: The Pathway to Social Transformation and a New Future for India*, Bombay: The Hunger Project, 1999.

3

Problems faced by the Elected Women Representatives

Introduction

Ever since the enactment of the 73rd and 74th Amendments to the Constitution of India, "empowerment of women at the grassroots" has become a popular concept that is used by many, (Batliwala, 1996; Batliwala, Anita, Gurumurthy and Wali, 1998; Sharma, 1992) with varied meanings and explanations. One-third of the seats at the three levels of grassroots institutions[1] have been reserved for women of all categories. This has raised expectations among different sections of the community that this group of women will become a critical mass, which, in turn, will make an indelible difference to the management of these institutions at the grassroots level. Such an expectation has grown to the extent that the existing development paradigm will undergo a drastic change in the system of benefits (Buch, 1998).

Women elected to grassroots institutions have been performing their roles and functions since 1996. The impact and the implications of the management of these institutions by women leaders have been felt in many spheres. It was expected that the newly formed critical mass of women who got power through reservation would perform a critical function. But the women leaders who assumed responsibilities are not in a position to perform the critical function as they face a volley of problems. Despite their struggle they continue to make efforts to address the problems of people (Krishnaswamy, 2001).

An in-depth analysis will show the systematic effort on the part of the mainstream system (bureaucracy of the State Government) to project the failures of women leaders rather than their problems in handling power and institutions. It is also observed that in the Government training institutions in the name of training and capacity building, women leaders have been oriented to be submissive to the bureaucracy and obey the instructions of officials. The women leaders' vision and their sense of self have been eroded. This has been evident since 1996 and women grassroots leaders have been silently made subordinates to officials.

A conscientious move has been made to equip women leaders to be self-reliant by Gandhigram Rural Institute, founded as an institution for empowering women by the disciples of Mahatma Gandhi at the dawn of independence. This new initiative has also highlighted scores of problems faced by women representatives on various fronts. In order to overcome these associations for elected women representatives have been formed and they have been federated with other associations of elected women representatives in South India.

The problems, issues and encounters of women leaders dealt with herein are location specific and are confined only to Tamil Nadu. These observations, analyses and explanations cannot be generalised. All these problems are to be seen against the backdrop of the environment of the State of Tamil Nadu. This chapter, therefore, seeks to illuminate the problems faced by women representatives of the grassroots institutions of Tamil Nadu. Further, it highlights some of their experiences while trying to achieve their avowed goals. It also indicates some suggestions on the type of support needed to sustain their position of power in this space created for them.

Data on the problems of women representatives were collected from two sources. First, while conducting training programmes for women representatives, a specific dialogue session was arranged in which all the problems faced by them were discussed and documented in detail (G. Palanithurai, 2001). The second occasion was when the women representatives formed an association and federated themselves with the support of Gandhigram Rural Institute, they organised regional meetings in several places in order to consolidate the demands of women representatives in the local bodies. The above exercise was carried out in four zones and the exchanges and interactions with women leaders have been documented (Palanithurai, 2000, 2001).

The Reservation Debate and Process

While looking at the issues affecting women leaders, one has to bear in mind the environment in which the institutions have been created through 33.3 per cent reservation of seats for women and how they have carried out the duties and responsibilities assigned to them. Right from the 1941 Report of the Sub Committee of the National Planning Committee[2] to the recent report of the Committee on Status of Women in India, every report (Government of India, 1975) has emphasized that the condition of women is unacceptable and that they have been denied their rights and opportunities. While commenting on women's predicament, Justice V.R. Krishna Iyer observed: "Rethinking on the separate terms from the perspective of women who, despite the constitutional guarantees, had not achieved real justice or liberty or equality or dignity produced the holistic concept of gender justice which united all the principles into one to challenge the persistent denial of these promised objectives to the overwhelming majority of the women of India within a quarter of a century after the birth of the Republic" (Kasturi and Mazumdar, 1994).

It is true that Indian history (Altekar, 1978) provides ample proof that the rights and freedom enjoyed by women change in inverse proportion to the status of their families, especially the men in their families, within the social hierarchy. Further, it is horrifying to note from the observation of an IAS officer, based on the latest two censuses, (Agnihotri, 1996) that the only segments of India's population, which neither destroy their baby daughters before or immediately after birth, nor allow them to die in infancy through discrimination in nutrition and health care are tribals whom the rest of us have been taught to regard as the most backward and least civilized members of our nation. There have been a series of reviews and observations (Moser, 1989; Sen, 1994) about the conditions of women based on which new schemes and programmes have been chalked out for the welfare of women. Yet, one cannot see any significant impact on society. The marginalisation of the majority of women in the economy and the consequent neglect and demonstration of gender, class and urban bias led to a complicated situation in the general political framework of society.

It is also true that even the opportunities that have been provided to women have not been properly used by them for their upliftment as they are trained to be insensitive towards their own issues (Narasimhan, 1999). In a democratic country, power rests with the people and they should have the strategy to handle power. It is not the Government that gives power to people, it is the Government which derives power from the people.

To liberate oppressed women, steps have to be initiated from the point of view of the oppressed and not from that of the oppressor. The Government in a patriarchical society looks at issues only from a patriarchical perspective. To overcome these problems, feminists have fixed two long-term goals—freedom and empowerment (Asia Pacific Centre for Women and Development, 1979). Freedom from oppression for women involves not only equity but also the right to freedom of choice and the power to control their own lives within and outside their home. Control over their lives and bodies is essential to ensure a sense of dignity and autonomy for women. 'Power' refers to the sense of internal strength and confidence to face life, the right to determine choices in life, the ability to influence the social process that affects their lives as well as the direction of social change (Sahay, 1998).

Empowerment of women is a concept which has gained prominence and currency among academics and policy-makers now. Empowerment has been defined differently by different scholars contextually (Batliwala, 1995). But, at present, most scholars (Sen and Grown, 1987) have come to give a broad meaning to the concept. It is a method of tackling powerlessness in encountering and combating personal and social problems. It is distinguished by its focus on developing critical awareness, increasing the feeling of collective and self efficacy and developing skills for personal, interpersonal or social change. In other words, empowerment can be defined as control over material assets, intellectual resources and ideology. Thus empowerment is a process of awareness, capacity building, leading to greater participation, to greater decision-making power and control and to transformative action.

This process takes shape in two forms, internal and external. Women should realise their inner worth and should be made to realise their worth. In order to perform the above tasks, the problems faced by the powerless should be first eliminated from the social environment. In the 1970s and 1980s, systematic steps were taken through the five year plan proposals (Government of India, 1976; 1980). Consequent to the pressure brought on the Government by the women's movement at the national and international levels commissions were constituted.[3] Yet, the struggle is still on to acquire a legitimate space in all spheres of life for women. The position of women has changed neither drastically nor dramatically. The problems of women representatives at the grassroots have to be looked at against this background.

Problems faced by Elected Women

To empower women, first the elected women representatives have to be empowered by building skill, capacity and support structure. In this process, it is essential to understand the problems faced by women representatives while performing their roles and functions and to evolve solutions to these problems to the extent possible.

Women representatives elected to grassroot level institutions have been facing numerous problems, within their families, in their social, political and administrative settings, which will be spelt out hereunder. This has often led to ineffective administration of these bodies by women leaders. They do not have a common platform to express their grievances and get them redressed. Experiences from capacity building exercises conducted in various parts of the State have enthused us to prepare an action programme for empowerment of women leaders at the grassroot level. We thought that this can be done by forming an association of women representatives and federating it with similar associations of women representatives in local government in different parts of the country and making them articulate their issues on their own.

In the Indian context empowering women is a herculean task, as social and cultural moorings have established strong roots in the belief system of people. As a result, there has always been an uncommon disparity in the upbringing of women and men. All social reconstructions take place only through political activities, that too through political systems. Democracy provides enough scope for such reconstructions through polity. Hence every social segment is moving towards power. Yet, women hesitate to take part in politics as if it is a male space. In order to break this barrier at the micro-level, a new device has been worked out through the 73rd Constitutional Amendment Act. Women had been made ineffective in administration since they came to these institutions as freshers. But there are instances of women having achieved a great deal of success in managing panchayat responsibilities.

Women leaders in Panchayats are engaged in a constant struggle. Many leaders are insensitive to their own, and gender issues in general.

They have been oriented to lose their identity and only serve as instruments to operationalise certain processes for others. This process has made them sink in localism and become voiceless. As a result, their space is still severely limited. In order to overcome all these hurdles, an attempt has been made to bring women leaders into a federation in order to address all the issues which they face in administration and to focus on issues of special relevance to women.

Need for this Programme

The finding of the capacity-building programme is that women leaders are in need of an alternative arrangement for the continuous flow of information and consultancy to stabilise their activities for development. The requirements of women leaders are not adequately fulfilled by their organisations. Hence, the demand for a full fledged professional organisation to assist women leaders of local bodies. Against this background, a series of programmes covering the entire State of Tamil Nadu was organised in four zones. The details of the programmes are given in Table 3.1.

Table 3.1: Network Meetings of Elected Women Representatives

Sl. No.	*Category of Participants*	*Programme*	*No. of Leaders attended*	*Venue*
1.	Panchayat Union Chairmen, Village Panchayat Presidents, Ward Members and Self-Help Groups	South Zone Network Meet on Associating Women Representatives in Local Bodies	25	Madurai
2.	Village Panchayat Presidents, Ward Members and SHG Leaders	North Zone Network Meet on Associating Women Representatives in Local Bodies	32	Chengulpet
3.	Village Panchayat Presidents, and Ward Members	East Zone Network Meet on Associating Women Representatives in Local Bodies	23	Tiruvarur
4.	Panchayat Union Chairmen, Village Panchayat Presidents, Ward Members and Self-Help Groups	Central Zone Network Meet on Associating Women Representatives in Local Bodies	48	Karur
		Total	128	

Source: Computed.

A facilitating centre for grassroot women leaders is being considered at the Gandhigram Rural Institute.[4] Before proceeding further, it is necessary to take a glance at the problems of women leaders.

The problems are drawn from the elected women representatives who have attended training programmes organised by Rajiv Gandhi Chair for Panchayati Raj Studies funded by various agencies. The details of these programmes are given in Table 3.2.

Table 3.2: Details of Training Programme Conducted for Elected Women Representatives

Sl. No.	*Training Programme*	*Funding Agency*	*No.of Participants*
1.	Empowering Panchayati Raj Institutions on the issues of Population, Health and Social Development	Population Foundation of India	6834
2.	Capacity-Building for Gram Panchayat Presidents	CAPART Hyderabad	681
3.	Training of Presidents and Vice-Presidents on Panchayat Administration with Special Reference to Water and Sanitation	DANIDA Villupuram	815
4.	Training of Presidents and Vice-Presidents on Panchayat Administration with Special Reference to Water and Sanitation	DANIDA Cuddalore	416
5.	Training of Women Presidents of Gram Panchayats	Social Welfare Board	825
6.	Training of Elected Women Representatives of Urban Local Bodies	Tamil Nadu Institute of Urban Studies	2150
7.	Training of Trainers in Multi Level Planning	State Planning Commission	71
8.	Capacity-Building for Weaker Sections in New Panchayati Raj System	CAPART Hyderabad	425
9.	Capacity-Building for Gram Panchayat Presidents	CAPART Hyderabad	317
10.	Training Programme for Panchayat Leaders in Nilgiris District on Ecological Empowerment of Panchayats	Rural Development Organisation The Nilgiris	102
11.	Training for Village Panchayat Presidents and Vice-Presidents in Total Rural Sanitation	DRDA Cuddalore	682

Source: Computed.

Total number of elected local body leaders trained	=	13,318
Total number of panchayats covered	=	2,354
Total number of urban local bodies covered	=	294
Districts covered	=	17

Increasing Workload

The moment the women filed their nomination for election to the grassroot level institutions, their workload doubled and so did the constraints. No woman representative from the rural areas reported that her workload on the home front decreased due to her work in the public space. In a joint family system, attention to routine work cannot be reduced. At every stage, the elected women representatives have to tackle problems of the family carefully; otherwise, they face trouble. The family burden, coupled with the workload in the Panchayat, created a stressful situation for these women in their office. Their efficiency could neither be exhibited nor improved as they had no time. On most occasions, the elected women representatives opted for a joint workshop with the males of their families. Instead of discussing the problems faced by them among themselves, a workshop could be organised to which the elected women representatives and their husbands or other males in their families could be invited. All the issues affecting women representatives could be discussed in the open and that could bring about change in their attitude.

Varied Concerns of Women Leaders

Politics has its own ramifications and dimensions—whether it is at the State or at the National level. Till they entered grassroots institutions, women had confined themselves to voting. After the reservation of seats for them in grassroots institutions, they have also assumed the role of players in the political game. So far, they had not been dragged into this game and hence they are novices in this art. In order to acquaint them with politics, they need the support of men. But, while drawing upon the support of men for their work, they run the risk of men trying to make women representatives submissive.

Illiteracy

Illiteracy is a basic problem among the newly elected women representatives. They are not able to write and read, but they are allowed to file their nomination. After they are elected to positions, they feel annoyed about their inability to read and write. They have the aspiration to read and write and are prepared to undergo training. But, their husbands prohibit this, since many of them are now operating the Panchayat on behalf of their spouses. Wherever the elected women representatives establish contact with NGOs, they are properly oriented and trained to manage the institutions on their own by the intervention of NGOs. To maintain thirty one records as a representative of Panchayati Raj Institutions every one requires adequate skill. The training programme is intended to impart skill in the art of management of Panchayat Institutions, for which literacy is a prerequisite. Nearly 9 per cent of the participants lack this skill. Hence they have to rely on others for managing the Panchayats.

Usual Shyness

Having traditionally secluded themselves from public spaces, especially the menfolk, women face difficulties in interacting with men in office and in public life, after being elected to Panchayati Raj Institutions. They have had no previous experience of working with men but when they become leaders they have to interact with both men and women of the community. Women leaders are, therefore, inhibited in their interaction with men in public contexts. When Gram Sabha meetings are convened, women representatives have to conduct the proceedings as chairpersons of the Gram Sabha, sitting along with men in a crowd, a rather unusual situation in remote villages. According to Ponnikailasam, the President of the Women Panchayat Leader's Federation, in the first three or four Gram Sabha meetings, she did not feel comfortable sitting with men.

Domination of Males

It is clear from the experience of these elected women representatives that their capacity has not been recognised by males of their families. After their election, women representatives have been attending meetings and training programmes, where they learn many things. Initially the men in the family, in the guise of helping them, accompanied the elected women representatives to offices and public places. Over a period of time, the women learnt the art of administration through interaction and training. But the males would not accept that their family women, who have been elected to Panchayats, have equipped themselves to manage institutions. It is an irony that though the elected women representatives feel that they can manage the affairs of the Panchayat on their own without the help of any male from their families, they cannot say so to the males in their families. Further, elected women representatives face problems in Panchayats when the men of their families interfere in administration. In the absence of interference in administration by males in the families of elected women representatives, trouble from male representatives would be minimal and negligible. This is partly so because men generally feel that women are not elected on their own merit but because of their support. This sort of attitude is very difficult to change since the women leaders too are of the belief that they have been elected to Panchayat Institutions only because of the influence of their husbands or other men in their families. While narrating her experience, Minnalkodi of Adhanur Panchayat reported that the men in her family take decisions and impose them on her. She said that she did not have adequate courage to change this.

The women representatives pointed to yet another problem: the restriction placed on their movement. The people of the village are used to approaching their Panchayat representatives with their problems at any time. Although the women representatives indicate their willingness to attend to such work at any time, they are not permitted to do so by their husbands or other family members. They need the permission of their husbands or in-laws if they want to go to the police station or the hospital at night. On such critical occasions, people want the support of leaders. If women, as leaders, do not come forward to help the people, they have to face criticism.

Forced not to Raise Issues of Women

Although women in rural areas face a multitude of problems, men ensure that such problems are never raised openly in public fora. Women representatives feel suppressed by this. Neither women affected by problems nor their women representatives muster enough courage to raise issues affecting their lives. The family members of elected women representatives, however, prevent elected women representatives from articulating women's problems in public.

Environmental degradation and depletion of natural resources are affecting the life of women in rural areas, especially the poor women. Even though elected women representatives are aware of the gravity of the problem, they are unable to raise the issue in public fora as some mafia gangs are involved in such despicable activities. Only NGOs are creating awareness about this problem among the *Dalit* women and the poor in the rural areas.

The menace of alcoholism breeds all sorts of troubles for the family, especially women. Women face innumerable problems in the family and in society because of alcohol. Every woman and every child is affected and yet nobody has the will to oppose this practice, since everybody knows that this illicit trade takes place with the active support of politicians and with the connivance of the police. No one need create awareness about this menace among the people as they are all aware of it, but are afraid of the police who are behind it.

The health of womenfolk is an issue, which is not seriously viewed in rural areas by men. Women themselves do not realise the importance of their health. In every respect, women are discriminated against in the family. No one dares to create awareness among women. Even in carrying out activities in the Panchayat, men are not sensitive to issues confronting women. Worse, women are not sensitive to their own issues, be it guiding pregnant women to avail themselves of ANC or motivating girls to go to schools. In such circumstances, elected women representatives who take up these issues are not appreciated. Instead, they are criticized by the males in the Gram Sabha meetings.

Negative Attitude of Officials

Elected women representatives find it difficult to convince officials in government offices as the latter have a poor opinion about women representatives. The officials feel that elected women representatives are in position simply because of the reservation policy and that they do not have any opinion or vision of their own and assume that women representatives are already to accept whatever they advice they give.

Consequently, women representatives who go to offices with aspirations and expectations feel frustrated. Ponnikailasam, the President of the Federation of Women Panchayat leaders, while presenting the report about the plight of women leaders in her presidential address in 2001, indicated how officials were indifferent towards the demands of women representatives of local bodies.[5]

Ill-treatment

It is a sorry state of affairs in Government offices where elected women representatives with a high social and economic background get respect while poor elected women representatives, especially *Dalits,* face only ill-treatment. To illustrate the tragedy of *Dalit* leadership, a case is narrated here. A poor *Dalit* woman who served as a construction worker assisting the mason got elected as the Gram Panchayat President. She went to the Panchayat Union office to clear a file for her Panchayat. The moment she met the concerned clerk, she was asked to bring a cup of tea from the nearby tea stall by the clerk. She readily agreed to do so and picked up a glass tumbler and got a cup of tea for the clerk without a murmur. Later she was asked to meet him at his residence. She went to his residence and she was asked to do some work in his garden. She attended to that work also. Later, she got the cheque from him and went home happily. When she narrated the incident in the training programme she was asked why she did not resist. She said that previously it was her practice to bring tea to the mason at the construction site. Now she was asked to do so by an official and so she obliged. Ill-treatment continues unabated, despite the *Dalit* movement. Another Gram Panchayat President, Reeta, narrated her experience with officials and police in a dialogue session at the annual convention of elected women representatives of rural local bodies in Tamil Nadu. She explained how she responded to the challenges.[6]

Information Blockade

There are several hurdles and barriers to the process of women's empowerment. Information blockade is the most powerful weapon used by officials to disempower women. Generally, women do not have access to newspapers. Moreover, all Government information is transmitted from one department to another only among officials. The officials circulate information booklets and details only among men and not among women. Even elected men representatives are not willing to share their knowledge with women representatives. Susila, Karungulam Gram Panchayat President, narrated in her presentation in the group discussion in a training programme sponsored by the Social Welfare Board that she was discriminated against by officials and male Gram Panchayat leaders in giving copies of the Government Orders on Rural Development and Panchayati Raj.[7]

When women representatives are invited for training programmes, permission to participate in these programmes is not accorded by many of their families. When elected women representatives insist, they are allowed to attend training programmes along with their husbands or other males of the family. Now, the Government insists that elected women representatives should not be accompanied by their husbands or others while attending training programmes.

Domination of Caste Panchayats

Traditional caste Panchayat leaders are yet another barrier to elected women representatives as they impose conditions and restrictions on women leaders. If the elected woman representative belongs to the caste of the traditional Panchayat leader, they extend all support to her to remain in power but not to attend to the work on her agenda. The traditional Panchayat leaders expect that the elected women representative should adhere to the advice of the traditional Panchayat leaders. She is expected to carry out her work from the agenda of the traditional Panchayat. If the elected woman representative belongs to any other caste, particularly *Dalit,* she cannot do any work at all. Invariably, she has to be under the control of the traditional Panchayat leader, or else she has to face problems.

Party men also expect the same. Normally, women in the Panchayat do not have any political identity and hence they look at issues on the basis of reality. On the contrary party men want elected women representatives to look at issues from the party angle, failing which they face problems from the party high command. Why do party men take such a stand? Because, it is the normal practice that when a seat is reserved for a woman, a male of the party gets permission from the party to field his wife or sister in that place. Hence, the party men feel that it is the responsibility and duty of the elected woman representative to adhere to the dictum of the party men at the local level. Issues such as domination of caste Panchayat leaders over the formal Panchayats headed by women and the control of political party leaders at district level over women Gram Panchayat leaders, repeatedly figured in the training programme while women Gram Panchayat Presidents narrated their experience in Panchayat Administration.[8]

Lack of Communication Skills

Communication skills are very important for the success of any leader in the modern era. Elected women representatives never had a public space experience and hence they lack communication skills. They have to manage the council and the public with effective communication skills. Since they feel that they lack skills, they can not achieve what they want to. Even the Federation President Ponnikailasam stated in the training programme that she was conscious of her poor communication skills.[9] But now she speaks for an hour in meetings along with ministers and higher level officials. When elected women leaders preside over the Panchayat council, some men use unparliamentary words with the intention of making them nervous.

Poverty Prevents

There are elected women representatives from the working class who have to rely on their daily wages. Though elected women representatives have been entrusted with many responsibilities and duties there is no means of reimbursing their loss of wages. This deprives them of their livelihood and hence some are forced to use proxies in their office. V.R. Kalaiyarasi of Veppangulam Panchayat argued that the Constitution has created a space for poor scheduled caste women to occupy positions in a Panchayat but it has not created a conducive climate for them to work as leaders. She explained her plight in managing her family without economic compensation.[10]

Oriented to Lose Self

We generally expect women to be sensitive to gender issues. However, it is not true in the case of elected women representatives as they have been continuously oriented formally and informally not to be sensitive to women's issues. In the same way, *Dalit* women representatives are insensitive to *Dalit* issues. One argument put forward is that they are representatives of not only women or *Dalits* but the entire village community. Therefore, they neither address all the women's issues nor the issues of *Dalit* women effectively. Most of the training programmes concentrate on procedural matters and not on developmental issues. So there was further training in team building and vision building (Palanithurai, 2001).

Interference of MPs and MLAs

Elected women representatives face yet another problem in administration i.e., the interference of MPs and MLAs. They feel that every one has his or her own domain of action. Roles are different for representatives of different institutions. MPs and MLAs feel that the Panchayats are under their control and that local body leaders have to accept whatever they say regarding rural development. This has been raised in many fora (Palanithurai, 2000).

Lack of Managerial Skills

Managerial and administrative skills are essential for any successful administrator. Elected women representatives lack accounting and managerial skills. So they are misguided by officials and males of their families. Sometimes women are trapped on this count and thereby get involved in many cases of official misappropriation. They say that they need managerial and accounting skills to overcome such problems. To this end, the Hunger Project in India offers leadership training to women leaders in which accounting and auditing procedures have been given a major thrust. [11]

Women Leaders as Tokens

When elected women representatives meet officials with males of their family, the officials talk to the males and not to the representatives. Even the reserved seats are offered to their husbands and other males of their family and not to them. Initially, they felt humiliated, but, gradually, they started taking these insults in their stride. Only after attending training programmes, they have realised the mistake. Most of the matters transacted between their husbands and officials were not known to them. The training programmes which they attended made them understand the key issues in administration. The ignorance of women representatives is exploited at every level.

However, in local politics, muscle and money power have an upper hand. Hence, all activities are planned in the context of managing the muscle and the money. In order to overcome this problem, women have to rely on the family/caste/party leader. At a later stage, whoever comes to the rescue of the woman representative comes to the Panchayat for personal favours and obligations. When such obligations are denied, women representatives are criticised and castigated. This was reported by the Federation leader Ponnikailasam in the network meeting organised at Thiruvarur.

Social Cleavage

The caste division in villages has been another kind of hindrance to elected women representatives. While forming Self-Help Groups (SHGs) all women are united and do not entertain any cleavage. But, after forming the same and functioning for a period of time, the women are compelled by their menfolk to look at issues from the perspective of caste. As a result, many SHG groups have collapsed. In the same way, while distributing benefits to the poor, women leaders are compelled to go by caste considerations. Caste has entrenched itself everywhere and become a barrier to the smooth functioning of Panchayats. Elected women representatives often find themselves in trouble because they look at issues beyond the perspective of caste.[12]

Lack of Motivation

To perform any job, motivation is important. Elected women representatives are new to this job. All of them have not taken up this assignment willingly or voluntarily. Further, they have been facing problems without any support. There is no motivation for them. As a result, many elected women representatives are in a state of mental depression. How is this problem to be solved? Nobody knows the solution. The problem has reached such a stage that there is a search on for a counselling centre for mentally depressed elected women leaders.

Elected representatives are asked to carry out a variety of programmes and schemes. Before one starts one's work, one should know what role one has to perform. They filed their nominations not of their free volition but out of compulsion. They are not aware of the 73rd Amendment to the Constitution of India and the State Conformity Act of 1994. Without knowing the basis of decentralization of powers, they have been assigned the task of realising it in practice. Normally one would expect women's organizations to start the exercise of pepping up elected women representatives. In the absence of such an initiative, elected women representatives have taken steps to form their own associations through which they have decided to articulate their grievances and the problems they have been facing in Panchayat administration. Gandhigram Rural Institute has decided to support such activities since women's empowerment is one of the basic objectives of Gandhigram Rural Institute. Periodical meetings of women leaders have been arranged for which the institute has willingly extended its support.

Caste Discrimination

Untouchability is in practice in rural areas. For *Dalit* leaders, it becomes a problem. Whenever a *Dalit* heads the Panchayat Council and Gram Sabha, we may witness a pandemonium. *Dalit* leaders are not respected and, in many villages, the traditional leaders conduct the proceedings. In the meeting elected women representatives merely serve as spectators. Further, the two tumbler system prevails in rural areas where *Dalit* leaders are Presidents. They are not able to speak on those issues as they have developed a sense of fear. It is the duty of the Panchayats to administer social justice but, in reality, they are not able to do so. Only a few political parties highlight the issues and the plight of *Dalits*.

Dalit Women Leaders Marginalised

Dalit women representatives, unless backed by some political party, are powerless and voiceless. *Dalit* leaders are not allowed to speak and that too about the problems of *Dalits*. Even if some *Dalit* oriented decisions are taken in the Panchayat, they are not allowed to be executed. Genuine and basic facilities to *Dalits* are not allowed to be provided. In certain areas, the traditional Panchayat leaders ask the *Dalit* women representatives to hand over the office to them. In many places, the Gram Sabha is organised and conducted by the traditional Panchayat leader and the elected woman representative remains one among the spectators. She has no voice and she has to sit along with other *Dalit* women among the audience. Kalaiyarasi of Veppangulam Panchayat explained that in Sivagangai District wherever the *Dalit* leaders are able to make compromises with caste Hindu traditional Panchayat leaders, there is no problem in Panchayat administration and where there is no cooperation between the traditional and formal Panchayats, *Dalit* Panchayat leaders are in trouble.[13]

Husbands Made Tools

When the husbands of *Dalit* women representatives work on the farms of traditional or caste Hindu leaders, it is all the more easy to take over the Panchayat. The husband insists that she has to obey the dictum of the caste leaders in order to avoid conflict and to lead a peaceful life. Officials, on their part, terrorise *Dalit* women leaders to execute whatever programme they want to be executed in the rural areas, without taking the priorities into consideration. *Dalit* women representatives are easily trapped in the corrupt administrative system without any resistance. Whenever the misdeeds are found out, the poor *Dalit* women are penalised and not the officials.

Non-Cooperation of Police

It is a well known fact that police officials are most often under the control of upper classes or upper castes. Despite repeated steps being taken by *Dalit* women representatives, nothing favourable happens to *Dalits* from the side of the police. Police officials do not take cognizance of genuine grievances of *Dalit* representatives. *Dalit* representatives complain to the police about the encroachment of common properties by caste Hindus and influential party men in rural areas. As per the Government order, the police have to take action and eviction has to be carried out. But, no action is taken against the encroachers despite repeated complaints. Common property resources are the lifeline of the poor. But now several hundred acres of common properties have been encroached upon by party men. When they are identified, action is initiated by the Panchayat President. But there is no action from the police. But the police act in accordance with the Government order in Panchayats headed by caste Hindu women leaders. The basic question here is why do we have such discrimination? Caste hierarchies operate within gender hierarchies.

Design of Caste Hindus

Since *Dalit* women are poor, they hand over the Panchayat responsibility to others, mostly caste Hindu traditional leaders with a view to earning their livelihood. No one can refute this. But one has to look at the reality. Why is a poor *Dalit* woman preferred by the caste Hindu leaders, when a *Dalit* woman with a reasonably sound economic standing contests in the election? It is the design of the caste Hindus to elect a poor *Dalit* woman so that the woman could be easily co-opted in their design, whereas economically sound *Dalit* women do not succumb to their designs for exploitation since they have livelihood options.

Paucity of funds is a general problem for all Panchayats in Tamil Nadu. For *Dalit* women, it is a serious problem because they expect that a woman representing their community could do many things in favour of *Dalits*. But, contrary to expectations, elected women *Dalit* representatives can not do anything for *Dalits* due to paucity of funds. The caste Hindus do not allow elected women *Dalit* Presidents to carry out programmes earmarked for *Dalits* as they also need such programmes, for which there is no sanction from the Government. Even the allotted work for *Dalits* can not be carried out in rural areas. Hence, *Dalit* Presidents tend to acquire a poor image among the people of their own caste. They get the support of neither *Dalits* nor non-*Dalits*.

Dalit Problems not Focused

Dalit representatives face another constraint in all public fora. They realise that there are a large number of problems which have hitherto remained unattended but could now be addressed, in view of the reservation system. But it is deliberately ensured that elected women *Dalit* representatives do not take up *Dalit* issues either in the Gram Sabha or in the Panchayat Council meetings. This keeps *Dalit* representatives alienated from the *Dalit* community and they continue to be in the hands of others. Even if they are ready to take up such issues, their family members are not ready to support them as they are under the hold of the caste Hindu families. Thus, their expectations are belied and the *Dalit* youth are in an agitative mood, paving the way for social and communal conflicts in villages.

Non-Cooperation of Caste Hindus

Another significant attempt is made by caste Hindu leaders in their Panchayats through non-cooperation, which renders elected women *Dalit* leaders non-functional and unsuccessful. Thereby they declare that *Dalits,* especially women of that caste, are totally incompetent to manage public institutions. In many places they have successfully achieved this end. Wherever elected women *Dalit* representatives agree to cooperate with caste Hindus, they are allowed to carry out certain works which are not favourable to the marginalised.

Elected women representatives face yet another problem in Panchayats. The caste Hindus have cleverly created a design of usurping power from *Dalits.* Even during election time, in many Gram Panchayats, the caste Hindus resort to a ploy by which they get an assurance from among the candidates that the Vice-President would be elected from among the caste Hindus, and that too a male. After the election, the President is asked to accept the proposal that a male Vice-President could be elected from among the caste Hindus, so that they can get their cooperation. This renders the *Dalits* vulnerable as the Panchayat administration is virtually under the control of the Vice-President. The elected woman *Dalit* president has to accede to the proposals of the Vice-President. In many places, Vice-Presidents make the Presidents commit mistakes and bring them under the purview of Clause 205 of the Tamil Nadu Panchayat Act. Further, in these Panchayats infrastructure facilities are created in the settlements of caste Hindus and not in *Dalit* settlements. If this is raised in the Gram Sabha by the *Dalit* youth, the Vice-President gives a vague reply. The *Dalit* President is at the receiving end at the hands of the *Dalit* community.

Neglect of Vital Issues in Training

Training and orientation are given to elected women representatives by the Government but these programmes do not touch upon the vital issues affecting the lives of marginalized groups. In the training programme, orientation is given to the leaders to take up Government schemes and programmes. There is no scope for discussion on gender issues, issues of *Dalits* and participation of people in the planning process. Proper orientation is not given to women leaders in training programmes conducted by the Government and some of the non-governmental agencies. So, Gandhigram Rural Institute has designed a training module to train elected women Panchayat Presidents. This initiative was supported and approved by the Rajiv Gandhi Foundation (The training module which runs to 120 pages is available with the Rajiv Gandhi Chair, Gandhigram Rural Institute).

No Support Base

Another pertinent question discussed by women is the support base for women leaders. Discussions have been held on all relevant aspects based on which women leaders have taken the initiative to carry out certain schemes and programmes. They have faced a variety of problems in the field. To overcome these problems they are in need of some support organizations. But there is no such support base for women leaders. In the absence of such a support mechanism, one cannot expect exemplary achievements from the women leaders at the grassroot level.

Encroachment Encounters

As per the New Panchayat Act, the President of the Gram Panchayat can take action against encroachments. To evict an encroacher,

Panchayat Presidents have to get the village map from the village administrative officers. In many of the villages, the administrative officers do not give the village map to the Presidents of Gram Panchayats. With great difficulty the Gram Panchayat Presidents take the initiative to retrieve the common property from the encroachers. This act has incited encroachers to fight against women leaders. This is yet another challenge to elected women representatives. Menaka of Urapakkam Panchayat paid with her life for taking steps to remove encroachments. This issue was discussed in many meetings of the association of women leaders. Women leaders have exerted pressure on the Government to support the move of Panchayats to remove encroachments.

Crowd Management

Another problem that elected women representatives face is the problem of crowd management. Gram Panchayat Presidents have to convene Gram Sabha meetings four times during the course of a year. Our rural masses normally tend to shout in a crowd. Even the Speaker of the Lok Sabha is not able to manage enlightened representatives and the Legislative Assemblies do not fare any better. But in a Gram Panchayat, even if it is four hundred people in an open place, it is always a free for all. When women representatives are presiding, anti-social elements deliberately use unparliamentary words in order to drive womenfolk away. Nobody regulates the meeting, except family members of elected women representatives. When family members come to the rescue of elected women representatives other members of the Gram Sabha oppose it. But the same Gram Sabha members do not help elected women representatives while they face problems at the hands of anti-social elements. People under the influence of alcohol participate in and disturb the proceedings. But no one is ready to control them. What is the way out of this?.

Local body leaders are invited for public functions and they are asked to address the public. Many elected women representatives are not in a position to speak like others in public meetings as they do not have the required communication skills. Training in public speaking skills is the felt need of every elected woman representative. This deficiency is responsible for poor management of crowds also.

Representatives' Perception of Women's Issues

The above posited issues are problems faced by women leaders in Panchayat administration. They have perceived the problems faced by women in rural areas. The issues are classified and presented hereunder. Primarily, the aspirations and feelings of women are not respected and are not taken into consideration for decision-making. This is common both at the family level and in the community at large. There is not much difference between the rich and the poor. Gender discrimination prevails in the family, community, office, political parties, cultural and religious organisations. Women are discriminated against in providing facilities, services and benefits. From the family to the Central Government level one can find discrimination on the basis of gender. Girl children are poorly fed and malnourished. They are not given fair treatment on par with male children. Women are harassed in the family and sexually exploited in the workplace.

Girls are generally not permitted to go for higher studies or, for that matter, even beyond primary school. Women discharge dual responsibilities with great difficulty, yet, their burden is not appreciated properly. When women move beyond the routine, their workload increases with nobody to share it. For the poor women, there are no proper amenities in the workplace. Health facilities are not provided to women in the same way as they are extended to men. Women are also not sensitive to their health problems. Female infanticide and foeticide are the problems that women face in many villages. Due to non-availability of water, fuel wood, medical facilities, proper public distribution system, women are the worst victims. Women are denied property rights even though the Equal Property Rights Act has been passed by the Tamil Nadu Legislative Assembly. Women workers are paid poor wages as compared to men. Women are forced into a life of dependence. Assertive women are subjected to character assassination. Panchayats have no perspective plan for women's empowerment.

What do Women Need?

These are some of the vital issues women have perceived as problems of the elected representatives. Solutions can be found for all these problems. The women representatives themselves have identified some solutions. They are listed hereunder: (a) Proper orientation has to be given to elected women representatives by way of periodical training. (b) Women representatives are to be sensitised on issues concerning women. (c) They have to be organised at a larger level and enabled to address issues of concern on their own by creating a suitable support base. Institution-based legal support has to be provided to women who take up the struggle to administer social justice. (d) Periodic interface between successful women and women leaders who lead struggles, has to be organised. (e) Managerial skills, leadership qualities, accounting skills and communication skills have to be developed through periodic capacity-building exercises. (f) Comprehensive awareness programmes have to be conducted in rural areas on the problems of women. Information has to be provided to women representatives on all vital matters pertaining to improvement in the quality of their life. Women's participation has to be ensured in Gram Sabha meetings. (g) A Women's component plan has to be initiated at every level. (h) Stringent laws are to be enacted to deal with individuals committing atrocities against women. (i) Women segmented on the lines of political party, caste, religion and class have to be united and they should be helped to stand as a single entity. (j) As a prelude to this, elected women representatives have to be organised at state level and further federated with other state level organisations so that they will gain added strength. (k) If such a federation is organised, it can espouse the cause of women and legitimately claim political space in order to address women's issues effectively.

Where do They Stand?

Though elected women representatives face innumerable problems while discharging their duties, they continue their struggle to succeed in their mission. But their perception of their self and their desire vary from individual to individual and from group to group. There are six kinds of leaders, namely aggressive leaders, sober capacitated leaders, ambitious capacitated leaders, leaders with aspiration, leaders in a mood of withdrawal and leaders without an idea. A few party cadres and a few committed NGOs have been continuously orienting a set of leaders and extending all their support to women leaders having links with political parties and NGOs. They always exhibit an aggressive character which enables them to discharge their duties more effectively than other leaders. Twelve per cent of the representatives belong to this group.

There is yet another category of leaders, who have been oriented and trained but are not committed to any ideology or organization. But they are committed to their work. They have participated in the programmes organized by NGOs but they do not have continuous linkage with the NGOs. They are capacitated leaders concentrating much on their responsibilities and they have performed very well as they have enhanced their capacity. They have aspirations of continuing in public service, but do not aim for any specific position. Whether they win the next election or not they will remain in the public sphere. This group constitutes 22 per cent.

There is another category which is slightly different from the previous one. The capacitated leaders have concentrated much on enhancing their capacity continuously and performing their duties. While performing their duties, they see the response of the people, based on which they have a desire to continue in office. But this category has an ambition to continue in the same position, for which they have developed the art of managing people in local bodies. All their deficiencies are compensated by their public relations. Their linkages with people are strong as they have always been. Nearly 24 per cent of the leaders belong to this category.

The fourth category of leaders have a different aspiration. Though they have a number of deficiencies, by keeping themselves very active in discharging their duties, they want to demonstrate to their party leaders that they are the apt candidates for membership in the Legislative Assembly. They are always busy meeting people and building contacts. They consider the Panchayati Institution as a launching pad for their political career. Though their number is very small, they are certainly models for emulation. Eighteen per cent of the leaders have this type of aspiration.

Another category of leaders are unable to meet the challenges of their role and bear the pressures of society and their family. They have expressed their desire to withdraw from public life. These leaders were brought to public life forcefully by their husbands. In most of the cases the relationship between the husband and wife has undergone a change in the whole process of administering development through Panchayati Raj Institutions. Many husbands realise the fact that their wives have acquired the required capacity and, hence, they have to withdraw from the support space. But there is another segment of men who are determined not to allow their wives to attend to their duties on their own. Most women leaders have stated that they have been facing problems in the local body institutions because of the interference of their husbands. This factor cannot be explained to their husbands by women leaders of Panchayats on their own. This group constitutes 20 per cent of the leaders.

There is yet another category which has no idea of their role and responsibilities. They are in the hands of the males of the family, despite the pronouncements of the Government. The women leaders do not move out of their houses for public work. They do not meet people. Their husbands virtually run the show for them. They do not take this seriously. It is a money spinning device which is ably tackled by their husbands by their muscle and money power. Officials also cooperate with such leaders. They have no idea about the Panchayats and they have no aspiration to contest in the next election. If their husbands ask them to contest they will obey; otherwise, they will not bother about it. They are only 4 per cent; yet their cases have been repeatedly quoted in public. It is true that a withdrawal symptom is visible among many women leaders in local bodies. They face a volley of problems from officials, caste groups, family members and even their own political party leaders.

Yet, the majority of leaders have exhibited their determination to occupy public space. Having entered and tasted power, women leaders have come to the stage of enlisting themselves as members of various organizations to fight for their rights and legitimate spaces. In their struggle, they have identified the organizations and institutions which support empowerment of women and, through them, they are determined to continue their struggle. Further, they have started forming their own organizations and federating their organizations with other organizations. Another interesting development is that a large number of women are being trained in the Self-Help Groups (SHGs) to move over to this power domain. Women leaders have come to the public sphere and they will continue to keep their hold over institutions and try to expand their space.

Observation and Conclusion

Women have come to positions in the local bodies, as a provision has been made in the Constitution. The attitude of society towards women has started changing. But, in the process of empowering women, hurdles continue to remain. Steps are being taken by women, of their own accord, to overcome hurdles. It is a long drawn process. A structure which has been created over centuries to work against the interests of women cannot be dismantled within a short span of four or five years. It can be changed only by creating a women's movement for which this provision of one third reservation of seats for women will help. To fight against the designs of the structure, an organized movement of the masses is imperative. In order to make women achieve results in their positions an array of interventions is necessary.

Women need orientation, sensitization, capacity-building, information and counselling continuously through organizations. The on going experiments and experiences suggest that periodical training, orientation and sensitization make women leaders perform their assigned role in a better way. When women leaders respond to socio-political challenges, they are to be supported by organizations and institutions which work for their empowerment. Wherever such interventions are available, the achievements of women leaders are substantial and impressive. The Government will respond to the needs of these women leaders only when they are supported by organizations well-known for their credentials and are to be reckoned with as a force.

NOTES

1. Gram Panchayat, Block Panchayat and District Panchayats.
2. This report was published in 1941 but it was missing and later the Centre for Women Development Studies in New Delhi decided to republish the document.
3. The details of these activities are recorded in the article entitled "Women: From Equality Empowerment" by Vina Mazumdar in *Independent India: The First Fifty Years* (ed.) Hiranmay Karlekar, New Delhi: Oxford University Press. 1988, pp. 262-263.

4. A State Resource Centre would be created in Gandhigram Rural Institute. This centre would provide needed information to the Panchayat leaders through regional resource centers which would be created in different regions through NGOs.
5. For more details see Rajiv Gandhi Chair, *The Annual Convention of the Elected Women Representatives of Rural Local Bodies in Tamil Nadu*, Gandhigram: Rajiv Gandhi Chair for Panchayati Raj Studies, 2001.
6. *Ibid.*
7. Rajiv Gandhi Chair, *Report of the Training Programme Conducted for Women Presidents of Gram Panchayats in Five Districts of Tamil Nadu*, Gandhigram: Rajiv Gandhi Chair for Panchayati Raj Studies, 1998.
8. Rajiv Gandhi Chair, *Report of the Training Programme Conducted for Gram Panchayat Women Presidents of Madurai, Ramanathapuram and Pudukkottai Districts*, Gandhigram: Rajiv Gandhi Chair for Panchayati Raj Studies, 2000.
9. Rajiv Gandhi Chair, *Report of the Training Programme Conducted for Women Presidents of Gram Panchayats in Five Districts of Tamil Nadu*, Gandhigram: Rajiv Gandhi Chair for Panchayati Raj Studies, 1998.
10. Rajiv Gandhi Chair, *Report of the Training Programme Conducted for Gram Panchayat Presidents*, Gandhigram: Rajiv Gandhi Chair for Panchayati Raj Studies, 1998
11. Rajiv Gandhi Chair, *A Report on Elected Women Representatives Network Meeting*, Gandhigram: Singamma Sreenivasan Foundation, 2002.
12. Palanithurai, G. *Role of Caste Groups in New Panchayati Raj System: A Case Analysis of Tamil Nadu* presented in the UGC National Seminar organised in the University of Madras on 4th and 5th January, 2001.
13. Rajiv Gandhi Chair, *Report of the Second Annual Convention of the Elected Women Representatives of Rural Local Bodies in Tamil Nadu*, Gandhigram: Rajiv Gandhi Chair for Panchayati Raj Studies, 2002.

REFERENCES

Agnihotri, Satish (1996), "Juvenile Sex Ratios in India: A Disaggregated Analysis" *Economic and Political Weekly* (special number), 28, December.

Altekar, A.S. (1978), *The Position of Women: Hindu Civilization*, New Delhi: Motilal Banarasidass.

Asia-Pacific Centre for Women and Development (1979), *Feminist Ideology and Structures: Report of an International Seminar*, Bangkok, UNESCAP.

Batliwala, Srilatha (1996), "Empowerment of Women's Autonomy, Proceedings of a Consultation on Women's Health and Rights: Rethinking Population", *HIVDS Technical Report Series*, 1:4.

Batliwala, Srilatha, Anitha B.K., Gurumurthy Anita and Wali Chandana. S. (1998), *Status of Rural Women in Karnataka*, Bangalore: National Institute of Advanced Studies.

Batliwala Srilatha (1995), "The Meaning of Women's Empowerment", *Women's World*, pp. 23-34.

Buch, Nirmala (1998), "Decentralized Governance, Women's Participation and Poverty Eradication, *Women and Political Empowerment* (eds.), B. Mohanty and S. Haider, New Delhi: Institute of Social Sciences, p. 82.

Government of India (1975), *Towards Equality: Report of the Committee on the Status of Women in India*.

Government of India, *The Fifth Five Year Plan*, New Delhi: Planning Commission, 1976.

Government of India, *The Sixth Five Year Plan*, New Delhi: Planning Commission, 1980.

Kasthuri, Leela and Mazumdar Vina (1994), *Women and Indian Nationalism*, Delhi: Vikas.

Krishnaswamy, P. (2001), "Women Panchayati Leaders More Sinned Against than Sinning", *The New Indian Express*, 22, Aug, p. 3.

Mazumdar, Vina (1998) "Women: From Equality to Empowerment" in *Independent India: The First Fifty Years* (ed.), Hiranmay Karlekar, New Delhi: Oxford University Press.

Moser Caroline (1989), "Gender Planning in Third World: Meeting Practical and Strategic Gender Needs" *World Development*, Vol. 17: No. 11.

Narasimhan, Sakuntala (1999), *Empowering Women: An Alternative Strategy from Rural India*, New Delhi: Sage Publications, pp. 44-45.

Palanithurai, G. (2000), *Report on Capacity-Building for Gram Panchayat Presidents*, Gandhigram: Rajiv Gandhi Chair for Panchayati Raj Studies.

Palanithurai, G. (2001), *Report of the Workshop on Networking of Associations of Elected Women Representatives in Local Bodies*, Gandhigram: Rajiv Gandhi Chair for Panchayati Raj Studies.

Palanithurai, G. (2001), *Report on the Capacity-Building for Weaker Sections in New Panchayati Raj System*, Gandhigram: Rajiv Gandhi Chair for Panchayati Raj Studies.

Palanithurai, G. (2001), *Capacity-Building for Local Body Leaders*, New Delhi: Concept Publishing Company.

Sahay, Sushama (1998), *Women Empowerment: Approaches and Strategies*, New Delhi: Discovery Publishing House, pp. 8-9.

Sharma, Kumud (1992), "Grassroots Organizations and Women's Empowerment: Some Issues in the Contemporary Debate", *Samya Shakti*, Vol. 6, Delhi, CWDS.

Sen, Gita (1994), "Poverty, Economic Growth and Gender Equity : The Asian and Pacific Experience" in *Gender Economic Growth and Poverty* (ed.), Heyzer Nocleen and Sen Gita, New Delhi: Kali for Women.

Sen, Gita and Grown Caren (1987), *Development Crises and Alternative Visions: Third World Perspectives*, New York: Monthly Review Press.

4

Leadership Training for Elected Women Representatives

Introduction

The enactment of the 73rd Constitutional Amendment Act in India has created a significant change in the political life of rural women. 33.3 per cent reservation of seats in the rural local bodies for women has provided opportunity for women to exercise the political power for the socio-economic development of their area. This critical mass of women is expected to perform a critical function, and thereby, the process of development would take a new turn and women's participation in governance would produce far-reaching implications in the lives of the people. The decentralization process has opened up opportunities for women and other marginalized groups to influence the process of governance. This is the greatest experiment in the contemporary situation by transferring decision-making power to one million elected women local-government representatives. The new dispensation has opened an opportunity for many women with different socio-economic background to climb up the ladder of power with different set of limitations and disabilities. However, there are a variety of barriers to women hailing from marginalized sections exercising their powers[1]. Really, it is a challenge to work for the social, economic and political empowerment of women, particularly those from marginalized sections. No doubt, it is necessary to work for the goal of empowering women for which the oppressive power of the existing gender relations is to be exposed and challenged.[2] Further, the gender relations have to be reshaped.[3] The critical mass will be able to perform the critical function only if they are oriented, conscientised and trained in the methodology of deconstruction and reconstruction of gender relations. Since most of the women representatives have been first timers in occupying political spaces, it is imperative that they be given opportunities for training and capacity-building that informs them, strengthens and recontextualises their skills and capacities, and empowers them to become effective leaders. Given the fact that the Panchayat reforms were the product of Government fiat, the extent of which women benefited from these reforms depended upon their prior history of activism [4]. Since most of the women are new to political space, a range of factors hinder women's participation in politics including inexperience in politics and lack of exposure to it, illiteracy, family responsibilities and objections from family members, restrictive social norms, lack of enabling environment for women and lack of confidence for interacting with the public. Therefore, in order to ensure women's performance better in the governance, capacity-building measures and support systems for women should be made available. It is unfortunate that, in India, capacity-building is not a serious issue for the representatives of the people who determine the fate of millions of people. However, in the Panchayati Raj scenario, it has been felt that, to manage the Panchayats, training is essential even though there is no training policy and no conscious steps have been taken by the Government to build the capacity of the elected representatives of the people in the grassroots institutions.[5] In this situation, the Rajiv Gandhi Chair for Panchayati Raj Studies at Gandhigram Rural Institute took a series of steps to prepare a training manual to train the Panchayat leaders. The Chair decided to give training for Elected Women Representatives separately because if they were combined with men they felt that men will dominate the whole proceeding and they won't allow women to raise their doubts and clarifications. Moreover, the input given to the women is different from men as they are new entrant arena to the political.

Collaboration

To increase the efficiency of an individual in performing assigned roles and responsibilities continuous capacity-building is imperative. The success of the first Government, Local Self Government, depends on a number of factors in which capacity-building plays an important role. In Tamil Nadu the Gram Panchayat Presidents have to perform twin roles, namely that of the elected Panchayat leader and that of the executive authority. Unless their managerial skill is improved there can be no effective delivery of services to the people in the Panchayats. It has been the lament of the leaders that they are not properly oriented in Panchayat administration and they are not provided with needed information. To overcome this obstacle, the Rajiv Gandhi Chair has conducted capacity-building exercises for Gram Panchayat leaders of thirteen districts.

> Before the commencement of this exercise in the eight districts, an order was issued by the Director of Rural Development of Government of Tamil Nadu by which the District administrations were asked to make use of this opportunity and conduct the capacity building exercise for Gram Panchayat leaders. The District Panchayat Secretary was made the nodal officer for training to help the Rajiv Gandhi Chair. Accordingly the District Collectors were approached by the Coordinator of the Rajiv Gandhi Chair to help the team ensure attendance in the training programme. Highly enthusiastic, energetic and committed District Collectors took steps through their officials to mobilize the leaders to attend the training programme. They insisted that, in the training programme, social development issues had to be discussed and the Panchayat leaders were to be sensitized on social development issues.

Orders were passed and instructions were given to the Assistant Director for Panchayats and Block Development Officers that they had to send the Panchayat leaders for training. For each Block, one Deputy Block Development Officer was assigned the duty of ensuring attendance in the training programme on all the three days. Every day the earmarked officer took attendance and reported to the Assistant Director of Panchayats about the progress of the training programme through phone.

Frame Work of Capacity-Building

The Rajiv Gandhi Chair for Panchayati Raj Studies Women Leadership workshop aims at building-capacity among Elected Women Representatives to the maximum. It adopts the above framework for building-capacity.

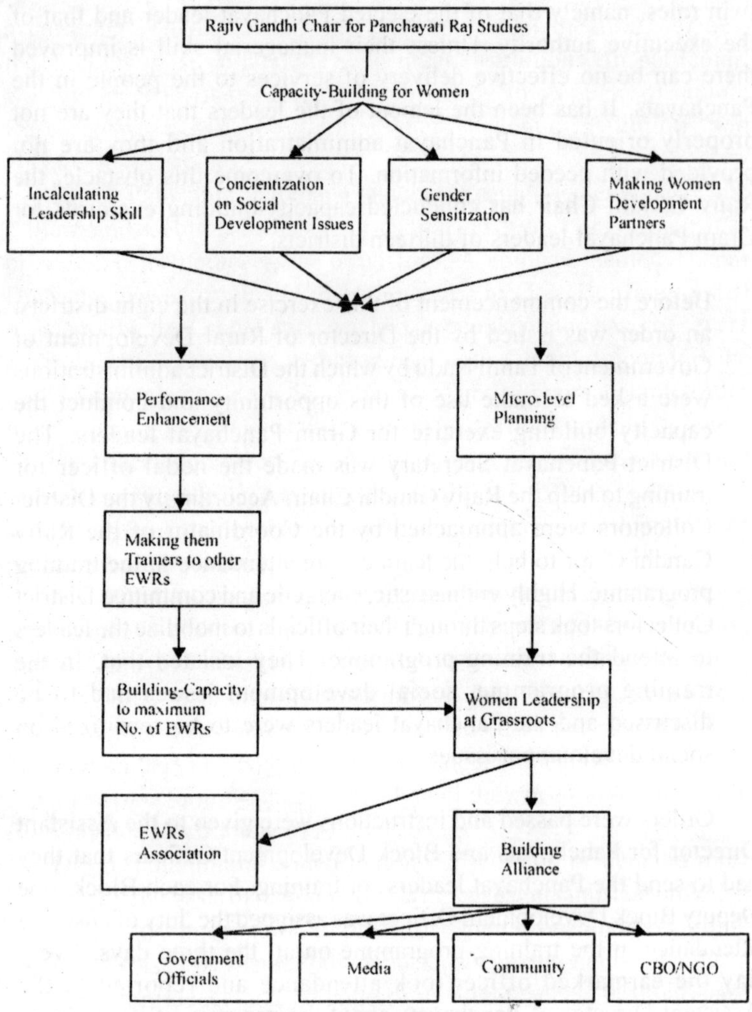

Rajiv Gandhi Chair for Panchayati Raj Studies acts as a catalyst in women representatives and empowers them to bring necessary changes in their lives as well as the life of the community at the grassroots, where they are elected as leaders. Rajiv Gandhi Chair for Panchayati Raj Studies also sensitizes and concretizes the mindset of the Elected Women Representatives on gender issues and social-development issues. Rajiv Gandhi Chair for Panchayati Raj Studies aims at not only creating vision for the Elected

Women Representatives but also creates vision for the future of the community. To convert these visions into reality, the Elected Women Representatives are expected to take the process of planning. In the planning process, they explore the different stages. In the first stage they were made to realize the present scenario and then they were made to create a vision for the future. The vision is a statement of the future that is possible to achieve and it brings them to a new level in the quality of life. Based on their vision, the Elected Women Representatives are assisted in creating a micro-level planning for their Panchayat to address the issues like malnutrition, under weight birth of the child, equal status for women and children, health of women and children, freedom from exploitation, education for all, income generating activities, food security, importance of realizing a plastic-free society, importance of caring pregnant women, steps to be taken by the Panchayats regarding health of all adolescents and children, personal hygiene, how to dispose human excreta safely, how to dispose solid wastes, importance of nutrition, role of women in social and economic development, realizing women subjugation is not their fault but it is because of the social conditions prevailing for so many years and this is an opportunity to realize this and make other women in the society to realize this. Rajiv Gandhi Chair for Panchayati Raj Studies also educates women on the importance of building alliance with the media, CBOs/NGOs, Government Officials to carry out the activities successfully and also to access the information and to disseminate their successes and grievances to the other members of the society. In the meantime, the Elected Women Representatives realized the importance of forming informal groups among themselves to share their experiences and also to gain strength among themselves. This group, in the course of time evolved as a pressure and formal structure. Thus, Rajiv Gandhi Chair for Panchayati Raj Studies helps the women at grassroots to create a vision for the future of the village through PRIs and Rajiv Gandhi Chair for Panchayati Raj Studies made women leaders realize that they have equal opportunity, power and responsibility to ensure the well-being of the entire community and they can address all the social-development issues to improve the living condition of the village. Rajiv Gandhi Chair for Panchayati Raj Studies has given Elected Women Representatives an opportunity to build an alliance with other agents in the society to fulfill their commitment towards society.

Objectives of the Capacity-Building

The main objectives of the programme is to enable the Elected Women Representatives to realize their commitments in the political space. This can be outlined as follows:

- Develop a sense of self-esteem and dignity.
- Make a shift from a mindset of "I cannot" to "I can".
- Instill a sense of political citizenship, fundamental rights and responsibilities that is crucial in making them effective leaders.
- Articulate a vision for their communities.
- Acquire the skills needed to be effective Panchayat leaders like familiarizing them with the rules and regulations, various schemes and programmes of the Government, management of finance and accounts of the Panchayats etc.
- Emphasize the importance of the participation of women in regular meetings of the Panchayats and Gram Sabhas.
- Create a sense of solidarity with others (e.g. Self-Help Groups) committed to this cause.

Based on the above said objectives Rajiv Gandhi Chair for Panchayati Raj Studies is expecting to create the following results:

- Enhancing the leadership qualities of the Elected Women Representatives by eliciting leadership skill in action, and empowering them to bring about the necessary changes in their lives, their villages and their country, through the Panchayati Raj Institutions.
- *Dignity and self-hood*: Women taking the capacity-building exercise develop a sense of self-hood, self-esteem, dignity, power and importance.
- *Subjugation and lack of progress*: That the women came to see that the subjugation that all women are subjected to is not their fault—but is a systematic, societal condition—and it is holding back progress in their country.
- *Personal role*: That the women have the feeling of not being able to back away from who they are and their key role for the future of their families and of India.

- *Personal potential and ability*: That the women come away with the feeling that this can be done, that they will do it.
- *Grounding and connectedness*: That the women are located in their villages and in India, and feel a sense of connectedness to the other women in the country.
- *Political citizenship*: That the women experience being citizens of a great country with basic rights and responsibilities.
- *Opportunity*: That the women see that they have been chosen by their fellow villagers and entrusted by the Constitution to lead their villages to achieve a healthy and productive life. They have the opportunity, power and responsibility to ensure the well-being of everyone in their villages.
- *Vision*: That the women create a vision of the future, and work to make this vision a reality by exploring the statutes in the planning process.
- *Support structure*: That the women leave the capacity-building programme with a system of on-going support and empowerment in place, including the creation of women's collectives and access to powerful information etc.

Methodology

It was a fully residential programme. The Elected Women Representatives had to stay for five days in the campus of Gandhigram Rural Institute. Of the five days, three days would be devoted to Panchayat administration and two days to social development issues. Subjects such as the bases of decentralization of powers in the context of the globalization of the economy, Panchayat, finance, common-property resource management, people's participation, micro-level planning, economic development, accounting and auditing procedures, Gram Sabha and its implications, social justice and the implications of reservation of seats for women and *Dalits* were covered in three days. Social development issues such as sanitation, water supply, gender bias, child care, pre- and post-natal care, school enrollment, child labour, RCH and other issues were covered in the remaining two days of the five-day programme.

Originally, the capacity-building programme initiated by Rajiv Gandhi Chair for Panchayati Raj Studies was only for three days. In order to create a cordial atmosphere efforts were taken to introduce the women leaders to each other and to get to know each other as people with common struggles and experiences. Then their role as political citizens and social citizens were explained. The vision building exercises, opportunities of Panchayati Raj Institutions and steps in the planning process and making vision a reality were taught. Thirdly, the development of an on-going support structure was discussed. The Rajiv Gandhi Chair for Panchayati Raj Studies which has committed itself towards the empowerment of Elected Women Representatives extended the training programme for two more days to sensitize women on social development issues and management of Panchayats.

Trainers delivered lectures in the beginning of each sessions. After the lecture there was a discussion among the trainers on the lecture. Apart from these lectures, focused-group lectures were also given in the particular topic and they discussed intensively. Role plays, games, one to one discussions also were arranged. The trainers were divided into groups to prepare a vision document for the Panchayat. Doubt clarification sessions on Panchayati Raj Administration were conducted in the late evenings. The trainees also came up with their own solutions for various problems in group discussions. It is very difficult to understand the Government rules and orders even by the literates. So, special sessions were arranged for them to understand and interpret those Government rules and orders. Role models like the President of Kuthambakam Village Panchayat Mr. Ilango, the President of Keerapalayam Panchayat Mr. Panneerselvam were invited to share their experience and this motivated the Elected Women Representatives. The Dindigul District Watershed model was considered as one of the best models in Tamil Nadu. So, field visit was arranged to the watershed areas in Dindigul. Apart from this, many innovative models of Rural Development have been developed in Gandhigram Rural Institute and Gandhigram Trust and the trainees were taken to these places to get inspiration. Overall, the workshop was a participatory exercise where trainees were not treated just as "learners" but as "leaders-in-the-making".

Table 4.1: Capacity-Building Exercise of the Elected Women Representatives

Day	*Contents of the Programme*
1	1. Registration and Personal Counselling
	2. Principles of Decentralization, 73rd Constitutional Amendment Act
	3. Tamil Nadu Panchayat Act, 1994
	4. Gram Panchayat Administration: Duties, Responsibilities and Power
	5. Gram Sabha and People's Participation
2	1. Multi-level planning in Gram Panchayat—Discussion
	2. Integration of Panchayat Plan and Sectoral Programme
	3. Common-Property Resource Management
	4. Protection of Natural Resources
3	1. Financial Management, Finance and Financial Resources
	2. Maintenance of Accounts and Records and Audit Procedures
	3. Social Development and Social Justice
	4. Vision-Building Exercise
	5. Leadership-Building
4	1. Status of Indian Women/Rural Women
	• Social Citizenship
	• Society and Family Related Issues faced by Women
	• Problem Solving Process
	• Gender Equality Role of Individual
	2. Total Rural Sanitation
	3. Social Development
	• Listing of issues
	• Role of Women in Social Development
	• Role of Panchayat in Social Development
	4. Reproductive Child Health
	5. Role of Panchayat in Economic Development
5	1. Computer Orientation
	2. Exposure Visit to Village Panchayat

Apart form the above said input, the trainers briefed the Elected Women Representatives about the changes which they need in their behaviour, like how to keep their surroundings clean, use the toilets in their houses, how to sit in the meetings, how to behave in the crowd, interact with officials and how to ask questions in the meetings and also the trainers regularly interact of with them about the new culture that they have to bring about in their Panchayats.

Resource Materials

Rajiv Gandhi Chair for Panchayati Raj Studies considers this workshop not only for training women as leaders but they also want to provide all necessary information to the women leaders to run the Panchayat administration successfully to bring overall development in their Panchayats. The participants were given a manual written by Dr. G. Palanithurai entitled "New Panchayati Raj System in Tamil Nadu : Rules and Schemes". This manual consists of the updated Tamil Nadu Panchayats Act, Government rules, Government orders pertaining to Gram Panchayat administration, State and Central Government schemes for rural development. Apart from this manual, a small booklet containing the roles and responsibilities of the Gram Panchayat Presidents were given for easy understanding of the administration. The Charter of the new Panchayati Raj Institution system was also given to the trainees. While handling classes the trainers used flip charts and OHPs. To realize their roles and importance of being grassroots leaders, a film entitled "Namma Ooru Panchayat" was screened.

Table 4.2: Number of Elected Women Representatives who attended the Capacity-Building Programme

Sl. No.	*Name of the District*	*Total No. of Women Presidents*	*No. of Presidents Attended the Programme*	*Percentage of Women Presidents*
1.	Pudukottai	172	140	81
2.	Dindigul	105	100	95
3.	Tiruchirappalli	132	131	99
4.	Sivagangai	153	112	73
5.	Ramanathapuram	147	116	79
6.	Theni	48	43	90
7.	Karur	49	49	100
8.	Virudhunagar	144	103	72
9.	Tuticorin	140	67	48
10.	Cuddalore	229	168	73
11.	Tirunelveli	147	104	71
12.	Thiruvarur	147	62	42
13.	Erode	130	50	38
	Total	1743	1245	71

Source: Computed.

Resource Persons

The retired higher level officials of Rural Development were engaged in this programme to teach about the Panchayat administration. Apart from them, the professors of Gandhigram Rural Institute were asked to cover the focused topics like gender, governance, and social development issues, health and computer literacy. Rajiv Gandhi Chair for Panchayati Raj Studies Staff of Tamil Nadu dealt with the vision exercise and they stayed with the trainees throughout the exercise to ensure overall personality development. They also counselled them personally and made them realize their potentials and strengths.

Before the commencement of the training programme the participants were asked to fill up a questionnaire. This was done in order to assess their level of understanding on decentralized governance and Panchayati Raj Institutions. Similarly after the completion of five days training programme, their understanding on decentralized governance and Panchayati Raj Institutions is tested through a questionnaire.

Pre-Training Evaluation

A total of 1743 Gram Panchayat women leaders participated in the training programme. Of them 62 per cent had been elected for the first time. So they were not aware of Panchayat activities. The women leaders contested in the election and won with the support of their family and community. When they contested in the election, they were not aware of anything about the Panchayats. Only after assuming office and contacting the officials did they come to know that Panchayat leaders have to carry out certain activities in the Panchayats. They were not even aware of the major provisions of the 1994 Tamil Nadu Panchayats Act. By making use of this opportunity, they have developed leadership qualities and established contact with the officials. Their shyness and inhibitions have disappeared. Accordingly they showed awareness of many Government schemes and stated that they had received this information from Government officers. The majority of them did not know the meaning of the concept of decentralization. They thought that the new Panchayati Raj System is meant to implement the schemes and programmes of the Central and State Governments. Even though they knew a few of the provisions, they were not aware of the full implications of the Panchayati Raj Act of 1994.

When they were inquired about who motivated them to contest in the election, more than 50 per cent of the Presidents said that it was their husbands, family members or relatives and a very few only said that it was the people. More than 40 per cent of the Presidents said that they had been acting as proxies till then. Some mentioned NGOs while some said that they contested in the election out of their own interest. Some referred to motivation by the local MLAs because of their popularity in the village and their association with political parties.

When they were asked about what factors contributed to their success in the election divergent views emerged and some of them are listed below: (i) the confidence reposed in them by the people; (ii) familiarity in the village because of their involvement in public activity by performing social work; (iii) educational background; (iv) social and political involvement of the family members; (v) people believed that she was the right person to fulfil their desires and dreams to make their village a model one; (vi) village and family members' support; (vii) their strong will power and their desire to perform in public; (viii) their honesty and confidence in themselves; (ix) involvement in grievance redressal of the people; (x) they were honest and led a disciplined life; (xi) public cooperation, their approach to the public, personal character; and (xii) fulfilling the basic needs of the people.

Making use of this opportunity they had developed their personality and acquired the following new traits: (a) leadership quality; (b) realizing the roles and responsibilities of the President; (c) respecting the village people, treating all equally, being kind to people; (d) confidence, perseverance and endurance; (e) serving the poverty-stricken people and helping them lead a decent human life; (f) functioning on the principle of consensus and inculcating the spirit of tolerance; (g) functioning without any bias and working for the welfare of all sections of society; (h) qualities which are very much required to continue in social life; (i) functioning as an agent between the Government and the people; (j) administrative capacity; (k) bringing about justice for suppressed women and concentrating on their upliftment; and (l) readiness to take on any contingency.

Next, their idea about the new Panchayati Raj System was enquired into and many were not able to spell out the basic structure of the new Panchayati Raj System. Their answers were varied: (i) to fulfil the basic needs of the people since the Central and the State

Government could not do it; (ii) for safeguarding common property resources; (iii) to implement Government schemes through the Gram Sabha; (iv) three tier system of local government, (v) list of 29 subjects in the Eleventh Schedule; (vi) ensuring social justice and economic equality; (vii) reservation for SC/ST people; (viii) reservation for women; (ix) importance of women's participation in political life; (x) power devolution to make Panchayats as self-governing institutions; (xi) Tamil Nadu Panchayats Act 1994; and (xii) State Election Commission.

The next question asked was about the 73rd Amendment. About 40 per cent Women Panchayat Presidents were aware of the features of the 73rd Amendment Act. The other didn't know them and they were attending the training programme to learn them. A few clearly mentioned some of the basic features as: (a) Gram Sabha; (b) reservation for women and *Dalits;* (c) election every five years; (d) three tier system; (e) self-governing institutions; (f) devolution of powers on 29 subjects (11th Schedule), and (g) planning at grassroots, planning by the people in the Gram Sabha for the village.

The next question was about the roles and functions of the Gram Panchayat Presidents according to the Local Government Act of Tamil Nadu. Of the total participants, very few spelt out their roles and functions and they were: (a) to provide basic amenities like safe drinking water, roads, streetlights, health and sanitation; (b) construction of public toilets for women and sensitizing people towards constructing individual toilets; (c) the main function of the Gram Sabha is to decide the basic facilities for the Panchayat with the participation of the people; (d) creating consensus among the people to enable the President of Panchayats and the members to pass resolutions is the function of the Gram Sabha; (e) the Gram Sabha is a forum to share individual opinion among others; (f) the Gram Sabha is a forum to create awareness among people about social issues; (g) the Gram Sabha is convened to inform the people about the income and expenditure of the Panchayat; (h) to convene and to chair Panchayat meetings every month and to convene Gram Sabha meeting for four times in a year; (i) to collect taxes properly, to regulate and to monitor the functioning of the PDS, to plan for the Panchayat (long-term and short-term plan); (j) to maintain and properly utilize common property resources; (k) to implement the projects and schemes of State and Central Governments; (l) the main function of the Gram Sabha is to select the beneficiaries for Government schemes; (m) the Gram Sabha has to pass resolutions on various demands of the people; (n) there is a mandatory quorum for the Gram Sabha meeting; (o) participation of SHGs in the Gram Sabha is important; (p) the Gram Sabha is convened to share divergent views and to work for consensus; (q) the Gram Sabha takes care of social audit, preparing annual plan; (r) the Gram Sabha meets to inform people about various Government schemes and plans; and (s) the Gram Sabha gives a good opportunity to the backward and weaker sections and women to voice their problems and take decisions.

The next question asked was about the people's participation in the Gram Panchayat. Most of the women Presidents were satisfied with the people's participation in the activities of the Gram Panchayat. Some were very much concerned about the disturbance in the Gram Sabha. Because people are very enthusiastically and eagerly participating in Gram Sabha meetings people say that all rural development schemes must be implemented through Panchayats. People are coming forward to put forth their requirements in the general meeting and particularly, women are more articulate in expressing their needs. The Panchayat Presidents are very much concerned about embarrassing situations like some of the resolutions passed in the meeting not being implemented due to lack of cooperation from the officials. Due to financial constraints the Presidents could not fulfil their demands. People used to ask the Presidents about the action taken on the resolutions passed in the earlier Gram Sabha meeting. But the Presidents couldn't fulfil their demands. In spite of all this, people are cooperating with the Panchayats fully. This shows that cooperation from the Government is required to fulfil their dreams. As for their attendance at previous training programmes only 20 per cent of the Women Panchayat Presidents had attended training programmes conduced by various Government departments and Gandhigram Rural Institute. The remaining were new to the training programme.

Next, they were asked about the various schemes offered by the State and Central Governments. All the participants answered this question and mentioned a few schemes as given below: (a) SGRY and SJRY; (b) Swajalthara; (c) IAY; (d) TRSP; (e) rainwater harvesting; (f) Indira Awaz Yojana; (g) Sarva Siksha Abhiyan; (h) PMGSY; (i) TANWA; (j) schemes related to the disabled; (k) Rural Sanitation Programme; (l) Namakku Naame Thittam; (m) Chulah; (n) Women and Children's Sanitary Complex Scheme; (o) MLA and MP constituency fund; (p) Anna Marumalarchi Thittam; (q) housing facilities; and (r) drinking water scheme.

Post-Training Evaluation

With the help of resource persons and specialists the utility of the training programme was assessed through a questionnaire which was administered at the end of the training programme. The women Panchayat Presidents responded to all the questions. The first question was about the objectives of the Panchayati Raj System. The responses of the Women Panchayat Presidents are given below: (a) to provide the basic amenities in the village; (b) to plan for the welfare of the people in the Gram Sabha with the help of the people; (c) to create a village based on the vision of the late Prime Minister Rajiv Gandhi; (d) to ensure the participation of women and weaker sections of the society in governance; (e) to make sure to take the Government schemes to the needy; (f) to create a just society with economic equity; (g) to create awareness about common property resources and to maintain the same; (h) to provide good governance in grassroots democracy; (i) to create awareness about education and provide education to all; (k) to empower the people to prioritize their own needs; (l) to ensure the development of each family; (m) to devolve powers and finances directly to the people; (n) to develop the village socially and economically; (o) to attain self sufficiency and to be self reliant; and (p) to conduct election for grassroots governance without any lapse.

A few respondents noted that the financial position in the Panchayati Raj Institutions is very bad because the disbursement of funds is delayed. They also said that political parties tend to interfere in the New Panchayati Raj System. The second question was about "what is meant by the term 'decentralization'? The responses of the women Panchayat leaders were: (a) Constituting State Election Commission, Finance Commission and Planning Committee; (b) reservation for weaker sections of society such as *Dalits* and women in the Panchayats; (c) power given to weaker sections of society to take decisions on the issues affecting their life; (d) roles and responsibilities relating to governance are relevant to the community as a whole, not to just the elected representatives; (e) to plan for those who live below the poverty line; (f) three-tier system; (g) work on 29 subjects; (h) ensuring people's participation through the Gram Sabha; (i) to implement Government plans and schemes; and (j) to mobilize funds on their own to perform their functions.

Despite decentralization of powers inadequate devolution of finance prevents Panchayats from fulfilling the goals of development in such areas as education, drinking water supply, environment protection, women and child welfare and health facilities. A few respondents also stated that they had trouble in mobilizing participation. The third question concerning the impact of decentralization drew the following responses: (a) Panchayats can provide the basic amenities to people; (b) Panchayats can alleviate poverty through economic activities; and (c) Panchayats can solve problems and evolve good solutions to them.

The fourth question was about their roles and responsibilities. After the training, the participants were more conscious of their roles and responsibilities than before. They knew the roles and responsibilities to be discharged by the Presidents, especially women leaders. They admitted that, even without power and money, the Presidents can play a positive role in transforming the rustic folk. This they felt was the impact of the training. Now they realize their role in propagating the importance of pre-natal and post-natal care, because this is very much required for a healthy society. Awareness about health and sanitation should also be created and this will be the sole responsibility of the Panchayat Presidents to free society from chronic diseases. They can seek assistance from the medical officer and sanitary inspectors. They also know about the importance of SHGs and other social organizations like youth club and they have acquired basic information on how to work with them and use them for developmental activities. The other functions and responsibilities that they indicated were: (a) providing basic amenities is the primary role of Panchayats; (b) resource mobilization and management; (c) managing common properties; (d) managing natural resources; (e) proper channelization of functions and giving priority to urgent needs—value neutral administration; (f) to work for the cause of gender equality and solve gender related issues; (g) to perform the obligatory functions; (h) to give attention to the provision of quality education; (i) to implement Government schemes and programmes and monitor them through the Gram Sabha; and (j) to conduct regular Panchayat meetings and Gram Sabha meetings effectively.

The fifth question was about the roles and responsibilities of the Gram Panchayat. The participants were more conscious of the Gram Panchayat's roles and responsibilities than before. They mentioned the following: (a) convening the Gram Sabha meeting regularly; (b) proper implementation of Gram Sabha resolutions; (c) working towards creating a healthy society; (d) to create awareness about the Gram Sabha; (e) sending all children to schools and balwadis; (f) proper implementation of plans/schemes of the Government; (g) public grievance solving mechanism; (h) making the official concerned participate in the Gram Sabha meeting; (i) making women join various committees; (j) propagating the importance of Gram Sabha to the people; (k) working on consensus based public opinion in preparing annual plan; and (l) district administration has to recognize the resolutions passed in the Gram Sabha meeting.

With regard to making the people participate in the activities of the Panchayat to improve the Panchayat administration, they suggested the following: (a) mobilizing people to undertake environmental activities; (b) providing amenities like road, light, drainage, streetlight and involve the people in maintaining them; (c) involving the people in the maintenance of sanitary complex, burial and burning ground, library building, recreation building etc. (d) mobilizing the people through SHGs and youth clubs; (e) making the people participate in some crucial activities, e.g. maintenance of OHT, road, common property resources; and (e) various committees may be organised and village people may be appointed to each Committee, e.g. Peace Committee, Vigilance Committee, Health Committee, Education Committee, Planning Committee and Agricultural Committee.

The next question asked was about the maintenance of the common property resources. They gave the following replies: (a) to start agriculture and small industries in the poramboke land; (b) to implement wasteland development programme in the poramboke land; (c) to grow plants for better yield for the Panchayats; (d) creating awareness among the public to safeguard public properties; (e) to prevent encroachment on common properties; (f) auctioning and licensing the common property resources for proper maintenance—the amount realized can be used for welfare activities; (g) avoid exploiting resources like sand and mines; (h) hand them over to the village committee to manage the same; (i) making use of poramboke land with the help of the Revenue Department; (j) giving power to the Panchayat to punish the misusers and exploiters of the common property resources; and (k) maintaining sacred groves.

To the next question on how one should go about augmenting the financial resources of the Gram Panchayats, the respondents gave the following suggestions: (a) revise taxes and ensure their prompt collection; (b) people's contribution in the form of donations; (c) increase the number of small scale industries and plant trees on Panchayat land; (d) encourage and collaborate with SHGs to start economic activities; (e) increasing the number of fishing ponds; and (f) find out the various Government schemes and financial assistance available for Panchayat activities.

Most of the Presidents stated that their performance was affected due to lack of funds. After attending the training programme the participants were confident because now they knew about various sources and methods for increasing revenue. The next question was about the steps that should be followed in the planning process. Most of the respondents gave suggestions, on what to do in the planning process and who should be included in the planning process: (a) the Planning Committee should plan for basic needs; (b) plans should cover 5-year periods; (c) convening Gram Sabha to prepare a plan; (d) the needs should be prioritized before detailing of the plan; (e) the availability of resources must be taken into account; (f) identifying the beneficiaries in the Gram Sabha meeting; and (g) the Gram Sabha should be convened to prepare the plan.

The next question was about the attention given to equipping themselves to maintain accounts and records. Before the training 80 per cent of the Panchayat Presidents did not know the accounting procedure. They thought that the accounts are to be maintained by the Panchayat clerk. But now the Presidents know that they are responsible for properly maintaining accounts. They gave the following suggestions for proper maintenance of accounts: (a) maintain bills and vouchers properly; (b) atleast twice a month check entire accounts, i.e., 31 registers, bills and vouchers; (c) proper and regular collection of house tax and immediately deposit it daily in the bank, updating the pass book regularly; and (d) proper inspection of activities/records.

With regard to social development, the respondents suggested that the following activities are to be undertaken in each village: (a) create awareness about girls education; (b) ensure child health care, immunization and nutrition; (c) ensure public health and sanitation; (d) ensure pre-natal and post-natal care; (e) maintain harmony in the society; (f) increase awareness about cleanliness among school children; (g) increase the number of Self-Help Groups; (h) develop the weaker sections, particularly Dalits and women; (i) ensure proper understanding among various communities and caste groups; (j) work against the practice of dowry, female infanticide and foeticide; (k) sensitizing women regarding gender issues; (l) enhance the production of all agricultural commodities; (m) promote cultivation of medicinal plants; and (n) utilize the assistance and guidance of NGOs, SHGs and other social organizations.

The next question was about how to develop leadership qualities. Their suggestions were as follows: (a) working for the whole community without bias; (b) ability to convince people; and (c) self confidence, listening capacity.

The next question was about the strategies to enhance the economic position of the Panchayats. The participants suggested the following: (a) increasing and collecting 100 per cent taxes properly; (b) establishing more number of SHGs and giving training to people to establish small business; (c) arranging self-employment for youth; (d) associating with organizations concerned with economic development such as NGOs; (e) increasing agricultural productivity in Panchayat lands; (f) ensuring the participation of the people in social development; (g) propagating the importance of family planning; (h) planning to make use of dry land and poramboke land; and (i) developing orchards/groves and generating income through them.

The next question was about the means of developing the Adi-Dravidan community. On this 90 per cent of respondents said that it is important to understand the problems of the Adi-Dravidans and SC people before trying to solve them. They also stated that it is important to implement Government welfare schemes properly. Efforts must be made towards the creation of awareness about education, child marriage, environment and sanitation. These efforts should also focus on employment opportunities.

Next came the most important topic of women's empowerment. All the women Presidents were concerned about the upliftment of their own segment. They came out with important suggestions to empower women. They were: (a) forming SHGs to motivate women to achieve economic development through access to loan facilities; (b) creating awareness about women's education, child marriage and other related issues; (c) improving women's self-confidence to make them capable of decision-making; (d) implementing Government's Women's Welfare Schemes; (e) creating employment opportunity for the youth; (f) creating awareness about female infanticide as the first step towards its eradication; (g) creating awareness about health and hygiene, pre-natal and post-natal care, child education and child care; (h) creating awareness about rainwater harvesting and toilet usage; (i) creating awareness among women about the implications of illicit liquor; (j) acting primarily President and only secondarily as executive authority; (k) regularizing the Panchayat electricity fees; (l) special plan for women's upliftment in the Gram Sabha; (m) training women in self-employment and educating them about the importance of family planning and small savings; and (n) implementing special upliftment plan for destitute women and disabled ones.

The final question was about the list of priorities of Panchayat activities. On this 90 per cent of the respondents said that the following were their primary concern: women's development, children's development, education, toilet culture, avoiding of plastic, savings promotion, rainwater harvesting, ending child labour, health and hygiene.

The women Presidents' opinion about training was also asked. Most of the participants stated that they preferred 10 days of training. A few participants were satisfied with a 7 days another 10 per cent of the participants stated that they needed training once in 6 months.

Most participants stated that they needed training once a year. Regarding the training programme they said: (a) it was very much useful to women Gram Panchayat Presidents to perform effectively. (b) it gave them direction for taking bold steps in Panchayat activities; (c) they gained knowledge about Panchayat administration and social development issues; (d) they learnt the details of Acts and GOs; (e) they gained knowledge about administration, audit, role and responsibilities of Panchayat Presidents; (f) they learnt about financial and functional devolution of powers; (g) they should be trained in the technical aspects also like how to harvest rainwater, develop waste land development etc; and (h) they should be trained in the technical aspects of small scale industries through exposure visits to all such units.

Finally, their way of functioning in solving issues was analyzed. Most of the participants took decision after analyzing the cause of the issues and the problem and also sought the assistance of the departments concerned. Many worked on consensus to avoid problems and some sought the assistance of the police if the situation went out of control, e.g., communal conflicts, anti-social activities etc. A few said that there won't be any problem at all if there is more money. However, many of them were not satisfied with the powers given to them, because the powers were only on paper and not in practice. If more power were given they could solve any type of problems. Some said that the Gram Sabha was their operational ground to solve problems.

Every one felt and indicated that the training which is being given now should have been given immediately after the election. When training information was given, representatives were reluctant to attend. It was only the Block Development Officers, who have driven the representatives to the training programme. After reaching here and attending to one or two sessions, they have realized the importance and worth of the training programme. The Panchayat President opined that the elected representatives have realized their roles, responsibilities, powers and even worth only after attending training programme. They understood the official procedures to be followed in Panchayat administration. They have learnt the art of establishing relationship with officials and the people.

They informed that their fear over section 205 of Tamil Nadu Panchayat Act has gone. They felt that they have realized their potentialities and worth only through this training. They consider the

Panchayat as a space for development. Till they attend the training they said they thought that Panchayat is a space for politics. They further informed that Panchayat officials should be given training. Panchayat institutions are in trouble because of the officials confusion over the new dispensation. Here only they have realized how effectively the facilities could be utilized to achieve development. It provided self confidence to the *Dalit* leaders. Earlier they were not conscientized on social development. Only after training they have realized the implications and importance of social development.

Integrated Analysis

Of the two-phase training, the second phase was scientific as it was conducted with the guidelines of the manual and by a good training team. The participants, namely the Panchayat Presidents, attended the programme with a volley of questions. The precise roles and responsibilities to be performed by the Panchayat leaders and the resources and grants which are due to Panchayats were clear. Information to be supplied to the leaders were compiled and distributed to them. In the training programme they were briefed about their destination and where they are now and how they have to reach their destination. In the first phase the women leaders were groping in the dark but now they were enlightened leaders with a sense of commitment. Finding the environment not positive towards devolution of powers to Panchayats, the women leaders had formed their own associations region-wise and integrated them into a federation. Women leaders had formed their own federation and *Dalit* Panchayat leaders had formed their own outfit. Gram Panchayat Presidents have formed a Federation which is called the Federation of Gram Panchayat Leaders of Tamil Nadu. Women Gram Panchayat Leaders have formed their own federation called the Tamil Nadu Federation of Women Panchayat Leaders. *Dalit* leaders in Panchayats have for their federation. These three federations periodically meet and discuss their problems. They are drawing the support of NGOs. These federations are independent and not politically affiliated. These associations and federations demanded powers. Further, to clarify day to day administrative problems, Gandhigram Rural Institute with the collaboration of a popular vernacular (Tamil) daily, namely,

Dinamalar had started a weekly supplement (every Monday) under the caption 'Panchayat Malar' which carries Panchayat news and information. For the 'Panchayat Malar' the Rajiv Gandhi Chair does all the work for the entire page, recording the struggles and the successes of Panchayats, providing useful information for effective Panchayat administration, and, giving answers to the questions of the public and Panchayat leaders on the affairs of Panchayats. Gandhigram Rural Institute, with the support of The Hunger Project, New Delhi, conducted a workshop for journalists and sensitized them on the issues of Panchayati Raj and development. Now the media is focusing attention on the successes and struggles of the Panchayats. Gradually the grassroots movement is emerging as a popular movement, gaining momentum from the people, wherein training plays a major role.

Capacity-building and information dissemination are the two prerequisites for the effective functioning of local bodies at present. But it is unfortunate that serious thought has not been given to training since there is no policy on training. Conducting training programmes is not easy as it requires several facilities and a well trained team of trainers. Further it requires a volley of information pertinent to Panchayat administration. By imparting training, the skills and the capacity of the Panchayat leaders have been enhanced. The existing conditions and the way in which Panchayats are being administered have been identified only through the training programmes. Steps which are to be taken to put the Panchayats on the proper track have been identified. From the experience of Gandhigram Rural Institute it is perceived that by building the capacity of the leaders of grassroots institutions, a movement can be generated with the active participation of the people for the establishment of the Panchayati system as an institution of self government. One need not wait for the initiative of the Government either for the preparation of a manual and a module for training and for conducting capacity-building exercises. If a few NGOs join together the right kind of leadership can be developed at the grassroots and through them people could be mobilized for the establishment of grassroots institutions. Through the capacity-building exercise, the leaders can be sensitised as to where they are now in terms of devolution of powers and where they have to go in consonance with the spirit of the Constitutional Amendment for devolution of powers and a strong people's movement can be mobilized with the initiative of the grassroots leaders. As a result Panchayats can move to the right track to reach the destination.

Conclusion

The main aim of the capacity-building programme through women leadership workshop was to develop the skills, habits, knowledge and aptitudes in selected fields and also to increase their effectiveness and prepare the trainees for future position. The Elected Women Representatives who were trained through this programme are now acting as resource persons for trainees in the State Institute of Rural Development. The impact of the training of a Woman Panchayat President results in the uplift of her village Panchayat. This can be seen in many village Panchayats headed by the trained Elected Women Representatives. While observing their performance after the capacity-building programmes one can notice the following changes in their functioning: (a) they are well-versed in accounting procedures; (b) they are working towards social justice and gender equality; (c) they have gained leadership qualities like vision, values, strategic thinking and planning, augmentation of resources, accountability, relationship building, transparency, gender consciousness, empowering the disadvantaged and marginalized people, managing the Panchayat system by collaborating with higher level officials; (d) managing common property resources; (e) understanding the importance of SHGs; (f) learning how to carryout micro-level planning; (g) ensuring more concentration on environment protection; (h) knowing schemes and programmes for rural development; (i) learning the importance of participation of people in development process; (j) learning how to work for the welfare of the society even with limited money and power; and (k) women leaders have shown the way to others in innovations and have developed strategies to build alliances to overcome barriers.

The capacity-building exercise shows that the Elected Women Representatives can convince the policy-makers that the Panchayats can perform beyond expectations. Women leadership at local level is a space for development and not a space for politics. They realized the importance of training and continuous flow of information. Finally one can conclude that empowering women through such a type of capacity-building exercise addresses the social issues and ensures socio-political uplift of the whole country.

REFERENCES

1. G. Palanithurai, *Empowerment of Women: Problems Faced by the Elected Women Representatives in Tamil Nadu*, Gandhigram: Rajiv Gandhi Chair for Panchayati Raj Studies, 2001.
2. G. Palanithurai and V. Ragupathy, *Building Alliance and Capabilities Among the Elected Women Representatives of Grassroots Institutions*, Gandhigram: Rajiv Gandhi Chair for Panchayati Raj Studies, 2003.
3. S. Wieringa, "Women's Interests and Empowerment: Gender Planning Reconsidered", *Development and Change*, 25, 1994.
4. Amrita Basu, "Gender and Governance: Concepts and Contexts", in Martha Mussbaum *et al.* (eds.), *Gender and Governance*, New Delhi: UNDP, 2003.
5. G. Palanithurai, *Capacity-Building of Grassroots Leaders*, Gandhigram: Rajiv Gandhi Chair for Panchayati Raj Studies, 2004.

5

Building Perspectives for Networking

Elected women representatives to the grassroots level institutions have been facing numerous problems in their social, political and administrative settings apart from their families since their entry into the local bodies. This has led to ineffective administration of the bodies by the women leaders. They don't have a common platform to express their grievances and get them redressed. Experiences of capacity building exercise programme conducted in the various parts of the State have propelled us to prepare an action programme for empowerment of women leaders at the grassroots level by federating themselves with similar women representatives association in local government in different parts of the country and make them speak their issues on their own.

To perform this activity a State level consultation was conducted on 26th August, 2000 at Gandhigram Rural Institute, Gandhigram by the active involvement of women activists, gender specialists and feminists. This programme was part of the major action project "Associating Women Representatives in Local Government" sponsored by the Ford Foundation through Singamma Sreenivasan Foundation, executed by the Rajiv Gandhi Chair for Panchayati Raj Studies, Department of Political Science and Development Administration, Gandhigram Rural Institute, Gandhigram.

Why this Programme?

The outcome of the capacity-building programme is that women leaders are in demand of an alternative arrangement for the continuous flow of the information and consultancy to stabilize their activities for development. The existing grassroots leaders' organisations are not providing space for grievance redressal of women leaders. Moreover, the requirements of the women leaders are not adequately fulfilled by these organisations. Therefore, it has resulted in demanding a fullfledged professional organisation to assist the women local body leaders when they are on the job. Against this background, a facilitating centre for grassroots women leaders is being thought of at the Gandhigram Rural Institute. Rajiv Gandhi Chair will facilitate the women leaders to form a federation. When Rajiv Gandhi Chair is facilitating the elected women leaders to form a federation, what perspective the federation has to keep is a major issue and for which a feminist meet is arranged in Gandhigram Rural University.

Consultation

To get the problems faced by the EWRs rectified and to make the women leaders empowered and effective in functioning with the Gender and feminist perspective the State level consultation was organised on 26th August, 2000, by inviting women activist, feminist scholars, academicians, lawyers, and representatives from women organisations working for grassroots women leaders development. Dr. V. Ragupathy highlighted the pioneering attempts made by the Gandhigram Rural Institute in the context of empowerment of grassroots leaders since the inception of New Panchayati Raj Institution in the State. Dr. G. Palanithurai initiated the consultation by giving a brief account of the proposed programme. They are :

(a) To sensitise the Women Leaders periodically on Gender and Social development issues;
(b) To activate, strengthen and network the organisations of leaders of Women Panchayat Leaders;
(c) To provide necessary information for their organisational activities;
(d) To interact with the leaders of the organisation and aggregate their demands for policy advocacy;
(e) To build the capacity of the Leaders of the organisation to manage their organisations and to address the issues of the Women Panchayat Leaders;

(f) To process their problems and to take them to appropriate bodies for reddressal; and

(g) To extend legal guidance to women leaders when they face problem while performing their role and function legitimately.

Major Activities Proposed

1. Networking the women leaders' organisation,
2. On request, organising interface programme for the office bearers of the organisations in other States—e.g. Kerala and Karnataka,
3. Supporting the women leaders' organisation while organising conferences to discuss their problems annually,
4. Organising periodical meetings to sensitise the women leaders on gender and social development issues,
5. Performing the role of policy advocacy—aggregating the problems of the women leaders and transmitting the same for policy and decision-making at the appropriate level,
6. Organising counselling for the leaders who are under mental depression,
7. Organising capacity-building exercise for office bearers of the Association to manage their organisation,
8. To provide necessary information to the office bearers for their conduct of their role and responsibilities as leaders of Panchayats,
9. To bring all the issues of the women leaders to the media for wide publicity, and
10. To provide legal assistance to women leaders through their organisations whenever they demand. (Women Lawyers Association of Tamil Nadu has agreed to provide such assistance).

Expected Results

1. Building a Women Panchayat Leaders movement in Tamil Nadu to address their issues on their own,
2. Making their organisations stronger and sustainable in the years to come to function on their own even after our withdrawal,

3. Establishing an information dissemination Centre for Women Panchayat Leaders in Gandhigram Rural Institute, and
4. Women Leaders will be made sensitive towards gender and social development issues.

Deliberation

Dr. G. Pankajam initiated the discussion and said that the women members of the grassroots institutions must be involved in a full-fledged way in all the activities of the Panchayats and they must be activated with necessary information. Then only we can expect efficiency and effectiveness in their functioning. Gram Sabha meetings may be used to mobilise large number of women members and by which they can gain the organisational support.

Ms. Mythili Sivaraman opined that, women are made victims in most of the occasions as there are lot of loopholes in the existing Panchayats system. But certain women leaders function effectively due to organisational backings. Even with the support of the organisation they are not able to function. The best example is Mrs. Leelavathy. This shows that women leaders have an array of problems, hurdles and barriers. Women can function effectively only with the support of institutions or organisations. In the absence of such support women will be in the hands of the male member of the family. So, it is a must to organise grassroots women leaders. Secondly women leaders face yet another crisis in the Panchayat due to the caste consciousness of the people. For example, a women leader from the SC community finds it very difficult to function as the president.

She interestingly quoted a typical case from Villupuram district. A Women Gram Panchayat President hailing from SC community has been relentlessly fighting against the atrocities of the party leaders. He is able to respond to the challenges only because of the backing of the organisations. The need of the hour is some supportive organisation to the women leaders to assist them continuously.

Dr. G. Palanithurai while sharing his experiences from the training programme brought the following: (a) Women leaders are not ready to share their ideas and even if they are ready they are not allowed to do so; (b) They are not in a position to understand the existing problems from a proper perspective; (c) They are not ready to speak out the issues because they feel that they will become victims without organisational support. Rarely they speak issues and if they speak, they have orientation and perspective; (d) Women leaders who have come to power through an organisational background of any kind are successful, because for every action they are being supported by the organisation; and (e) Women's problems will be highlighted and redressed only by the women leaders.

He also said that, the women leaders can organise themselves at the State Level and it can be linked with other state level organisations of the south. The outcome will be the reddressal of the problems faced by the women leaders through their organisations. For example, the difficulties in management of accounts can be sorted out by gaining experience from other States. The experience of Kerala is much useful in this respect as the Panchayats are in the hands of the people in Kerala where as the Panchayats are in the hands of officials in Tamil Nadu. Further, the issues of the women leaders can be addressed in a larger association and by which their issues will be highlighted. In the absence of their own associations and organisations women leaders are oriented to think and perceive issues from the perspective of Government and other organisations. They are always in the hands of others or they are made to be in the hands of others. Women leaders must look at themselves as leaders. They may be agricultural labourers or a coolie. They should perceive their role properly. At present the women leaders are to be oriented in the issues which are affecting the life of the poor and women. As long as the issues of the poor and women are highlighted by others, the problems will not gain momentum. Hence the problems should be highlighted only by the affected lot.

Hence, we can make women leaders function effectively by orgainising themselves. That organisation must be a fullfledged feminist organisation where the women leaders can perceive and prepare a plan of action according to their own perception. There is a notion among the politicians and officials that in the name of training programmes the women leaders are instigated to fight against the State Government. But it is not the fact. It is just a capacity-building exercise only. It is vital to note that Government is telling how a women leader should think? What women leader should think? This has to be removed and for this purpose and to make women leaders a full-fledged grassroots development workers, an orgnaisational structure is an imperative. Gandhigram Rural Institute is working on various dimensions for the enhancement of grassroots governance especially with women leaders in nine districts of Tamil Nadu. Gandhigram a long and cherished history on the part of empowerment of women and has its own strategy and programmes to work with them. This has made to see the issues in a feminist perspective and can look at the problems faced by the women leaders in a feminist perspective. This discussions will perfect the approach in this regard. Mr. Thirunavukkarasu said that a journal or a periodical carrying articles from women's perspective must be made available for women leaders. And Mr. Thangathurai said women leaders must be oriented in the issues of women and issues of development.

Dr. G. Pankajam felt that the burden of Indian women leaders has to be reduced because women leaders are under severe stress and it makes them not to be aware of their issues. They are not able to realise and express their difficulties. Secondly husbands of women leaders are ruling the women leaders and the women leaders made proxy of their husband hence, the suppression of women starts from the home or family itself. This is mainly due to the fact that the male members of her family are having sound political background and not having proper orientation. Thus women are not recognised and are not allowed to be conscious of their problems. In addition women are forced to take care of children and other domestic chores even after they become leaders and shouldering public responsibility.

The alternative for this can be: (a) Creating awareness among women leaders about the role, rights, duties, powers and functions of the women leaders; (b) Creating opportunity for effective functioning through organisational means; and (c) The concept of "all are equal" and 'information dissemination to all' must be put into practice effectively.

The ACP principle i.e., affective, cognitive and psycho motor principle can be adopted. The women leaders are not aware of the functioning of primary institutions in their locality. Women leaders must be sensitised on women-specific issues and about the primary institutions. They must be made to function totally independent of others. We have experiences in sensitising women leaders and changes in the same process. Women must be trained to conduct the Gram

Sabha meetings on their own. In practice husband's of women leaders are running the Panchayat Administration. We can quote as many examples as possible. Moreover, political backing or any organisational backing is a must for effective conduct of Gram Sabha. Today, we see women Self-Help Groups are functioning effectively in sensitising women's issues. So we can start with women Self-Help Groups. To make things effective, information dissemination is a must. An organizational support in the context of making women leaders work is important. The organisation which is to be established must be accepted by all. The organisation must be based on the principles of cognitive action, zero rivalry, and mutual trust among the members of the organisation.

Dr. G. Palanithurai further added that, the husbands' role has to be viewed seriously. There are husbands who assist their wives in the Panchayat activities by standing behind them. They are facilitating and enabling women leaders to perform their functions effectively. As long as the husbands of the Women Local Body Leaders are not taking the legitimate space of the women in the Panchayats, men should not be viewed as proxy. The experiences of Madhya Pradesh in training both the women leaders and their husbands is a milestone in strengthening the role of women leaders in Panchayats with the help of their husbands. This may be followed in the case of Tamil Nadu also. But in practice, the women leaders are not trained in the early days of their office. This practice has to be changed. The sense of individual management by women leaders is possible and this belief must be developed among the husbands of the women leaders.

Ms. Mythili Sivaraman stated that words like "Gender Sensitisation" "Feminism" have raised a sort of fear among the middleclass men. The resistance by the male has to be broken down in the area of ensuring women to play the role of leadership. This has to be done by giving a new definition, scope and shape to the leadership by the women. The notion created by male leadership is totally far away from the path of performance and administration. Women leadership must be viewed with into a new perspective i.e., a new leadership model has to be developed. This should be done by having a proper proportion of male and female components in the leader i.e., a male leader can have feminine characters and *vice versa.* So this new dimension has to be incorporated when leadership is discussed. The alternative for enlisting women leadership can be heard from the experiences of West Bengal. where a Women Minister who hailed from a women's association is functioning very effectively by giving a new definition to women leadership. Attitudinal change is a must for women leadership in the rural areas. Because caste and class differences are still existing among them whether she may be an upper caste or lower caste woman. Rubber Stamp Snatching Movement of North Indian Women is a best example to be followed by our women. We find many husbands are enthusiastically helping their female counterparts. This enthusiasm should not cross the limits. This should be supportive and not suppressive.

To make women leaders' performance more effective the working hours of women are reduced by four hours in Maharashtra in all Women Panchayats. This may be followed in Tamil Nadu also. The specific areas in which women leaders are to be sensitised are: (a) Public Distribution System; (b) Primary Education; (c) Primary Health Care; (d) Environmental Sanitation; and (e) Family Planning.

Women must have the access to all facilities at the primary health centre especially, family planning methods. Women should not be forced to adopt family planning methods. The attitude of the women leaders about casteism and feudalism must be changed.

The land reforms in Kerala and West Bengal have opened a new chapter in the life of Panchayats. This may be adopted by all other Indian States. Family burdens must be reduced by sensitising men and fear psychosis among men has to be removed. Women have to be seen as a part of the male gender sensitisation process. Humanness must be in practice in every action. A close liaison has to be established between the women's organisations in the village and the Panchayats. Interface programme has to be organised for women leaders. To make the women leaders aware of their roles, responsibilities, modules can be developed and they are to be administered. Finally, newsletter focussing on women's issues and women development has to be brought out in a simple way. The woman leader must change her life style apart from personal reservations and commitments. Another attitudal change has to be brought out among all and women leaders on their rights and duties.

Dr. M. Kuruvammal asserted that women leaders have to overcome the problems associated with their duties and responsibilities. They are: (a) Inferiority Complex; (b) Identity Crisis; (c) Social and Cultural Bondages; (d) Economic Dependence; (e) Fear of character assassination; and (f) Harassment of various kinds. Women must think that problems are nothing when they become leaders. Secondly, exclusive leadership training programmes for women must be organised. Women's issues have to be visualised separately. Self-confidence, courage and communicative skills have to be developed among women. Women need not expect appreciation. They must be mentally prepared for action.

Dr. Gabriele Dietrich raised a few questions like: (a) What is development?; (b) For whom this development?; (c) Why this development has to take place?; and (d) How this development is going to take place? And said that in the age of globalisation, development has to be in a new framework. Women component should be incorporated in the development process. Since women are closely associated with economic production and distribution, the various problems associated with these two economic activities are affecting the women especially in child care, health, education and domestic activities.

Today's technological development has created wider gap between the women and the reality. This will ultimately affect women in many spheres. This scenario has to be changed and women must be made the nucleus for development. For example traditional system of farming or production is closely associated with women. This can be put into practice today as an alternative. All the advancements must be pro-nature, pro-poor, and pro-women. A new outlook has to be made when development is talked about. Women must be made aware of the following aspects: (a) What is development?; (b) Basic economic problems; (c) Gender issues; (d) Enhancing efficiency; and (e) Problems associated with basic infrastructure facilities.

To achieve this, the relationship between man and women has to be changed. Supporting her view Dr. G. Palanithurai said that the concept of development should be redefined because there is an ambiguity in the concept that development can be achieved through people's participation or by technological transformation. People's participation is a must for any change. But leaders feel that technology can transform the society. Ms. Bimla Chandrasekar stated that situational analysis is a must for any activity. For example 50 years of independent life has witnessed a depletion of the natural resources, leading to starve for drinking water and water for irrigation and so on. Again globalisation process has created a wide gap between the micro and macro linkages.

To make women leaders effective, we have to create awareness on certain basic elements i.e. a change in the public distribution system must be brought out. Secondly the identity crisis of women leaders leads to non-functioning. This has to be changed. Importance is given for fulfillment of basic needs alone. This has to be extended to all other spheres. Existing disparity has to be removed and sense of oneness has to be made. Women must be brought out from the invisible position to the visible position. For all these things we have to exercise or perform physical and mental mobility of women. As we have lot of loopholes in the existing Panchayat system women are made victims.

The process of associating women leaders in local governance has to consider various aspects. Similarly women leaders have to be sensitised on various issues. The primary considerations should be given to the following aspects: (a) Review of the public distribution system (need based); (b) Integration of different organisation/ associations. For example a creche and a old age home in a village can be integrated; (c) Awareness about migration, feminization of poverty; (d) An exclusive leadership training for women leaders leading to perceptional change on the concept of leadership; (e) A sense of realisation that rights always go with responsibilities and duties; (f) An attitude that makes them to develop the idea that as "this is my village and I have to work for its betterment as I work for my family"; (g) Making the male counterpart understand that feminism is not for asserting one's own rights by denying other's rights. It is for protecting the rights of the women; (h) Documenting successful leadership and making it available for others as role models; (i) Media has to picture these components without affecting the performance of women leaders; (j) A clear cut idea about the rotational system of reservation has to be created; and (g) A clear cut understanding must be established among various segments especially during the Gram Sabha meetings to have better interaction.

Dr. G. Palanithurai further added that development indicators at the macro-level can be easily framed. Whereas at the micro-level it is very difficult to fix the indicators. Women leaders must be aware of existing environment and they should plan their course of action accordingly. To identify the problems persisting in the rural societies, the N.G.Os must collaborate with other institutions. In particular, women-specific issues can be identified by this course of action. Research work will be effective when academic institutions and N.G.Os join together.

Dr. G. Pankajam said that a Panchayat can do its level best what a State and Central Government cannot do it and only when it is provided with the necessary provisions. A company called Thapar Dupont Ltd was originally to be launched in Goa. But due to stiff resistance by the Gram Panchayat and its people on the basis of severe environmental hazzards, it shifted its site to Gummidipoondi. Like this a women leader must be a committed and support seeking leader in her functioning. Beyond this, women leader must create awareness among other women in the areas of resource mobilization and utilisation. Women leader should play the role of an educator i.e., she has to educate her women about democracy, and importance of people's participation.

Ms. Bimala Chandresekar stated that the mental block existing among the women has to be removed and they should have a feeling that they have a confidence that they are able to do or function independently with Panchayat administration. But they have a fear that how this message can be communicated to their husbands or family members i.e., who will tell the male members that women are capable of performing independently and they need assistance only from outside the framework.

Dr. G. Palanithurai added that any discussion or demand must be made on the basis of data support. Women leaders must be provided with necessary information to pressurise the Government regarding the issues raised by them. Only data can speak and get results. Data will give confidence and courage to women leaders. In this regard certain N.G.Os and academic institutions are very effective and they conduct research and create a data base which can be used.

Ms. Ramani Mathew said that today Panchayats are functioning like business centres or service centres. They give statistical information about income and expenditure on various activities. Their orientation is like contractors and it must be changed. Women usually neglect and avoid to take part in Panchayat activities as criminalisation and demoralisation of women is being done at the grassroots level in a massive way. We have to appreciate and extend a supportive hand to the women who come out of these hurdles and function in the Panchayats. Certain other women leaders try their level best to overcome the hurdles. But they lack supporting base. The establishment of forum to support and assist the women leaders gains considerable momentum. It is a difficult task to create a support base for women. But continuous effort in this regard must be undertaken. This supporting base must be created at various levels. In addition this base must make the women leaders think, act and react. A second support structure at the family level must be made. These support structures must make women leaders committed with the common agenda for action. Nature of the common agenda must be made in such a manner that, we can do this on our own, we can do this with the joint effort of others. Modules on self empowerment, conflict resolution, capacity-building and leadership qualities has to be developed in a way that it will fulfil the needs of the common rural women. A consistant and continuous need-based training must be planned for women leaders. These training programmes must create a deep sense of convictions and course of actions among the women leaders. In addition to this, they must be made to know about the utilisation of power, finance and personnel. For this, the Kerala model campaign can be adopted.

Ms. Rajini said about the caste system and women leaders are made victims out of caste differences. The alternative is migration from rural areas to urban areas as stated by Ambedkar. Since modernisation is faster in the urban areas. To make *Dalit* women leaders into overcome the difficulties, small Panchayats must be clubbed together and made as town Panchayats/satellite towns.

Dalit Women Panchayat Presidents are ineffective in Panchayat administration and they are removed from office due to caste differences. This has to be changed totally. Because of this fact, the functioning of women leaders are limited. For the effective functioning of the Gram Sabha, Women Presidents have to be given protection. To make the empowerment process very effective, there must be proportional representation, multi-seat constituency in the contexts of women and *Dalits.* Ms. Shenbagavalli substantiated Ms. Rajini's statements and said that special attention should be given to *Dalit* women leaders also. In practice, we find rivalry and revenge even after *Dalit* women leaders acquire office. They experience non-cooperation, disturbance of different kinds in their office. This situation must be changed by providing certain measures which safeguard *Dalit* Women Leaders.

Dr. G. Palanithurai added that associating *Dalit* Women Leaders is a must in the present context. We find people are working together in various places without any hierarchy. But when they come out from the organisation, the social hierarchies will emerge. This makes much differences among women as majority of them are labourers. This situation has to be changed. Economic emancipation of women is a must. It is very difficult to achieve development on a massive scale. To empower women leaders, they must be educated or as an alternative, educated women have to come into politics. Secondly, an organisational support must be made for women leaders. Husbands of women leaders have to be oriented in such a way that the women are having all the abilities and potentials to function as leaders. There is a need for creating a space for women leaders to express their views. Dr. M. Kuruvammal also supported this view and said that women who are treated as untouchables assert their rights and become powerful. This is taking place slowly. This process has to be speeded up. A quorum must be insisted for women and *Dalit's* presence in Gram Sabha. This will ultimately enhance the empowerment process of women.

Dr. G. Pankajam gave her idea to empower *Dalit* women. She stated that education and employment should become accessible for *Dalit* women. Making access alone is not important but also providing opportunities to make use of the facilities is much more important. N.G.Os can play a pivotal role in this regard. Dr. G. Palanithurai finally said that specialized Government schemes for *Dalits* are not reaching the targets. Information related to the schemes are not disseminated. We have people's charter everywhere but in practice they are not being circulated. Dr. G. Palanithurai stated that it is important that how we are going to provide opportunity for *Dalit* and women to make use of the facilities. We can take the *Dalit* and women to the next phase of development by extending the opportunities, to make use of the various kinds of common property resources. He urged that the women should be empowered and they should become a part in the process of development by educating them and creating awareness, providing opportunities and support. We have to work for these aspects.

Proposed Agenda for Action

- Awareness Creation.
- Sensitisation.
- Information Dissemination.
- Association Formation.
- Creating Supporting Base—Information Centre.
- Organising Interface Programmes.
- Tie-up with N.G.Os.
- Documenting Success Stories other Women Related Issues.
- Conducting Women Convention Meetings.
- Policy Advocacy.

The Highlights of the Deliberation

- Women are shy, ignored and not ready to share their ideas and this mind set has to be changed. To change this, information dissemination is an imperative. Information dissemination will empower the women.
- The prevailing fear among men out of gender sensitisation and feminism can be removed only by sensitising both men and women and make them realise that every individual should have the charter of a man and women.
- The prevailing leadership in our polity should not be the role models for the new women leaders. They are to be oriented and sensitised in a different way and they should be the role models for others. Hence we have to recognise the tough task ahead.
- To make the women leaders function effectively in the Panchayats, their burden has to be reduced to a larger extent. Secondly, the role of women leaders' husbands will be supportive. If they stand behind them, without occupying their space, i.e., women leaders can be drawn easily from the invisible position to visible position.
- Women leaders' performance can be analysed from the perspective of the organisational/associational backings. As

a leader with sound organisational or associational backing the performance is more positive. It makes the women leaders overcome several hurdles. Hence organisational support is a must for the empowerment of women at the grassroots.

- Women leaders must have a tight hold over Public Distribution System, Primary Education, Primary Health Care, Environmental Sanitation and Family Planning, as the major issues affecting the women in the rural areas. Access to these basic facilities will make the women leaders sensitise various problems faced by women.
- Awareness through dissemination of information about the clear objective of reservation of seats for women and its implication, the role expectations of the women leaders will make them realise the importance of their role in the development process of women and children in the society.
- Overcoming the personal hurdles like inferiority complex, and identity crisis become inevitable for a women leader to realise herself as leader. This realisation will enhance the women empowerment process at the grassroots level. They should realise their worth.
- Access to education and employment will make women overcome the social and cultural bondages which they have inherited from tradition.
- NGOs, academic institutions and activists can bring specific issues more effectively to the women leaders and can assist them to resolve the issues. Periodical sensitisation can be done by these institutions. Collabcrative work is possible between a women leader and said institutions.
- Women leaders function does not end with the Panchayats alone. She has to integrate different organisations in her locality and add efficiency in administration, settlement of disputes and sharing of resources to maintain equity. We need more number of role models. Hence documentation of such role models is essential. The dissemination of information about such role models will be immense use for women empowerment. Women leaders must be provided with opportunities to learn about the successful leaders.

- Periodical training is an imperative for the women leaders. They need information for their functioning and for which a newsletter or a magazine is very essential.
- Women leaders must be oriented and made to know, what is development? For whom this development is meant? Why this development has to take place? and how this development is going to take place?
- Situational analysis is a must by the women leaders to get long with lasting results. In addition, all the information about the various schemes have to be disseminated to women leaders. Right to information will empower the women leaders and enhance their performance as the leader of a Panchayat.

What Next?

Women leaders of local bodies have to be sensitised on the women issues. They should have orientation to look at issues perspectively otherwise they will be lost and their identity will be lost. Further, they should know clearly what is development in the context of Globalization and for whom the new economy is being pursued and the linkage between the resources and institutions. Sofar in all training programmes representatives are oriented towards ensuring participation of the people in the process of governance. At present, they are to be sensitised on what for participation? They should go beyond participation.

The issues which are affecting the people even to ensure their entitlements are to be taken up for sensitization. When the women representatives are oriented towards issues, they will acquire their grip over the problems and methods to be adopted to fight against all kinds of exploitation. Further, sensitization is needed not only for the women leaders but also for their husbands or the male members of their families. Issue based activities have to be designed and higher level linkages have to be established. Unless the women leaders are not linked with the issues, the women association will became a get together clubs not as an organisation of the marginalised who are struggling for decent life in the society. It is equally important that the women leaders organisations should find a critical mass by expanding its activities horizontally all over the State and for which partnership building is essential and imperative. With whom partnership could be developed is a basic question. There are NGOs who have deep commitment on women empowerment, grassroots democracy and empowering marginalised and they will be accommodated with the women leaders' organisation. The linkages are activity based. Till concretising the organisation of the women leaders in the society for women empowerment, it is necessary to rope in organisations which are coming forward to help this kind of activities. Periodical interventions, sensitization, capacity-building and extending support to their activities and struggles are imperatives. The women leaders' organisations can take up location specific issues and more in their own mode with their issues. Issues need not be the same all over the State. Associations will mutually help each other to realise their objectives.

Deciding upon these strategies the feminist meet came to an end. Even though the activity of associating women together to form a federation was carried out in a sporadic way by different organizations, after this meeting Rajiv Gandhi Chair took an earnest step to bring women leaders under one umbrella. This led to the formation of Tamil Nadu Elected Women Representatives Association. The federations started functioning as a mass movement and large scale and coordinated action were organized over a large geographical area. On many occasions, they provided the leadership for women to get their legitimate demands fulfilled. They were sensitized and conscientised on social development issues. As a result, they came out from the mindset imposed by men to one of their own and took up the causes of women. In consequence of this, they had to face problems on many fronts from the family to the Panchayat office. The resultant struggle gave them momentum and they became visible. This process propelled many sectors, including the media, to create a support structure for them. In the course of the struggle the women leaders scored success in terms of performance. The success and the struggle brought them to the centre stage where problems arose in building up the alliance further. Many of the women elected representatives would like to become leaders of the federation. The representatives being large in number, the present leaders could not provide the leadership needed to manage the entire group. Further, region-wise federations have now been formed to focus on local issues and act independently. Political parties, excepting the left, are luring prominent leaders of the federation by promising them tickets in the next assembly elections. Because of poor consolidation of the association activities throughout the State, the federation is weak at the local level while it is strong and visible at the State level. Due to lack of perspective at the State level the leaders fail to analyze the issues properly. To overcome this problem many meetings were arranged for sensitizing them on social development issues, particularly the issues of the women.

It is a well known fact that such kinds of problems would crop up in every organization when it emerges successfully. To proceed further the Rajiv Gandhi Chair for Panchayati Raj Studies, with the assistance of the SSF, planned to evolve an appropriate approach to take the federation further based on the inputs of the colleagues working with women and their problems throughout Tamil Nadu for the past three decades. So, a State level workshop was organized to discuss the problems involved in strengthening the federation for empowering the women to take up issues of social development. Women activists from various backgrounds participated in the workshop to share their valuable views. As scheduled the programme began at 10.30 in the forenoon of 21-10-2003 with a prayer followed by a welcome address, by Dr. Celine Rani, Reader, Department of Political Science and Development Administration, Gandhigram Rural Institute (GRI). Dr. V. Ragupathy, Reader, Department of Political Science and Development Administration, GRI, briefed the participants on the origins, objectives and activities of the women's federation. Ms. G. Uma, Programme Coordinator of the Hunger Project, GRI, presented the activities and the problems faced by the Women Panchayat Presidents' Federation. She also presented the problems faced by the facilitators in strengthening and supporting the activities of the federation. Dr. G. Palanithurai, Coordinator, S.S. Foundation Project, initiated the discussion and Ms. Kalpana, who represented CRY (Child Relief and Youth), at the moment concentrating on local bodies and their role in child development, added punch to the discussion by saying that the Federation of Women Panchayat Presidents had failed to concentrate on problems faced by women and Dalits even though the Federation had won political recognition. She also said that integrating the grassroots women representatives in one single organization is not possible as it requires a vast field exercise. Her idea of training was quite positive as she argued that through training, accountability, values and issues should be taught to the women representatives. Regional level federations, district level federations and Dalit federations are bound to crop up and are essential.

Ms. Vasuki, General Secretary (Tamil Nadu), All India Women Federation, passionately listened to the proceedings and, when her turn came, she analyzed the problem critically and suggested possible solutions. She said that leadership crisis and identity crisis cannot be seen as problems since these are common in any organizational setup. She suggested that joint action by different factions can be thought of while focussing on specific issues. Networking of associations working in different places in different spheres with different backup organizations on specific issues will be useful. Practical difficulties will also crop up while coordinating the women representatives' work on issues. Therefore, it is not necessary to get support from all women representatives on every particular issue. Coordination can be obtained from other organizations working on a particular issue. Apart from these things the main task is to sensitize the women to their own issues. Her solution to party politics was subtle in nature. She said that women representatives who have different political affiliations can be brought together based on the issues and work towards a consensus which may lead to fruitful results. To achieve a desired result different strategies may be adopted even though a single approach is followed. Her suggestion for strengthening the federation was to have a localized network in all areas and to have effective communication with NGOs and other women's organizations. She also suggested releasing a newsletter about Panchayats by the Rajiv Gandhi Chair for Panchayati Raj Studies so that information can reach all the women representatives and their opinions can be shaped. Quoting from the famous historian K.M. Pannicker, she said, "make local community a secular community".

Ms. Vasantha from GUIDE discussed the importance of alliance building among the elected women representatives, NGOs, women's organizations and other volunteers who work on these issues. She said that the creation of a formal structure will strengthen the Federation. Ms. Kameswari from the Women's Collective Forum suggested having an association at the block level so that it will be able to focus on local issues. Ms. Ramani Methew of EKTA said the EWRs should be asked how to strengthen themselves. Alliance building with NGOs and SHGs will also be helpful while focusing on issues. Ms. Suriyakanthi, Director, ACE&E, GRI, also suggested building alliance with NGOs and SHGs. She said that SHGs are powerful everywhere and their support for collective action will yield good results. She added that training for the family members of the EWRs is also a must. This view was supported by Ms. Vasuki also. Mrs. Celine Rani said that the structure of the Federation should be flexible in nature and frequent meetings will strengthen its base.

Mrs. Salma, Chairperson of Thuvarankurichi Town Panchayat, said that the Federation should be built up from the bottom so that long-term functioning is possible and insisted that its members should know their responsibility and accountability. An artificially created Federation will wither away in the course of time. Dr. V. Ragupathy proposed a three point agenda: his first point was to create a sustainable and self-governing Federation; the second was to ensure a broad-based alliance with civil society, community-based organizations and SHGs; and his third point was to create a broad based platform of people interested in the Panchayats. Finally Mr. M.A. Thirunavukkarasu summed up the whole proceedings.

The following are the points discussed in the workshop:

- Based on the ideological perception and the felt needs several types of federations/associations among the elected representatives are bound to emerge. This is a welcome move and there is no need to be worried.
- Field realities vary from district to district and strategies have to be evolved to suit the field requirements.
- The EWRs are showing interest in and positively respond to any organization and make proper use of the facilities extended to them. They need more numbers of organizations to tackle their problems at different levels.
- The visibility of the performance of the EWRs Federation has drawn the attention of the media and the political parties. This trend has induced the political parties to lure the EWRs to higher positions.

- NGOs play an important role in organizing the EWRs but their capacity is limited. The NGOs' varied interests and approaches sometimes put the EWRs in trouble.
- The EWRs quickly understand the developmental issues and are ready to work in a proactive manner on these issues within the limited guidance and facilities provided to them.
- Casteism is not considered a serious issue by the EWRs. They have accommodated the *Dalit* women leaders in the Federation at the office bearers' level.
- The EWRs Federation is strengthened as a non-party forum, properly representing all the EWRs in Tamil Nadu since Federation draws representatives from the Gram Panchayat level.
- The EWRs are keen to sustain their leadership and have made use of the opportunities during their meetings with political leaders and succeeded in their attempt. The reservation has been extended to one more term only in Tamil Nadu. This success has made them continue their lobbying with political parties.
- In general the leaders of grassroots governance view the political leaders as models.
- Several outstanding role models among the EWRs are emerging in many districts.
- Particularly in the area of social development, the EWRs are performing well and work innovatively on these activities. They draw the attention of the media.
- The EWRs feel handicapped to attend centrally organized events due to several constraints. Normally they attend district level and block level meetings only.
- Interface with and exposure to EWRs of other States are very useful and educative. Women leaders from northern districts could not have the opportunity to attend the meetings as they are organized either at Chennai or at Gandhigram.
- Leadership and identity crisis are unavoidable. People working with women leaders need not worry about these as they are bound to occur.
- More consultation/orientation and facilitation are needed on many critical issues.

- Care and attention should be ensured when promoting leadership among the EWRs. They have to be oriented in the right sense of leadership for common causes and not for parties or caste institutions.
- Each and everyone has her own political perceptions. It is a reality. In general, the politically oriented EWRs would not raise their voice against the Government or political parties.
- Zone-wise/district-wise consolidation of the Federation's activities is necessary though it can be a Federation at the State level.
- Necessary orientation should be given to the leaders of the EWRs Federation to build close association with other local institutions.
- Instead of thrusting our ideas on them, we should learn from them and act on their ideas if they are workable.
- A newsletter for mass consumption is necessary along with other publications.
- Capacity-building exercises have to be conducted continuously based on the needs of the EWRs then and there.
- Casteism is a strong issue. Tackling it is not an easy task. Public mobilization and pressure are necessary to combat casteism. To address social development issues the EWRs must have a broad alliance at the local level.
- Religious fundamentalism is rooted everywhere. It is essential to build a secular community at the local level. It could be achieved at the local level by the EWRs.
- The EWRs have realized the strength of the traditional institutions and other CBO, and succeeded in bringing them together for common activities.
- Though they hold power, the EWRs could not deliver the goods against the anti-social elements. Ms. Menaka was murdered and nobody could protect her in spite of her revelation of the threat to her life. What is the scope of the support base? It was only the Federation which made the police file an FIR.
- Coordination of a loose network with a semi-structure is always a problem. It is better to consolidate the district level association.

- Poverty and under-development are witnessed in many villages. The EWRs should be properly equipped to work out an integrated strategy to bring about socio-economic development. Successful experiments have to be publicized through a periodical newsletter.
- Issues like conducting election in Papapatti, Keeripatti and Nattarmangalam, the State policy on PDS, CPR Management, pressure from their own family members are emerging as challenges to the EWRs.
- During the first tenure, the EWRs had the backing of their family members to face the election. In the second election they projected their performance. Many EWRs decided to contest for the open seats in the next election.
- The bureaucracy at the lower level has not changed its mindset towards the EWRs. They prefer to deal with the males of the EWRs families. Though there is a Government Order to prevent transactions by proxy the officials do not strictly enforce the GO in this regard. It is a drawback that the males of political parties both the DMK and the AIADMK do not allow the wife or other females elected to function independently. This should be intimated to the top level leaders of the concerned parties. It is an irony that these same parties vociferously clamour for gender equality and women's empowerment.
- If public pressure is mounted effectively the males of the EWRs' families will desist from acting as proxies in the Gram Sabha and the Panchayat Council meetings. The SHGs can play a constructive role in this respect.
- Orientation to both the husband and the EWR can be arranged as it is being done in Madhya Pradesh.
- There are cases of mutual understanding. The husband helps the EWR by looking after the children and some family chores.
- A survey reveals that the work at home is not reduced for the EWRs. The family is the foremost support structure to the EWRs. Hence, proper orientation is necessary to all concerned.

- In the context of social and cultural barriers in rural areas, complete independence of the EWR is not possible. Hence, role clarity is needed. Facilitation and support to the EWR by the family males should be inculcated.
- Attention is necessary to prepare an agenda for the EWRs to face the next election for the PRIs.
- Localized alliance will be more useful to the EWRs Federation for maintaining sustainability. Local issues can be sorted out very easily.
- SHG members have effective leadership and they are knowledgeable also. More link should be created between EWRs and SHGs.
- A pressure group is necessary for policy advocacy even though the EWRs' Federation functions independently. Panchayat friendly associations can be meaningfully tied up with EWRs.
- It is better to have a loose federation approach or semi-structured one than a *pucca* structured federation which requires time and energy.
- A supportive platform is needed in the context of Tamil Nadu where the goodwill of Government is limited in respect of the Panchayati Raj System.
- The EWRs can not depend solely on the media as the media has it own priorities and also its own business mindset. But the provided space should be properly utilized by the EWRs.
- Unlike in Kerala, Karnataka and Andhra Pradesh in Tamil Nadu the Panchayati Raj System is still being evolved. In those States the Governments have acted proactively to strengthen the PRIs. In Tamil Nadu the perception of the public as well as the elected representatives regarding Panchayati Raj Institution is improving gradually. It is a conducive climate to move further.

Integrated Analysis of Deliberations

The wrong perception of society regarding women's leadership is refuted by establishing the performance of the EWRs in Panchayati

Raj Institutions. The reservation provided to women and *Dalits* in Panchayati Raj Institutions paved the way for thousands of women to develop aspirations. The EWRs who assumed power and position newly felt handicapped in discharging their functions. Lack of knowledge of the concept, system and rules and regulations of the Panchayati Raj System, the negative mindset of the bureaucracy, the parochialism prevalent in society and the non-participatory inclination of the public are the main threats to the EWRs.

Capacity-building is an important factor for the EWRs to face the challenges. During the common training programme, they could not get an opportunity to share their feelings. Hence, a capacity building exercise exclusively for women was organized. It was an eye-opener to both the trainers and the trainees. Based on the lessons learnt and realizing the village atmosphere, the EWRs understood the scope of and the opportunity for associating themselves as an organization. The institution involved in empowering women in general and the EWRs in particular has already experience with SHGs and their federation though not at the state level. Hence an attempt to associate EWRs and federating them up to the State level is feasible.

A constant study on EWR leadership, delivery of services, skills and techniques of handling issues, innovative strategies for tackling the bureaucracy and managing dual role is an imperative. It is here that the imperative need for a strong support base to facilitate the organization and the strength of the federation of the EWRs is perceived.

Decisions Arrived At

- Allow all the associations, irrespective of whether they are at the block level or at the district level, to grow and carry out activities which will facilitate this.
- All the members and leaders need orientation on the issues affecting the women and the poor.
- For State level activities all associations can be invited and involved.
- Since the political predicament shackles some of the women leaders an appropriate strategy has to be worked out by which those who are willing to project issues can be encouraged.

- The EWRs can work with political parties which take up the issues which are projected by the EWRs.
- Regional meetings can be organized at the district level.
- Periodical capacity-building exercises have to be conducted.
- A Small newsletter can be thought of for dissemination of information related to successes and struggles of the EWRs as it has been done in *Dinamalar* (a popular daily in the vernacular).
- Innovative practices developed by the EWRs in tackling issues and managing the affairs of the Panchayats should be documented scientifically and initiatives have to be taken for their wide dissemination.
- More number of interfaces could be organized for the EWRs to address issues by drawing the attention of the officials.
- The Federation can have periodical dialogues with SHG leaders by which the SHGs can be made to perform a complementary role.
- The Federation can allow the SHG members and leaders to become members of the EWRs' Federation. This will bring sustainability to the Federation.
- The EWRs can retain their membership of the Federation even after their tenure ends. They can play a supportive role to the EWRs' Federation.

6

Partners Meet

Empowering women is a herculian task in Indian context as social and cultural moorings had established their strong roots in the belief system of the people. As a result, there has always been an uncommon disparity in the upbringing of women and men. All social reconstructions took place only through political activities that too through political systems. Democracy provided enough scope for such reconstructions through polity. Hence, every social segment is moving towards power. Yet women hesitate to take part in politics as if the space is for men. In order to break this barrier at a micro-level, a new device has been worked out through 73rd Constitutional Amendment Act. This Act provided the women with one-third reservation of seats at all levels in all positions of the Panchayat Institutions. But this provision has not yielded the expected results as this space is not perceived properly by the women leaders. Because the elected women representatives of grassroots institutions are facing a variety of problems in their social, political and administrative settings, apart from their personal family life. They have been made ineffective in administration since they have come to these institutions as freshers. Yet, laudable achievements are made by women leaders in Panchayats. To achieve things in Panchayats the women leaders have to face plethora of problems and infact the leaders are overcoming all those difficulties by taking series of efforts. They are in struggle. The leaders have been made insensitive towards their self and women issues. They have been oriented to lose their identity. They are made as instruments to operationalise certain things for others. This process has made them sink in localism and voicelessness. As a result their space expansion is severely limited. In order to overcome all those hurdles, an attempt is made to associate the women leaders on their own to address all those issues for the general cause of the women in their functioning. Moreover, as discussed in the previous chapter gender specialists and feminist suggested the following: (a) awareness creation about their space; (b) periodical sensitisation of the women leaders on women issues; (c) information dissemination; (d) federating the existing associations; (e) association formation; (f) creating supporting base information centre; (g) organising interface programmes; (h) tie-up with NGOs; (i) documenting success stories and other women related issues; (j) conducting women conventions; and (k) policy advocacy.

How to do the above suggested activities? We need more number of institutions and organizations to perform the above activities. NGOs are the major players in the process of empowering the communities and the Panchayat Institutions.

Why NGOs?

NGOs have a long cherished history in working at the grassroots for the betterment of the people. In the fifty three years of democratic governance both at the Centre and State, opportunity had not been provided for peoples participation. This has resulted in a wide gap between the ruled and rulers. Hence, all the initiatives by the Government did not reach the people. As a result, an intervention by an outside agency becomes inevitable in the process of facilitation. NGOs have intervened in a massive way to implement some of the Government programmes and exhibited success with the participation of the people. So the role of NGOs was realised at the grassroot level for their contact with people.

NGOs play a crucial role in mobilising the mass for development activities in the rural areas. They have a supporting networking system at the grassroots. So these grassroots NGOs will play a commendable role in empowering women and simultaneously associate women leaders at the grassroots level. Hence, NGOs of this kind came forward for a tie-up activity with Gandhigram Rural Institute as they have direct contact with the people at the grassroots level.

Some leading and professional NGOs are doing Panchayat activities in their areas for the past four years in awareness creation among the people about the New Panchayati Raj System and conducting capacity-building exercise for the grassroots leaders. Hence they are invited to take part in this programme. They are expected to perform certain functions to facilitate the women leaders to federate themselves and to offer training to them.

The Meet

To explore the possibility of the NGOs role in this endeavour, they are asked to look at the issues of the women leaders as they are working in the same field for the past four years. They have been asked to react on the following points: (a) what are the problems faced by the women leaders in performing their role and function?; (b) how to help the women leaders to break the barriers in their way to achieve results?; and (c) to what extent they can work with the women leaders organisation as facilitators?

Dr. G. Palanithurai, in his introductory remarks gave a detailed picture on "why this decentralisation of power" and the work done by Gandhigram Rural Institute in creating awareness on New Panchayati Raj System. He added that awareness creation is not done at the time of election alone. It is a continuous process and hence it has been continued till now. Ever since the Government of Tamil Nadu passed the confirmity legislation, academic exercise had been started in Gandhigram Rural Institute to study the act and assess its position in the State. It made several recommendations. After the conduct of the election, training programme was started and thereby rural and urban local body leaders have been trained. In the whole process of training, we have learnt the dimensions of the problems of the leaders especially the women. The problems are so acute for *Dalit* women leaders. Those problems have been documented and done policy advocacy and yet there is no sign of qualitative improvement. Their problems are being presented by us and other NGOs. But the issues remain unsolved as we speak for them. Hence we have decided to make them to speak on their own.

When they speak, they would take up issues based on their perception and understanding. But in reality, the women leaders have been oriented to think in a different pattern as expected by others. Sometimes the women are insensitive towards their own issues. A careful analysis of the women leaders would suggest ways and means to achieve empowerment of women. Our experiences with the women leaders and their functioning in the past four years in Tamil Nadu bring a lot of issues to the front for discussion.

Types of Women Leaders in Position

(a) Women oriented by NGOs
(b) Women oriented by political parties
(c) Women oriented by families
(d) Women oriented by community
(e) Women oriented by women organisations

What enabled them to make an entry into the local bodies?

(a) Caste
(b) Political party affiliation
(c) Family
(d) Organisation
(e) Relatives
(f) Peer groups
(g) Money
(h) Past service
(i) Own reputation

Nature of Women Leaders

(a) Aggressive women leaders
(b) Capacitated and sober women leaders
(c) Leaders with *status quo* aspiration
(d) Leaders with the aspiration of upward mobility
(e) Depressed leaders in the process of withdrawal.

Problems faced by them are due to

— Non-cooperation of the officials
— Non-cooperation of their own party leaders
— Influence by family members
— Influence by caste leaders
— Influence of MLAs and MPs
— Interference of political party leaders

Against this background an attempt is made to sensitise them on their own issues and to rise up to the occasion to speak out their issues. They in fact form their association and get collaborated with other organisations and associations in other States. In this exercise, we are exploring the possibility of involving the NGOs for federating the women organisations as facilitators. After the presentation of status report by Dr. G. Palanithurai, Dr. N. Markandan (Former Vice-Chancellor of Gandhigram Rural Institute) in his intervention stressed that people must be made aware of what is going on in the world and only then we can achieve development. For the effective functioning of grassroots institutions, proper orientation of leadership is an imperative. Otherwise, they will be oriented to work as a contractor for the Government. Even people are not ready to participate in any of the activities relating to their development as they are not sensitised on their issues and the new Panchayati Raj System. Secondly, NGOs who are all involved in this process have to be accredited as they have to be at the back of the women leaders organisations in their struggle. The role of the NGOs and the capacity of the leaders are essential components of this empowerment process of the women. To carryout this task, the orientation must be done on non-violent basis. Non-violent techniques have to be taught. This alone can bring peace at the grassroot level and Panchayats can achieve desired ends in a sustainable way.

The programme was inaugurated by Dr. G. Pankajam (Executive Secretary of Gandhigram Trust). In her inaugural address she stated that it is a right time now to take stock of the situation after four years of the functioning of the Panchayati Raj Institutions under the leadership of the women folk in the society. For this we have to take into consideration the following aspects: (a) in the past four years how far these institutions under the leadership of women have functioned?; (b) what were the problems faced by the women leaders in their institutions?; (c) are the women leaders sensitized and conscientised?; (d) how far the Self-Help Groups are helping the functioning of women leaders in Panchayats?; (e) how far the other associations function with the Panchayati Raj Institutions?; and (f) what were the developments achieved in the past four years by the women leaders?

Other States Experience

Dr. B.S. Bhargava, Senior Fellow, Institute of Social Sciences, shared the experiences of women leaders in grassroots governance in Karnataka with the participants. The following are the key points: (a) Karnataka is a pioneering State for democratic decentralization; (b) women constituted 25 per cent in Panchayats when they were given opportunity in 1985 there is a well documented literature available for grassroots governance in Karnataka; (c) a well established information guide for the Panchayat Leaders on Panchayats is available; (d) proxy leaders are yielding to corruption; (e) women are still on old prison and they move from critical mass to critical action; (f) women leaders have acquired positions more than 42 per cent in the local bodies; (g) there are numerous NGOs working at the grassroots for empowerment of women; (h) at taluk level there is an association for Panchayat Leaders; (i) women still are experiencing gender discrimination; (j) they worry much about money and muscle power; (k) many women want to withdraw from their office because of non-cooperation of officials and their own colleagues; (l) Government is devolving powers through Governments orders but not through the act and this itself is a set back for the effective functioning of the women leaders; and (m) radical change has been made in Karnataka by women leaders.

He stressed that in order to make the local body institutions more viable and vibrant the local list has to be added to the Constitution like the State list and Central list. After 73rd Constitutional Amendment Act of 1992, the bureaucracy is on the upper hand and the peoples representatives are at the lower level. The alternative can be, the District Panchayat President must be made the real executive and all the ordinances must be made in his name only. He concluded his sharing with one observation that for the empowerment of women leaders, interface programme between Tamil Nadu and Kerala and Tamil Nadu and Karnataka will be very useful and effective. Experiences of the others will be lessons for the Tamil Nadu women leaders.

In terms of Panchayat Administration, the problems faced by the women are not different from those faced by the men. They face more problems as they are women. The crucial question is how the women leaders are going to mitigate the sufferings of the women living in the rural areas. At every sphere women faces problems starting from the parents to workspot, they have been treated as second rate citizens. Even for the female infanticide, women are the worst victims. They commit such a crime since they were under severe stress in the family and they were terrorised by the family members. Poor women coolie doing the work on par with men getting low pay yet no one is to ask for the women folk. In the same way maid servants were harassed sexually and there was no protection. Due to the influence of alcohol, women are tortured in the family by their husbands. Who will speak about their cases? And where are they heard? Instances and events can be listed. But all those issues are not finding place in the agenda of the discussion of Gram Sabha. It was only a money business in Gram Sabha. If it is a people's forum all the issues of the people whether they are connected with children or women or *Dalit,* they are to be discussed and decision has to be taken. These are some of the points highlighted in the inaugural session.

Session I

The theme for Session I was "Assessment of Women Leaders Performance in Panchayati Raj Institutions and the problems faced by the Women Leaders in Panchayats". Sri Vallinayagam, Retd. Additional Director of Rural Development, Government of Tamil Nadu and an advocate chaired the session. In his introductory remarks he highlighted the following issues:

(a) 73rd and 74th Constitutional Amendment Acts have created a space for women but the maintenance and expansion of the space depends not on the acts but on the efficient management of the institutions provided to them and conscientising themselves properly to keep up the space. It was hoped and believed that with the inclusion of the marginalised sections the misery of the women folk would be mitigated. The newly recruited women for the leadership have to prepare themselves to face the challenges in many fronts. They have to respond to the multipronged attack and for which they have to qualify themselves by enhancing their capacity. To safeguard themselves, they have to rely on the strength of the organisations.

(b) Officials especially the District Collectors use the Section 205 in the Tamil Nadu Panchayat Act to remove the Gram Panchayat leaders. Till date 98 Panchayat Presidents have been sacked from office and out of the 98, 66 are women. This has created a sense that women leaders are incompetent. It is not the fact, women leaders are not aware of their rights, powers and functions. So a small deviation creates a big confusion. Awareness creation is a must on the part of the women leaders and the people. Enlightenment is empowerment, so women leaders must be enlightened. People have a notion that effective laws will create wonders in the society. Law cannot create wonders. It is the people who handle the law can bring wonders. Hence "participation" has been considered as a key for social transformation.

(c) Women leaders at the grassroots level cannot change the existing syndrome all of a sudden. They have to equip themselves to demonstrate their competence. They have to be conscientised properly to address the issues. They should cultivate the habit of working in an organised structure to galvanise the support of the organisation for their struggle in the society. They have to be supported by the women leaders at the higher level and for which reservation for women in the State Legislature and National Parliament was sought.

(d) Against this background, it is thought that awareness creation must be the primary aim of the organisations and institutions towards the women leaders.

There is a comment everywhere about the women representation. The women representation in the country that too in the grassroots institutions is only a proxy and they are the instruments of the male members of the families. Partially there is truth in it. But the conditions are changing fast that has to be recognised. It is the responsibility of the Government to take initiative to build the capacity of the women leaders and see the powers of the leaders should not be encroached. There are explicit and implicit forces working in the system to project the women are incompetent to manage these institutions. And this has been taken as an advantage by the family members in the name of helping the women presidents, they transact all those activities. Even the officials are cooperating with them for this proxy leadership as to quicken the process of carrying out their activities without much trouble.

It is demonstrated in many places that the capacitated women leaders are carrying out their activities on their own without the help of the male family members. It is true in the case of the women leaders oriented by the party and NGOs. So, what is needed is the capacity building.

There is yet another issue which has to be taken note of seriously. In the name of training the women leaders they have been oriented in such a way to forget about the self and made to think in a form which is suited to Government and bureaucracy. Success and failures of administrations are in terms of the amount spent in Panchayats and not in terms of the issues that they have dealt with. There are a large number of issues being confronted by the people and especially the marginalised and excluded women and *Dalits,* but they are not taken note of. It is only the schemes and programmes of the Governments carried out in the Panchayats are considered as parameters of success. The basic issues remain dormant. They are made insensitive towards their own issues. Because they are not included in 11th Schedule and 12th Schedule and for all those issues the Governments have not allocated money and evolved schemes and programmes. These issues need only a change of mindset on the part of the leaders and the people to bring the needed change of mindset a struggle has to be waged and for which women leaders have to be prepared. It could be done not in isolation but through an organisation and a movement. As of now there is a legitimate political space created for women. It has come to a critical mass. It has to move into a phase of critical action. For critical action, the women leaders have to be prepared.

Gram Sabha is yet another legitimate space created for discussion of issues faced by the people, where people can bring their issues for discussion of the community. But time has not come sofar to bring the issues of the women folk. And women folk have not come to such a level to bring all those issues to the public for discussion. As agenda has been prepared by the Government officials, items relating to income and expenditure, proposal for schemes and programmes have been included in the agenda. No issues connected with dowry or unequal wage for women in farming operation or female infanticide or foeticide or education to women children or employment to women included in the items of agenda of Gram Sabha discussion.

Even the women leaders are not sensitive towards those issues. Because they have been oriented to treat all those issues as non issues. This is the saddest part of the whole exercise. Even if they are sensitised towards those issues, they cannot take all those issues because they have to meet the dire consequences from their own families. It requires an analysis and altogether it needs a new approach for those who work with Panchayat Leaders for empowerment of people and women. The above posited points have been discussed by the participants in the first session.

Session II

The focal theme of Session II is "How can we facilitate women leaders for their effective functioning in their space by keeping ourselves as outsiders". This session was chaired by Sri. Chidambaram, Retd. Additional Director of Rural Development, Government of Tamil Nadu. In his introductory remarks he stressed the following aspects:

There is no substitute to training. The women leaders have to be trained. This training might have imparted in the beginning of the term itself. Content of the training module must have due bias towards feminism and discriminationism. With a new content, women leaders are to be oriented on issues. It is a general trend that efforts should be taken to make the women to participate. The question is participation for what? It should be on an issue. More participation would reflect only the role of a spectator. Women leaders are not spectators.

Further, when women leaders take up the core and basic issues of the women, they need organisational support, otherwise, they will be terrorised by the vested interest in the society. It has been noticed from the women movement from Andhra Pradesh. Even the Government would not support. Hence, it is necessary to conscientise the women leaders on their issues. Train them to take up issues according to their capacity. When they deal with the issues they would be provided with all moral and legal support by the organisations.

The purpose of federating their organisations with the help of the NGOs is to keep their space in tact for the women continuously and to expand the space and they should deal with development issues, more specifically on issues affecting the women.

Dr. G. Palanithurai, in his concluding remarks stated that, before we plan for a course of action, we must be very clear about the issues. It should be noted that issues vary from region to region. Therefore, when we talk about the State level convention, we have to first work at the regional level and consolidate it at the State level. Orientation has to be given on the part of Panchayat Presidents and members. After the discussion, they have identified the issues which are to be dealt within the whole process. They are listed here.

Issues to be Considered

The issues to be considered while the process of associating women representatives in local governance are:

I. Social Issues

1. Female Foeticide,
2. Female Infanticide,
3. Malnutrition,
4. Domestic Harassment,
5. No Consideration for Feelings and Aspirations,
6. Sexual Harassment in Workplaces,
7. Gender Discrimination,
8. Education beyond Primary Level for Women,
9. Denial of Technical Education,
10. Dual Responsibility both at Home and Working Place,
11. Sexual Exploitations,
12. Increasing Work Load,
13. Denial of Basic Amenities in Working Place,
14. Lack of Health Facilities,
15. Food Habits,
16. Lack of Medical Care,
17. Domestic Situations such as Drinking Water, Fuelwood, Public Distribution System, Child care results in tension,

18. Forced Sex against their Will,
19. Liquor Consumption,
20. Viewing Women as a Child Bearing Machine,
21. Denial of Property—Non-implementation of Law,
22. Women are made Victims of Different Kinds of Violence,
23. No Security in Unorganised Sector, and
24. Widow Remarriage is Still Dream.

II. Economic Issues

1. Wage Disparity,
2. Over workload less wages,
3. Employed in Hazardous Industries,
4. Total Dependence, and
5. A notion is there that the work done by women are easy.

III. Political Issues

1. Voting rights are denied,
2. Name sake participation alone is allowed in political activities,
3. Not easy to form an organisation or association,
4. Very difficult to approach the political leaders,
5. Character assassination,
6. When women enter politics, they are not considered as leaders, they are treated as proxies,
7. Judiciary is still conservative. Judgments are mostly based on the judges, and
8. Women's rights are still on papers only.

Dr. V. Ragupathy, in his consolidated report observed the following:

- Out of certain difficulties women leaders are functioning effectively only in certain areas.
- Problems have to be identified region-wise and the women leaders are to be conscientised on those issues.
- When those issues are taken up for action at the micro-level, the experience of the leaders are to be documented.

- The whole transformation process has been visualised and observed carefully.
- Capacity-building exercise, for the women leaders and their members has to be done with a new perspective. Gender, discrimination and feminism should be the components in the perspective.
- Interface programme with Kerala and Karnataka has to be conducted.
- Document the successful leaders and make it available for as role model for others.
- The programmes should be proactive and constructive.

By federating the women leaders organisations, the documented issues have to be utilised for policy advocacy and they have to articulate their problems in their fora. All State level conventions are meant for politicising the issues for larger consumption.

Further a course of action was decided to proceed further as noted hereunder:

What to do?

1. Network the Women Leaders Association. Let them be first sensitised on women issues. Women are working solitarily at the grassroots level. They all must be brought under one umbrella.
2. Information dissemination.
3. Establishing a monitoring cell to monitor the activities.
4. Documentation of cases of conflict and achievement.
5. Projection of role models through documentation.
6. A sense of security must be given to the women leaders.
7. Legal assistance to be provided.
8. Policy advocacy has to be made.
9. Urging the Government to have gender analysis in its policy and programmes.

How to achieve these?

1. Tamil Nadu has 29 districts and they are divided into five zones namely:

Zone I

Erode, Namakkal, Coimbatore, Nilgiri, Salem, Dharmapuri

Zone II

Kanyakumari, Tirunelveli, Tuticorin, Virudhunagar, Madurai, Ramanathapuram, Sivagangai

Zone III

Dindigul, Theni, Karur, Thiruchirappalli, Perambalur

Zone IV

Tanjore, Tiruvarur, Nagapattinam, Pudukkottai

Zone V

Kancheepuram, Cuddalore, Vellore, Thiruvannamalai, Thiruvarur, Villupuram

1. In each and every district one or two NGOs will function as network agencies or partners and for every zone there will a coordinating agency which will work with Gandhigram Rural Institute.
2. These NGOs will identify the women leaders and associate them.
3. Zonal level meetings will be conducted and finally a State level convention will be conducted.
4. From the above said activities women leaders will be sensitised on the issues identified.
5. Necessary support would be extended from different spheres to the women leaders.
6. Documentation on every step will be done.
7. Role models will be identified and made available for others.
8. Interface and exchange programmes will be organised for them.

9. Finally the Tamil Nadu Federation will be associated with the federation of the other Southern States.

NGOS for tie-up activities

Zone I

1. **Erode**, Womens Organisation in Rural Development (WORD) 449, Thiruchengode Road, Pallipalayam-638 006.
2. **Namakkal,** WORD, 35, Middle Street, Post Bag 1, Pandamangalam Namakkal.
3. **Coimbatore,** Rural Development Organisation.
4. **Nilgiris,** Gramya Bhavan Aruvanakadu The Nilgiris.
5. **Salem,** Peoples Movement for Development Prof. Aruthur Nilayam (Opp) Ward : 8 Nangavelli Main Road Taramangalam-636 502.
6. **Dharmapuri,** ARCOD 4/637, Krishnagiri Road, Royakottai-636 116.

Zone II

7. **Kanyakumari,** ROAD, SAARATHY, 1-197/A, Kulasekaram Road, Marthandam-629 165.
8. **Tirunelveli,** CODE, Mahendrapuram, Radhapuram-627 111.
9. **Tuticorin,** AWARD, 10/20, Hameethia Nagar, Vallanadu-628 252.
10. **Virudhunagar,** KAJALS, Idhayam, 442, Main Bazaar, Virudhunagar-626 001.
11. **Madurai,** RCPED, 1-A/1 Ponmeni Periyavar Street, SS Colony, Madurai-625 010.
    EKTA, Plot No. 3, Lakshmi Nivas, First Cross Street, Bible Bhavan, By pass Road, Madurai-625 010.
12. **Ramanathapuram,** RCPED.
13. **Sivagangai,** GRAAMA IYAKKAM, Pudukattampur-630210, Tirupathur, Sivagangai District.

Zone III

14. **Dindigul,** CHERU, Vellbomman Patty, Vadamadurai-624 802
    PEACE Trust, New Police Colony, Trichy Road, Dindigul-624 005.
15. **Theni,** SIRPI, 1-A, Raja Street, Near Lakshmi Theater, Periyakulam Road, Theni-625 531.
    VIDIYAL, Karippanpatti, Rasingapuram, Valliyoor-627 117.
16. **Karur,** AREDS, Renganathapuram, Krishnarayapuram, Karur-639 108.
    ARPE, 42/3 Vanchinathan Nagar, Thanthondrimalai, Karur-639 005.
17. **Tiruchirapalli and Perambalur,** DOW, 18, Arulnayagam Street, Near Sakthivinayagar Koil, Crawford, Tiruchirappalli.

Zone IV

18. **Tiruvarur,** Bharathi Women Development Centre, 28, Kannaki Building, Thiruvarur Road, Thiruthuraipoondi.
19. **Tanjore,** Mulit Purpose Society.
20. **Nagapattinam,** SEVALAYA, Thirukuvalai (PO).
    SNEHA, Ilancheran Nagar, 55, Muthumariamman Koil Street, Velipalayam-611 001.
21. **Pudukkottai,** STEPS, Steps Women's Centre, Near Union Office, Pudukkottai:

Zone V

22. **Kancheepuram,** GUIDE, JCK Nagar, Chengalpet-603 001.
    LRSA, P.O.Box No. 20, Chengalpet-603 001.
23. **Thiruvallur,** SIGA, E.Block, F.21, PST Quarters, Anna Nagar 11th Main Road, Bharati Avenue, Chennai-600 040.
24. **Cuddalore,** PLUS.
25. **Villupuram,** Peolples Development Centre, Marakkanam-604 303, Tindivanam Taluk.
26. **Vellore,** CRHSE, A-11 Ashok Nagar, Tirupattur-635 601.
27. **Thiruvannamalai,** Rural Women's Development Agency, #1, New Muslim Street, Chinnakodai Theru, Thiruvannamalai.

Coordinating Agency for Five Zones

Zone I

1. **Rural Development Organisation,** Aruvankadu, Nilgiris

Zone II

1. **RCPED**
2. **EKTA,** Madurai

Zone III

1. **Rajiv Gandhi Chair for Panchayati Raj Studies,** Gandhigram Rural Institute.

Zone IV

1. **STEPS,** Pudukkottai

Zone V

1. **LRSA,** Chengalpattu

This project of Networking Elected Women Representatives with the support of The Ford Foundation was carried out in four States, namely Tamil Nadu, Kerala, Karnataka and Andhra Pradesh. These partners met at a workshop held at Gandhigram Rural University and shared their experiences. As a partners of the project they made the following observation before sharing their experience.

Major Observations Made

- After the project gets over the validity and viability of the association which is formed has to be assessed.
- The general response among the members and partner agencies interms of intra and inter-state federation across the Southern India has to be assessed.

- An introspection of what has been done and achieved during the past is essential to plan the future course of action.
- Sharing of reports and general communication among the partner agency was stressed.
- It is vital to spell out the modalities to form federation before March 2002 and propose next phase of action in terms of logical sequence.
- Converting the entire course of action in the two years into a well-knit document.
- The course of action or action plan after 2nd Inter-Agency meetings is to be decided by making a note on what is happening across the States.
- Solution has to be found out to solve domestic violence against the women.
- When the next level of action is decided research has to be done about what and how we have gone and what are the implications we have seen have to be seriously looked into.
- How the association is going to negotiate with Government at various level? is to be discussed.
- Training programmes should give adequate space for information dissemination.
- Sectoral approach has to be followed when the women in Panchayati Raj Institutions are studied.
- Globalization and its impact on women especially rural women has to be discussed with the representatives of the federation.
- The conventional system and approach of women development has to be changed.
- Globalization has made the things to move from the base not from the bottom. So as the project is from the base and not from the bottom.
- Only by creating needed awareness and concientisation of people, the objective of decentralization and development could be realised effectively. NGOs have a vital role to play in this process.
- It should be kept in the core that when the women in the Panchayat are affected, it is not the women who are affected, but it is the entire Panchayat system gets affected.

- Intervention at the village level has to be done.
- The organizational base and support alone can make the women to rise their voice high.
- An analysis of history of women organisation has to be taken into account, when the association of EWRs are considered.
- The type of association which is emerging out is to be studied carefully as it does not opt for more formalities.
- Unless satisfaction takes place on a larger side it is very difficult to bring the rural women under one umbrella as the existing scenario is highly complicated.
- As for globalisation is concerned that is no much resistance from the women. Women are made the victims hence women has to be sensitised on this also.
- Though globalisation has come to the doorsteps of every rural folk, all the women have come under the banner of SHGs to enhance their economic status and by improving their social status also. But the existing condition that the economic activities carried out by the women are of stereo type. Because of poor awareness their activities are centered around a narrow space. This reveals that there is a big question of sustainability and economic feasibility of the activities carried out by the women SHGs.
- Women in the rural areas do not think and act differently. This by changing the attitude or an attitudinal change by effective information dissemination alone can change the life style of the rural women.

Experience Across the States

Andhra Pradesh

As the elections for the rural local bodies are held recently, the first step of the project is yet to be launched. Inspite of the absence of local bodies, a series of programmes were organised on 'right to information'. 'Conduct of local body elections' and so on. It was stated that the three districts around Hyderabad will be the project operational area. Activities will be initiated soon.

Kerala

It was stated that to strong political affiliation and their dominant ideologies in Kerala did not permit them to form an independent association for the EWRs in Kerala. As there was no autonomous women's movement in Kerala and the planning board of Kerala had stolen a march over all the States in the country in launching the peoples planning campaign by devolving 40 per cent of funds to the local bodies and further reserving 10 per cent of the devolved funds for the purpose of 'women component plan'. Hence, building a gender network associations and mobilising elected women representatives of local bodies on a non-party plank gave a different kind of challenge to SAKHI. Thus a more strategic and cautious approach is needed to SAKHI. Against this background it was decided that information dissemination is an imperative need and no association is formed.

Karnataka

Apart from the execution of the project Singamma Sreenivasan Foundation has to prepare the interim report of the project and submit to the donar agency. Preparation of accounts and receiving the same from the partners and periodical reports and organising inter-agency meetings have become the core of the activities of the Singamma Sreenivasan Foundation. The interim report for the period March 2000-March 2001 was presented. It was expressed that Karnataka has taken its lead in the implementation of the project.

Tamil Nadu

As the project executed throughout the State, it was noted that there are independent associations at various levels and those associations are in loose forms and there is no well knit development throughout the State. But out of the project district level associations are formed with the help of NGOs and they are now trying the level best to shape it at the State level. It is felt during the formation of association that how these associations can be formed. EWRs has to realize themselves that they are in need of an association and hence they are made to realise the same and the associations formed at the district level to regional level and resulting at the State level.

Linkages Between Agencies

The partners also suggested the following means to have linkages among themselves:

- All the activities will be documented and the same will be shared among the coordinating and partner agencies.
- When public programmes are launched through the formed associations all the partners will be invited.
- People from different walks of life associated with local bodies will be invited to share their experiences during the interface programmes.
- Research will be conducted on key issues from the perspective of EWR and the same will be published and used for policy advocacy.

Behind the association of elected women representatives these institutions play a significant role in enabling them and facilitating the situation. Experience sharing of the partners will help each other in deciding their strategy. Likewise, seeking the help of committed NGOs will help the women leaders ultimately to fight for their cause and their empowerment.

7

Regional and State Level Meets

73rd Constitutional Amendment Act provided a legitimate opportunity for the women to enter grassroots politics. Women thus have made their entry into authoritative bodies and started participating in decision-making processes. It is evident from the past experience that women representatives are facing innumerable problems in the local administration as they are working in a closed community. Women representatives unlike the male counterparts do not have any platform on their own to express their feelings and problems. In a partriarchical social system, women representatives are bound by dictates of the male members of their families. To break the existing arrangement women are in need of a supportive system.

As majority of women representatives are not fully aware of the salient features of the New Panchayati Raj System, their activities in Panchayats are being hampered. It has become very difficult to overcome the hurdles. Secondly, the male representatives of various institutions at various levels have associations of their own to overcome the problems faced by them in the Local Body Administration. Whereas the women representatives do not have such a kind of association. If we want to make the women representatives to be effective, they must be sensitised on their problems and they must be organised. Thus, a programme was designed and carriedout to cater to the needs of the women representatives. As part of the programme of Associating Women Representatives in Local Governance in Tamil Nadu, it was decided to federate the existing associations and organisations of the women leaders in different regions of the State at the primary level and finally at the State level. After the consolidation of the federation at the State level, South Indian Federation has to be formed.

Zonal Meeting

As per the guidelines evolved during the State level NGOs network meet on 26th August, 2000 with the help of the coordinating agencies of the five zones, a regional meet was organized consecutively. EWRs, networking NGO representatives and the coordinating agency formed the core group in this exercise.

The Outcome

The outcome is presented in two different parts namely, women representative views and NGOs experiences.

Views of the Elected Women Representatives

1. Caste leaders in the villages do not permit women representatives to function independently and SCs are not permitted even to speak. If at all, if they speak they are heckled and silenced.
2. As male members are more in number in Panchayat, women leaders find it very difficult to carry out their duties.
3. Family members and relatives are becoming obstacles.
4. Since most of the women leaders are a political, they are being discriminated by the politicians at the village level.
5. Mostly the in-laws are not supportive of the activities of the women leaders when the women leaders want to take independent decisions.
6. Male members of the families of the elected women representatives have a very poor opinion about the capacity of the women representatives. Unless their opinion is changed, it is very difficult to expect independent action from the women representatives.
7. The dominant caste leaders also play a dominant role in the activities of the Panchayat by using their power. Hence, the elected women representatives have to move in a collusion course with the traditional Panchayat leaders.
8. Ilicit liquor and arrack play a dominant role in the decision making processes. In Gram Sabha meetings the women are

not able to speak about this issue as the anti-social elements are in the Gram Sabha in a drunken mood. They create problems.

9. Since people are ignorant about the development activities, they are always sensitised by the politicians on political issues rather than on developmental issues.
10. Information is received from the Government only after a prolonged struggle.
11. Government officials, especially men have not changed their attitude towards the women representatives.
12. Officials do not evince keen interest in meeting the genuine demands of the women representatives.
13. Officials are not cooperative towards the women representatives.
14. People do not recognise the women representatives as leaders.
15. Information regarding tender and related activities are not communicated to the women leaders well in advance by the officials.

Support Base

1. Committed NGOs are helping the elected women representatives.
2. Occasionally women clubs are helping the women leaders.
3. Some well meaning family members are supporting the EWR.
4. Some training institutions are also helping. The number is very less.
5. The SHG women leaders are coming to the rescue of EWR.
6. A few family male members are helping the EWR.
7. Rarely village elders help the women leaders.
8. Some of the political parties are supporting the EWR when they are in trouble.
9. A few higher officials use to help EWR.

Gram Sabha

1. Only SHG women participate actively in Gram Sabha meeting.

2. People suspect when income and expenditure statement is placed before Gram Sabha. In general, Gram Sabha attendance is very poor.

Suggestions

1. Gram Sabha has to be conducted hamlet-wise.
2. There should be match between the needs of the people and the financial allocation of the Government.
3. Gram Sabha members must be well informed about the Panchayats.
4. Ward members must be exclusively women. That is an all-women Panchayat can be made.
5. PDS should be accessible to people only when they pay the house tax.
6. Employment opportunity should be provided to those who have enough by the Government.
7. The cordial relationship must be made between president, members and the people.
8. Organic linkage must be made among the three tiers.
9. Gram Panchayat must have contact with the facilitating agencies.
10. Gram Panchayat should encourage youth to participate in Gram Sabha meetings.
11. Exchange of ideas must take place between the members of the Panchayat and the public.
12. Increase the financial status of Panchayats.
13. Reduce the Government official intervention.
14. Enhancement of the present Rs. 500 limit to conduct Panchayat meetings should be made.
15. G.Os must reach the Panchayat in time.
16. Tenders should be finalised in Gram Sabha.
17. MLA, MPs schemes must be executed only after getting the consent of Gram Sabha and by which wastage of money could be avoided.

NGOs Representatives' Views

1. Party intervention, male chauvinism, violence against women, caste factor, ignorance of the people, sexual harassment, neglect of women in decision-making process, are the difficulties faced by the women leaders in Local Bodies.
2. Training by NGOs and family members' cooperation are the supporting bases.
3. Gram Sabha gaining momentum due to participation of SHG women.
4. Training on New Panchayati Raj System and associating women representatives into a federation are the imperative needs of the time.

Panchayats are still functioning as contractors or agencies of the State Government. Till date, they have not realized their actual functions. For this, the argument put forth by the Panchayat Presidents is finance. Today, finance is not at all a constraint as the 18,000 crores of rupees meant for rural development was unspent and returned to the Government. Secondly Gram Sabha must function as general bodies of the Gram Panchayat and in turn Panchayat should change itself as the executive body. What the Gram Sabha decides must be carried out by the Panchayat. This is in practice in the States of Kerala and Madhya Pradesh. Thirdly, people's participation alone can decide the realities of economic development and social justice. West Bengal is the best example for this purpose. The programme for the conservation of the forest in West Bengal is very successful, because of the recognition given to the people and their involvement in the execution of the programme. Women Panchayat Leaders can be successful if they get a chance to learn to share and to manage the institutions on their own and by making them realise their strength and providing them with other needed support. They will reach the desired goals.

EWRs Association was formed in these five zones. Finally federation, was formed at the State level. In order to increase the membership of EWRs Federation, Regional Meets were organized at various places and under various contexts. A report of the meets are presented hereunder:

Regional Workshop at Thiruvarur

As a part of the larger effort towards organizing the elected women representatives of grassroots institutions, a regional workshop of elected women representatives was held at Thiruvarur on 27th December 2003. It was attended by the office bearers of the District units and Block units of the elected women. Representatives of Thanjavur, Thiruvarur and Nagapattinam Districts attended the meeting. After the formal welcome by Ms. B. Jeyashree, Dr. G. Palanithurai, put forth certain questions to the leaders. They were: Why should the women leaders be organized as a separate entity? What are the issues and problems to be tackled by the association of elected women representatives? How are all those problems to be tackled in the present context? He delineated the efforts taken so far in this regard.

He underlined the backdrop scenario, namely, globalization, patriarchy, feudal setup and caste hierarchy that prevail in India. Against the given background we have to visualize our activities to bring the women to the forefront by making use of the provisions in the Constitution. He underlined the point that if a woman elected representative is oriented properly on the issues of the people she will transform the scenario. It had happened in Tamil Nadu. He listed the major achievements of the women leaders in Panchayats. Many of the pathfinders are women leaders in the Local Bodies. What they need is a support structure. If it is provided, they will outdo the men leaders. What we have to do is to expand the activities of the Association. We have to explore the possibility of incorporating many leaders from the Panchayats into the Federation.

Ms. Ponni Kailasam mentioned the major achievements of the women's federation and highlighted some of the struggles of the women leaders. She appealed to the participants to discuss the steps to be taken to strengthen the Federation of Women Leaders to ameliorate the conditions of women and children. She listed the major efforts taken by the Federation and the solid results obtained by them.

To Strengthen the EWR Federation

The following are the problems indicated:

1. Visibility at a higher level (at State level).
2. No visibility at the grassroots as they are part of the Union Federation with men.
3. Existence of many associations at Block level, and District level.
4. EWR needed active support only on the ground as challenges are to be on the ground.
5. Women leaders are not aware of the problems of women.
6. No sensitization of the women leaders on gender and social development.
7. No proper capacity-building for women leaders.
8. Press is underutilized.
9. Women leader's achievements are not highlighted.

Solutions

- Activate the federation.
- Encourage the federation at lower levels.
- Partnership with press has to be created.
- Using the Government order issued earlier, periodical meetings have to be organized at the district level.
- For official intervention at the local level, District level leader has to be contacted.
- To contact the officials at State level, State level officials have to be contacted.
- While conducting the convention, the issues of women have to be discussed.

Good Panchayats

Though the consceintized Panchayat leaders work on development issues, and issues of women and children, they are conscious of the political role they have to perform according to the perception of the people. They argue that though the women leaders have to work for the development of women and children, they have to go by the perception of the people. According to the perception of the people good Panchayat leaders have to carryout the following activities:

- Street lights,
- Water supply,
- Roads,
- Transparent dealings,
- Inclusion of more number of beneficiaries,
- Less house tax on the people,
- More activities in the Panchayat which provide jobs to the people,
- Carry out the resolutions of Gram Sabha.

If the above are not carried out the Panchayat leader has to lose her popularity and popular support even though the leaders are conscious of the social development issues and the issues of gender.

People are not development oriented. People are oriented towards receiving doles from the Government. Politicians increase their popularity by asking the people not to repay loans, not to remit the house tax etc. In such a scenario, the Panchayat leaders have to tax the people heavily and earn the wrath of the people. One has to realize the difficulties under which the women leaders are working in the system. Men leaders are able to use their political and caste clout. But women cannot do as men do. In many of the places, men and communities have prevented capable women from coming to the post of the Panchayat President as they are likely to act independently. Only women who were well oriented already either through NGOs or SHGs or political organizations have come out openly.

Discussion Held on the Following Issues

1. Officials are allowing the husbands, fathers and brothers of the elected women representatives to act as proxy Presidents of Gram Panchayats by allowing them to attend official meetings and take cheques from the offices. As a result women leaders have been made to continue to be confined to their houses doing the usual domestic work. Leaders who have associated themselves with the Federation have come

out from the routine and work to act independently. The Federation has tried its best to influence the other women leaders. But they are not able to come out. As long as officials allow the males of the elected women representatives' families to act as proxy Presidents, women's participation in governance will be a farce. Women leaders who are in position are a critical mass but in action their strength is poor as their males never allow them to come out from the family shell. Moreover, the male family members feel that their powers and positions have been usurped. This trend can be changed only through the Government. The Government has to pass an order in this regard.

2. The Vice-Presidents (men from dominant caste groups) in many of the women and *Dalit*-headed Panchayats feel that they are the real power centres. They want to dominate over the women leaders and the *Dalit* leaders. As a result, the elected women representatives and *Dalit* leaders in Panchayats are not able to work independently. The problem has to be sorted out. Their open demand is that the women Panchayat leaders need women Vice-Presidents. Likewise, *Dalit* Gram Panchayat leaders want a *Dalit* as Vice-President. This demand is based on the experience in the past seven years.
3. The Central Government gives financial resources to the State Government for rural development activities but the sectoral departments are not in a position to execute works quickly and, as a result, they are not in a position to submit the accounts in time. Hence, Tamil Nadu had to forego certain grants. To avoid such delays, funds can be given to the Panchayats directly from the Central Government.
4. Due to escalation of unit charge for electricity consumption, Panchayats have to pay a threefold amount to the EB while Government of Tamil Nadu has stopped the house tax matching grant. As a result Panchayats have been brought to a tight spot in terms of financial position. Hence, they plead for more financial devolution to Panchayats commensurate with the responsibilities and activities entrusted to the Panchayats.

5. Common property resource management is an area where the women and *Dalit* Panchayat Presidents are evincing keen interest. They try their best to remove the encroachments and in the process they are put into difficulties and hence, they need strong support from the Revenue Department and the Police Department. Both are known for their discredits. They are the real villains in the whole tragedy. The leaders insisted that it is necessary for the Government to take earnest steps for a special drive through the Revenue Department as it is being done on Highways and in municipal areas for all encroachments to be removed and handed over to the Panchayats.
6. Women are not conscious of their own problems. They are to be conscientized on social development issues for which efforts have to be taken up by the State Government. Many of the service providers undertake activities as and when they want but they are not under the supervision of the Panchayats. For example, the primary health centre which is providing services to women and children has to be properly monitored and supervised by the Panchayat. But they are not doing so, as a result the poor are put to trouble and they even have to pay for such services. This could be avoided if these institutions are properly supervised for which the Panchayat leaders need proper training.
7. Non-cooperation of the officials with the Panchayat leaders has to be tackled. They cooperate only with party men and not with development agencies. Sectoral departments are carrying out several activities as they have got a budget for their activities. No one takes into consideration the demands projected by the people in the Gram Sabha. Many of the demands of the people can be met by the sectoral departments if they consult the Panchayats before carrying out their activities. But in reality, the Panchayats are not being consulted by the sectoral departments.
8. Village Administrative Officers have to attend to their duties from their office complex constructed very near the Panchayat office. They stay elsewhere and ask the people to move from pillar to post to get certificates. Village

Administrative Officers keep themselves aloof from the Panchayat activities and they consider themselves more powerful than the Panchayats. In most of the encroachment issues, Village Administrative Officers have involved themselves and worked against the Panchayats by not guiding the Panchayats properly or supplying correct information. In order to bring about coordination between the Panchayats and Village Administrative Officers that the office for the VAOs were constructed very near the Panchayat office. If they come to this office they will be in the public eye. They can respond to the people's demands and the Panchayat can also intervene. But the VAOs deliberately stay elsewhere and many of the offices are not in use. As a result the public are put to trouble.

9. Panchayat leaders, especially women and *Dalits*, should be given periodical training. Women and *Dalit* leaders need periodical orientation. They need more support in terms of information. Only general training is being given that too not as seriously as in Gandhigram. Gandhigram Rural Institute conducts a training programme for 5 days. It is fully residential. Gandhigram Rural Institute organizes periodical refresher courses also. This is the kind of training that they need.

Resolutions

1. Resolved to appeal to the Prime Minister of India and Chief Minister of Tamil Nadu to take earnest steps to provide adequate water from the Cauvery to save the standing crops in Thanjavur District.
2. Resolved to request the Government of India to pass a Bill in the Parliament to provide reservation of seats for women in Parliament and State Legislatures before the next general elections.
3. Resolved to request the Government of Tamil Nadu to incorporate a section on gender issues a special section in the training module and arrange in every training programme to deal with gender issues as it has been done by Gandhigram Rural Institute.

4. Resolved to request a special training programme for women leaders exclusively in leadership skills by all training institutions to bring out the elected women representatives from the clutches of the family and especially from the clutches of the males of their family.
5. Resolved to request the Government of Tamil Nadu to issue a strict order to Government officials not to transact any official business related to Gram Panchayats with males of the family of the elected women representatives. Further, an instruction has to be given to the officials, especially, at the lower level not to allow the males of the elected women representatives families in lieu of the elected women representatives in the official meetings arranged by the officials.
6. Resolved to request the Government of Tamil Nadu to take the initiative to help the Gram Panchayats to plan for integrated sustainable development of the communities and pass an order to the effect that all activities carried out by the Block Panchayat and the District Panchayat have to be incorporated in the plan itself so that the present enormous wastage can be reduced.
7. Resolved to request the Government of Tamil Nadu to provide annually Rs. 5 lakh to each Gram Panchayat as it has been given to MPs and MLAs to work for social development issues with special emphasis on women and children. Guidelines can be prepared by the Government of Tamil Nadu in this regard.
8. Resolved to request the Government of Tamil Nadu to simplify the administrative and accounting procedures with a view to enabling an ordinary citizen to understand the administration and the accounting procedures of Government institutions. The cumbersome administrative and accounting procedures only help the bureaucrats and middle men to breed corruption.
9. Resolved to request the Government of India to release funds which have been earmarked for rural development activities to the Panchayats directly instead of routing them through State Governments.

10. Resolved to request the Government of Tamil Nadu to release the grants which are due to the Panchayats for the last nine months.
11. Resolved to request the Government of Tamil Nadu to give sanction for schemes and release money at the earliest so as to carry out quality works. On many occasions they give sanction in the month of December and January and ask the Panchayats to complete the work before March. This kind of eleventh hour work spoils the image of the Panchayat Presidents and the quality of the work suffers.
12. Resolved to request the Government of Tamil Nadu to take firm action against the traditional Panchayats as they are the mafia who commit atrocities against women and children. They do not have community support also.
13. Resolved to request the Government of Tamil Nadu to launch a special drive by the Revenue Department to remove encroachments in Panchayat lands. The redeemed common properties can be handed over to the Panchayats.
14. Resolved to request the Government of Tamil Nadu to allocate resources to the Panchayats not on political considerations but on the actual needs.
15. Resolved to request the Government of Tamil Nadu to take steps to ensure that wherever a woman is the Gram Panchayat President the Vice-President is also a woman and wherever a *Dalit* is the President of the Gram Panchayat, the Vice-President is also a *Dalits* in order to overcome the existing practice of the Vice-President dominating over the Panchayat President.
16. Resolved to request the Government of Tamil Nadu to pass an order to fix a last date for the payment of house tax.
17. Resolved to request the Government of Tamil Nadu to take earnest efforts to see that the documents of the Panchayat are handed over to the newly elected leader by the outgoing President of the Panchayat.
18. Resolved to request the Government of Tamil Nadu to maintain a compendium of the original updated State Panchayat Act, rules relating to Panchayat administration, details of the rural development schemes and Government orders pertinent to Panchayati Raj and rural development.

Block Level Federation of Gram Panchayat Presidents

New Partner in Our Exercise

From the experience of the elected women representatives of Thiruvarur District it was learnt that the elected men representatives have extended a helping hand to the women leaders to perform their roles and responsibilities very effectively by forming a federation of Gram Panchayat leaders of a particular Block, namely, Kudavasal. On the basis of the request of many of the elected women representatives the President of the Association of Gram Panchayat Presidents of Kudavasal was invited to the regional meeting of the Tamil Nadu Federation of Elected Women Representatives held at Thiruvarur on 27th December 2003.

Mr. P.V. Sethuraman, President of Vikrapandian Gram Panchayat attended the regional meeting of the federation of elected women representatives as President of the Association of Gram Panchayat Presidents of Kudavasal Union. In Kudavasal Panchayat there are 49 Gram Panchayats. The basic objectives of the Federation according to the President Mr. P.V. Sethuraman, are:

1. Location-specific peculiar problems can be tackled locally and they cannot be tackled at the State level or at the district level.
2. When Government officials deal with Panchayat Presidents their approach varies from individual to individual. There is no perspective or uniformity in dealing with Panchayats. They give room for caste and political considerations in dealing with Panchayat matters. In order to avoid such variations and discrepancies an association is needed.
3. Information blockade is a major instrument through which Panchayat Presidents are made to tow the line of the officials. To disseminate information to all Panchayat Presidents an association is necessary.
4. In every Gram Panchayat, the weak and meek Panchayat Presidents have to face a volley of local problems. Local issues have to be sorted out at that level. They should not be brought out of that particular Panchayat area. Sometimes Vice-Presidents or at times Ward Members and on a few

> occasions the traditional Panchayat leaders create problems. On such occasions the federation should interfere and solve the local problem. Since the Federation leader is a local leader having much recognition in that area the problems can be tackled easily.

He listed the major obstacles which the Gram Panchayat leaders have been facing in the Panchayats. They are:

When a woman is the President of the Gram Panchayats and a man is the Vice-President, the Vice-President gives a lot of trouble to the President who is very weak. Being a lady, she can not manage the Vice-President individually. She has to depend on her husband. When her husband defends the Vice-President alleges that proxy work is going on in the Panchayat. Against this background the Federation should intervene to restore power to the Women Panchayat leaders. On most of occasions the men Vice-Presidents believe that the women Presidents cannot act independently and hence, the Vice-Presidents try to usurp the powers of the Presidents. In some places the Vice-Presidents wants to act as parallels by exploiting the ignorance of the women Panchayat Presidents. Likewise, the *Dalit* Panchayat Presidents are being dominated over by the non-*Dalit* Vice-Presidents. Wherever Presidents are woman and *Dalits,* Ward Members demand works to carry out in the Panchayat area as contractors. In the event of denial of such opportunities the Ward Members become non cooperative and pose a lot of problems to the Panchayat Presidents. There is yet another problem that the outgoing Presidents are not handing over the files and records to the new Presidents. The new Panchayat President has to start afresh.

The outgoing Panchayat Presidents give a lot of trouble to the new ones. Government officials are giving unequal treatment to the Gram Panchayat Presidents. *Dalit* and women Panchayat Presidents have to face a lot of problems as officials demand huge amounts as bribe. As they want to carry out schemes in their areas the women and *Dalit* leaders have to give the stipulated amount. For the same work other Panchayat Presidents give only a small amount. The weakness and the ignorance of the women and *Dalit* Presidents are being exploited by the officials at the lower level. Block Development Officers and Extension Officers fixed rates for inspection and audit.

After forming this Federation, women and *Dalit* leaders have approached the officials collectively. As a result the officials have fixed certain rates for their cooperation with the Panchayat leaders. 3 per cent of amount has to be given to the officials for correcting the 'M' book. For each inspection conducted by the EOP, they have to pay Rs. 100. For audit each Panchayat has to pay Rs. 1000. Officials suggest methods to the Gram Panchayat Presidents on how to siphon off this amount from the Panchayat funds. According to the perception of the Presidents smooth and cordial relationship between the elected leaders and the officials is necessary. This could be ensured only at the lower level namely, the Block level.

The Federation educates all the leaders on the roles and responsibilities to be discharged, providing necessary information to the Panchayat Presidents for their better functioning especially in delivering services to the people. This Federation mediates with political parties not to interfere in the Panchayat activities from the perspective of party considerations. Whenever the Panchayat Presidents are at loggerheads with the officials the Federation leaders intervene and settle the disputes amicably. The Federation leaders urge that the Gram Panchayat Presidents are elected not on party basis but on personal credentials and hence, they have to act independently without the interference of the party cadres.

Encroachment is a major issue which had been tackled not only through this Federation but also with the help of the community. While removing encroachments, women and *Dalit* Panchayat Presidents are facing a volley of problems and they even receive threatening calls from anti-social elements. Federation extends its full support to such leaders. The Federation insists on getting a copy of the village map from the Village Administrative Officer to keep it in the Panchayat Office. The Village Administrative Officers never cooperate with the Presidents and hence, the Federation has approached the Collector to give instructions to the Village Administrative Officers to supply the village map to all the Gram Panchayat Presidents.

The Federation collects Rs. 100 per individual per year for the activities of the Federation. They keep self-addressed post cards. Information is given through mail. Further the leader of the Federation used to contact the Presidents personally through phone. He feels that it is expensive as this Union has 49 Gram Panchayats. From this

Federation the maximum benefits are derived only by the women and *Dalit* Panchayat Presidents.

Officials favour only ruling party Panchayat Presidents and this practice was checked by the Federation since the majority of them are apolitical. The President of the Federation feels that Panchayat officials can be controlled by the Federation and not by individual Presidents. Such a kind of power is being given to Presidents through the Federation.

Mr. P.V. Sethuraman has quoted an important event that happened in three Panchayats in this Union. To remove the encroachment common properties by the influential individual, three Gram Panchayat Presidents, namely, P.V. Sethuraman of Vikkrapandiam, Palanimuthu Baskar of Setharkkamangalam and Dhanalakshmi Vaithialingam of Sethinipuram gave petitions to the concerned officials. As they did not get a reply, they printed hand bills informing the District Collector that the entire people of those villages would resort to dharna or road rokho. Finally, the District Collector intervened and settled the problem.

The State Level Women's Federation has established a partnership with a small Federation created at the Block level. While interacting with the Presidents of the Block Federation he said the Presidents are interested in carrying out the activities based on the schemes and programmes mooted by the Centre and State Government. They are not oriented in social development activities. Panchayat Presidents look at issues only from the perspective of the people. Why do Panchayat Presidents care more for service delivery? it is the basic question. According to the perception of the people the performers are those who deliver services like water supply, street light, roads and so on. Hence, Panchayat Presidents consider such services essential to get recognition among the people.

EWRs and General Election

Before the general elections, the federation representatives met the political party leaders and submitted petitions about the condition of the Panchayati Raj System in Tamil Nadu and the problems faced by the elected women representatives in local bodies. They met Mr. Vasan, the President of the TNCC and Mr. Anbazhagan, General

Secretary of the DMK and other leaders of the political parties and held discussions with them. The Federation leaders wanted to know the implications of their efforts. Incidentally, they were about to go to New Delhi to participate in a programme organized by the Institute of Social Science and in this connection they wanted to have a meeting at Chennai before their departure. Hence, they met on 21st April 2004. Nearly 55 representatives of the Federation from all over the State met at Chennai.

Objectives

- To review the election manifesto of the political parties and to highlight to what extent the political parties are sensitive towards the Panchayat and women issues in terms of keeping those issues in the manifestoes.
- To persuade the political parties to pass legislation for 33 per cent reservation for women in Parliament and Legislative Assemblies.
- To review the financial status of Panchayats in Tamil Nadu.
- To request the Government to release the SFC grant directly to Panchayats and not through the district administration.

Programme

The workshop started with a prayer. Ms. Ponni Kailasam, President, Tamil Nadu Women Panchayat Presidents Association welcomed the gathering. She listed out the financial issues of the Panchayati System in Tamil Nadu. She evaluated the manifestoes of all the political parties. She criticized the major political parties for the obvious omission of Panchayat and women's issues in their manifestoes. Ms. Kalpana Sathish, representative from CRY, delivered the inaugural address. She requested the EWRs to take their issues to the Prime Minister and the President. She also stated that the EWRs must be aware of the present status of the Panchayats and also identify the reasons for their sluggishness. They must know the views of the political parties on Panchayati Raj and try to change the mindset of the political parties in favour of decentralization. She put forth the following suggestions:

- EWR should meet periodically and discuss their activities and project issues to the political parties and they have to tirelessly work with them.
- EWR should cultivate the habit of mobilizing the people for Panchayat activities.
- EWR should set an example to others in terms of running a transparent administration.
- EWRs who are members of political parties should also consider whether the parties have a policy to strengthen the PRIs, and they have to lobby for it.

She also insisted that the Gram Panchayat Presidents must exercise their powers to implement Central and State Governments schemes to provide basic amenities, and to prepare the BPL list. They should not act as agents of Central and State Governments. The SFC grant has not been released for the last 18 months. The Government is adjusting the SFC grant against electricity bill arrears. Panchayat Presidents must realize that there is no transparency in the Central and State Governments. They are not properly disseminating information to the Panchayats.

She also raised the question of house tax matching grant. She advised the Gram Panchayat Presidents to assume powers without waiting for them to be given to them. Panchayats should not act as mere petitioners. Presidents should discuss the issues with the people in the Gram Sabha and Panchayat activities should be designed accordingly. The women Panchayat Presidents Association should act as a pressure group to change the mindset of the people, the bureaucracy and political parties. The Association also should take steps to retrieve common property resources of the Village Panchayats from encroachment. She appreciated the association for conducting a State level workshop like the current one to design the appropriate strategies for future action. Ms. Ponni Kailasam stated that the programme was organized for discussing various issues and to prepare an agenda for action. She mentioned that this programme was a special one to urge the political parties to bring in legislation for 33 per cent reservation for women in Parliament and State Legislative Assemblies. The political parties in Tamil Nadu never take up the local bodies issues in their manifesto.

The Government should arrange capacity-building exercises for the EWRs in financial management and accounting. The 29 departments of the Government should implement their programmes through the Gram Panchayats. They should also be accountable to the Panchayats. The Tamil Nadu Elected Women Presidents Association has decided that they would support the political parties who would take up their issues and who will work for the betterment of Panchayats. She highlighted the political parties' fear of the performance of the EWRs. The EWRs are working hard in their respective Panchayats to provide basic amenities, and also they are working with the following objectives:

- Ensuring transparency,
- Accountability to the people,
- Augmenting Panchayat resources.

She stated that Association has decided to strengthen the Federation at the Block level. She assured that the Association should act as a pressure group to strengthen the Panchayats. Ms. Jesumary, the President of Michael Pattinam Panchayat, highlighted the importance of strengthening the Federation. She appreciated Dr. G. Palanithurai for his support to the Women Gram Panchayat Presidents. She also thanked the Ramanathapuram District Collector and the officials of Ramanathapuram District for their support and cooperation for Women Panchayat Leaders. She requested the Association members to bring all Gram Panchayat Presidents into the Association to strengthen it at the district level. Ms. Rani Sathappan, President of K. Rayavaram Panchayat in Pudukkottai District, also insisted that the political parties should bring in legislation for 33 per cent reservation for women in Parliament and State Assemblies. She appreciated and thanked her District Collector for his support to the Panchayats. The District Collector of Pudukkottai District released a special fund to the K.Rayavaram Panchayat to desilt the PWD tank and, with his help, Ms. Rani Sathappan got an NOC from the PWD to desilt the same. By this exercise the PWD tank has come into the fold of the Panchayat. She stated that most of the pro-Panchayat officials are very cooperative and that it is the Panchayat Presidents' duty to identify such officials and to work with them.

Ms. Jamruth Beevi, the President of Devipattinam Panchayat in Ramnathapuram District, also insisted that the political parties must bring in legislation for 33 per cent reservation for women in Parliament and Legislative Assemblies. She said that among the three tiers of Panchayats, the Gram Panchayat is working for the betterment of the people. District Councillors and Chairmen do not know anything about the developmental activities carried out in the villages. She stated that the political parties are afraid of the EWR because of their performance. They fear that Women Panchayat Leaders are aspiring for the post of MPs and MLAs. She advised her fellow Panchayat Presidents that they must concentrate on sanitation. She narrated her experience with visiting Central Finance Commission officials from New Delhi. She clearly stated that the poor financial position of the Panchayats to the visiting officials from New Delhi. She urged that Panchayats should concentrate on confidence-building measures among the people in the beginning. Then only Panchayats can get peoples' support and contribution. The Government has instituted many awards for the best performing Panchayats. Panchayats should perform well to get the award money to implement many innovative measures. She advised the EWRs not to inculcate proxy politics. They must equip themselves to work independently and courageously. The EWRs should also equip themselves to get more information from the Government. She mentioned one example: the Mahalir Thittam has allotted 80 crores for SHGs, but no one knows about this.

Ms. Rajeshwari, a retired teacher, was proud of the 33 per cent reservation for women in Panchayats. She requested the EWRs to work cooperatively with the police during critical situations. Her area is known for communal violence and riots. She was threatened by goondas over phone. She mentioned that the people were not cooperative with the Panchayat in the beginning. Many of the common properties encroached upon by influential people have been recovered from them with the help of the police. The EWRs also should learn about the women-related laws and they should get legal support. Ms. Savithiriammal, Kadaladi Union, Ramnathapuram District, stated that rainwater harvesting helped her to increase the level of the water table in the village Oorani. Since her Panchayat is very near the sea, she wants to install a machine to convert sea water into drinking water. Ms. Padma from Trichy District stated that, due to drought, rich people also get loans from cooperative societies. Sand theft is still prevalent on the Erode-Trichy National Highways. She faces a lot of problems in getting the allotted money from the Block officials as they are demanding bribes. She also faces a lot of problems in preparing the BPL list. Officials themselves add or delete names in the BPL list without the knowledge of the Panchayat and the Gram Sabha.

Highlights

- Lack of support from political parties for devolution of powers.
- 33 per cent reservation for women in Parliament and State Assemblies becomes a point in the EWRs' agenda.
- Bring their demands to the notice of the Prime Minister and the President and the national parties continuously.
- Media should be made partners.
- Creating awareness among EWRs on proxy politics.
- Strengthening the federation at Union level.
- Creating good rapport with Government officials and identifying pro-Panchayat officials and working with them.
- Creating awareness among EWRs for the preparation of the BPL list.
- To exert pressure on the Government to provide house tax matching grant as it was granted in the earlier period at the ratio of 1:3.
- Creating awareness among EWRs to work with the people.
- Arranging interface programme with other State representatives.
- Creating awareness among EWRs to take up women issues.

Memorandum Submitted to President of India and Leaders of all Political Parties and the Resolutions of State Committee

Resolutions of EWRs on

- Political parties' poor attention to local body issues and issues of women are being highlighted and criticized.

- Poor financial status of the local body institutions has been highlighted and the State Government has been requested to ensure regular flow of funds to Panchayats.
- Village tanks and oranis have to be desilted and the channels have to be desilted and responsibility has to be handed over to Panchayats by the PWD as it has been done in Pudukkottai District.
- House tax matching grant has to be given to Panchayats as it was given during the previous period.
- Drought Relief Fund should be directly allocated to Panchayats and Panchayats should plan and execute the scheme according to the resolution of the Gram Sabha.
- Power devolution should be done meaningfully as it has been done in Kerala and West Bengal.
- Primary education, primary health and agriculture should be alloted to Panchayats.
- Section 205 of the Tamil Nadu Panchayat Act has to be removed.
- Arrears of EB charges of Panchayats have to be written off or the State Government has to bear the expenditure.
- Even though Gram Panchayats and Panchayat Unions have the right to monitor and issue licences for sand mining, the members of the Gram Sabha should not be allowed to take sand from the rivers for household purposes. The Government should ban profit-motivated sand quarrying. The cases registered against Government Order 4721, 1998 8 WMPN 7300, 7303, 7306, 1998 Industrics (MMCI) Department dated 02.01.1998 have been banned by the High Court of Chennai. This order has given the Panchayat Presidents the right to fix the lease amount which was earlier fixed by the District Collector. According to the G.O.Nos. 3, 4, 5 sand quarrying and mining (authority) should be handed over to Panchayats.
- Gram Panchayat Presidents oppose handing over waste lands to MNCs and other organizations. Land belonging to the Panchayat should not be given to the private sector. All the waste lands should be shared among the farmers (coolies) along with funds for cultivation (with proper documents).

Through Panchayats, wastelands should be equally distributed among the landless poor.

- All poromboke lands and common lands within the Panchayat area should be utilized for Panchayat activities for which a resolution should be passed in the Gram Sabha. This should be further ratified by the Government. The right of the removal of encroachment from the common property resources should be given to the Panchayat.
- The control and decision on usage and regeneration of all common lands, natural resources and water bodies should be vested with the Panchayat. The funds allocated for the maintenance of tanks, lakes, ponds and other water sources to the Agriculture and Public Works Department should be transferred to Panchayats with adequate staff.
- Panchayats should be given the freedom to reclassify any poromboke land which is not serving the purpose. All the poromboke lands in the villages should be entrusted to the respective Panchayats and if the State Government decides to reclassify any land or acquire any land the Village Panchayats and the Gram Sabha members should be duly consulted. The resolution passed by the Village Panchayat should be binding.
- All common water resources in the Village Panchayat like water courses, springs, reservoirs, tanks, fountains, wells and pipes etc., should be vested with and maintained by the Panchayats. The section dealing with this which was in the earlier 1958 Act has been omitted from the 1994 Act. Hence, the Government should insert Section 84 of the 1958 Tamil Nadu Panchayat Act into this new Act.
- Village maps, profiles and other related documents should be handed over to the Panchayats. Village map modification, land resource management, transformation of common property resources, all these activities should be decided upon in the Gram Sabha. When the resolution is passed, the activities should be undertaken by the Panchayats.
- The authority to issue licence to industries and production centres should be given to the Panchayats. The Panchayats are having power to renew these licences and to collect tax.

In the case of defaulting industries, the Panchayat should be provided with the power to disconnect power supply and other common resources.

- Any implementation of the Central or State Governments plans/schemes and MLA's and MP's schemes should get the prior approval of the respective Village Panchayat Councils and all Panchayat Presidents should be informed about the Government functions within their Panchayat limits.
- All funds allocated from MP's and MLA's fund should be spent with the approval of the respective Panchayats. Information on implementation of works under these schemes must be made public through District or Union Panchayats.
- The Departments of Revenue and Police should cooperate with the Gram Panchayat. According to the Kerala Panchayat Act, Article 252 the police should implement the resolution passed by the Panchayat. If the police bypass a resolution the Government can take action against them. This provision should be incorporated in the Tamil Nadu Panchayat Act.
- The police should not arrest or take any person for interrogating from a village without the prior permission of the Village Panchayat President.
- We find that the list of people below poverty line prepared by the Government department is irrelevant and several people who are actually below the poverty line are not included in that list. In this regard, the Central and State Governments should adopt the list prepared by Panchayats for their plans and policies without any changes.
- For the distribution of "Free Patta" the district administration should receive the list of eligible persons from the Village Panchayats. Any addition being made by the department authorities should get the prior approval of the Panchayat Council.
- Enforcement of land reform is very weak in Tamil Nadu. Thousands of acres have been encroached upon by dominant people, including panchami lands, temple lands and lands of irrigation tanks and ponds. Panchayats should ensure land rights for the common people by entrusting with powers for distribution of lands. Similarly, panchami lands should also

be taken possession of and transferred to *Dalits*. For this, Panchayats should have power to identify the lands encroached upon, to take possession of the same and restore them to the *Dalits*.

- The power of issuing community certificates should be vested with the respective Panchayat Presidents with the approval of the Gram Sabha.
- All restrictions regarding the nature of public works to be implemented with Central and State Governments schemes should be handed over to Panchayats. Panchayats should have the power to execute any work within their financial resources based on the decisions of the Gram Sabha.
- With regard to the disadvantaged groups and women, the Government of Tamil Nadu must take special efforts to create forums for them to express their opinions and evolve programmes which will be wholly managed by the Panchayats for the economic empowerment of these communities.
- The list faced by women and *Dalits* in Panchayat Institutions requires the Government's urgent attention. The Government of Tamil Nadu must take urgent steps to guarantee an environment in which women and *Dalits* are able to function in an atmosphere of dignity and freedom. Further, the Government should concentrate on supporting capacity building programmes, especially for women and *Dalits*, and take extra efforts to ensure that all information from the Government actually reaches Panchayats headed by women and *Dalits*.
- Complaints filed by victimized Panchayat Presidents with district authorities and Government functionaries against local dominant political and caste groups must be dealt with on a priority basis by the district authorities to stop the torture and threats.
- The Village President is an executive authority and also a Government functionary in the sense of a public servant. Any person obstructing the functioning of a public servant in the Panchayat Government should be proceeded against legally.
- All Government sectoral departments should produce an Action Taken Report upon the resolutions of Gram Sabha

meetings at least before the next Gram Sabha meeting. The days fixed for the Gram Sabha meeting viz., Gandhi Jayanti Day, Republic Day, Independence Day, and May Day fixed by the State Government should be abandoned. The Village Panchayats should have the power to decide upon the dates and timing for calling Gram Sabha meetings.

Meeting after Training

The Tirunelveli District Presidents were given capacity-building training by The Hunger Project in the month of June 2004. The EWRs of Tirunelveli District were federated during the training programme and office bearers from each block were also selected. Following the training, an interface programme was organized by SSF project for the EWRs of Tirunelveli, Theni, Ramanathapuram and Virudhunagar Districts in the month of August 2004. The exposure visit to model Panchayats motivated the EWRs. (a) strengthened the Union-wise Federation; (b) enhanced their confident on collective leadership; (c) learnt more ideas for effective Panchayat administration; and (d) they felt that it was a refreshing programme, which enriched their thoughts.

By these above continuous processes, the EWRs of Tirunelveli District, tried to organize Federation meetings on their own, not only for discussing their problems, but also for projecting their collective leadership. They also wanted the Government officials to pay attention to their demands and hence they organized themselves collectively in order to demonstrate their strength to the bureaucrats.

The members of the Tamil Nadu Elected Women Representatives Association planned to organize a one-day meeting to discuss the obstacles, constraints and crises which blocked them during the execution of their Panchayat administration. The Panchayat President of Thiruvenkatanathapuram Ms. P. Tamilselvi, felt that all the problems faced by them might be voiced through collective approach. Hence, she has decided to call Elected Women Representatives of Tirunelveli District and to list out the volley of problems which were discussed by them would be flashed through media. Local problems were planned to be discussed with the Collector and problems which could not be solved by the district administration might be brought to the notice of DRD. Gandhigram Rural Institute facilitated her by providing Union-wise responsible persons' list along with addresses and phone numbers for inviting several EWRs of Tirunelveli District. The programme was arranged by Ms. Tamilselvi with all available local resources.

The meeting was organized on 13.9.2004, the programme was started at 11 a.m. for the convenience of the participants, who travelled from various places of Tirunelveli District. The programme was arranged in Sivasami Trust Marriage Hall of Tiruvenkatanathapuram Panchayat. The entire programme was arranged by the Tiruvenkatanathapuram President. The EWRs from Palayankottai, Manoor, Alangulam, Kuruvikulam, Melaneelithanallure, Vasudevanallore, Papakudi, Thenkasi Unions were participated in the meeting. The Project Facilitators of SSF Project, Gandhigram Rural Institute were invited to participate in the above programme. The programme started with a self-introduction of the participants, the Project Facilitators briefing the activities of association, the need for an association, the importance of the association, etc. Then several problems were discussed by EWRs like: (a) The Panchayat has not been provided with sufficient fund; (b) Undue pressure is given by the politicians to Government officials, which reflects their non-cooperative tendency towards Panchayats; (c) No proper BPL list is prepared. The officials never give enough time to prepare the list and also they select people who are sponsored by the political parties; (d) The work allotted under MLA, MP fund has not been informed to the Panchayat administration; (e) The politicians are corrupted, the officials are not able to oppose them, hence the work earmarked by the Presidents, were not sanctioned. In order to fulfill the people's demands, the Presidents approached the contractors, to complete the decided work, on the Panchayat resolution of the Panchayats; (f) The appointment of sanitary workers are insufficient to clean the entire Panchayat, the salary provided for the sweeper is also less, hence, they do not work properly. To overcome this type of situation, they decided to take up solid waste management system which is being practiced in Ramanathapuram District; (g) The location selected for the work allotment under the Government schemes, is not suitable for the beneficiaries; (h) The EWRs should be provided with identity cards by the district administration; (i) The *Dalit* community is always neglected in providing several welfare projects and their needs are not fulfilled; (j) Undue support is given to party supported by the political parties; (k) The construction of buildings like sanitary complex, anganwadi, etc., the sites selected for these buildings are situated in an extension area, where the communities cannot able to utilize these amenities; (l) Several sanitary complexes are not utilized due to lack of water; and (m) SHGs were not properly involved in income generating activities.

The following resolutions were passed by the EWRs: (a) Resolved to request the Government of Tamil Nadu to release the grants which are due to the Panchayats from the month of September 2003 to January 2004; (b) Resolved to request the Revenue and Police Department to provide their cooperation during the removal of encroachments (within Panchayat areas); (c) MLA, MP and Union funds should be undertaken for the projects without the interference of political parties and the schemes which are going to be undertaken place should be initially informed to the Panchayat administration; (d) The allotment of IAY houses and *kaccha* houses upgradation should be provided to all the people living under below poverty line (which should not be reservation-based) and the allotment numbers should be increased; (e) House tax matching grant, funeral grant, stamp duty grant should be released in time; (f) The EB charges met out from the SFC grant should be conveyed to Panchayat with detailed cash receipt; (g) Meeting out the EB charges of the Panchayat from the SFC grant should be stopped and the money should reach the Panchayat directly. They also demanded decrease in electricity charges; (h) The sanitary workers allotted by the Government is insufficient, hence more number of workers should be engaged for sanitation work; (i) With reference to the G.O. No. 45387/2002/20.5.2002 the District Collector can meet the EWRs every month to listen to the problems voiced by them. But so far the Collectors have never met them, in order to remind this, the EWRs planned to meet the District Collector; (j) The Village Administrative Officer has to discharge his duties from his office constructed for the purpose and also has to supply the village map, land details and other Panchayat related information whenever is needed to Panchayats; (k) Motivate them to organize district meetings by themselves; (l) Importance given to Union-wise meetings every month; (m) Discussed and planned themselves for organizing the next district level meetings once in three months; (n) Build up a firm and good relationship with

Gandhigram Rural Institute and among themselves; (o) Their hospitality was amazing which showed the Indian tradition of treating others; (p) Decided to project every issue through media; (q) Needed alternative methods for increasing Panchayat funds through available local resources; (r) More interested in participating in several programmes organized by Gandhigram Rural Institute for the EWRs; and (s) Proper training should be given to SHGs, because they are the supporters of EWRs in several Panchayat activities.

Future Course of Action

This meeting is the initial step taken by the EWRs of Tirunelveli District. They decided on their own for organizing several meetings in the coming future. Following the meeting, the EWRs decided to attend the Annual Mela, which was planned for them at Gandhigram Rural Institute. They insisted that Gandhigram Rural Institute should inform such types of programmes. They wanted to render their services.

Ms. Suganya, the President of Vellimalaipattinam Panchayat of Coimbatore District, stated that most people in rural areas do not utilize the sanitary complexes and are not aware of the importance of sanitation. She insisted that the President of each Panchayat should provide the basic amenities to the community and become role models to the entire community. She insisted on the importance of the construction of individual latrines. She requested the participants to give priority to children's education. The President must be people-friendly. Even though transformation has occurred in a slow way the President has the responsibility to change the people's mindset. She urged the participants to approach several Government departments for getting the needed information. She encouraged the EWRs to face any kind of critical situation without fear and to take necessary action through the police department with the power provided to the Panchayat Presidents.

Thiru. Panneer Selvam, the President of Keerapalayam Panchayat, Cuddalore District, shared his experiences. He clearly narrated his 100 per cent provision of individual toilets. He stated that he invited all the members of his Panchayat and conducted a meeting for highlighting the importance of individual household toilets, but failed in the first attempt. Then he convinced the women and made them realize the importance of the use of toilets and they accepted it. He stated that he has attained cent per cent result in the provision of drinking water facility and education for the children. He proudly narrated his experiences at the time of receiving the Award for the Best Panchayat and meeting the President of India in New Delhi.

The people of his village contributed financial support and participated in every common Panchayat activity. He said that masonary training was provided to SHG members. Transformation of the people is a good process for development. Particularly sustainable development is the consequence of transformation. He said that many of the Presidents met crises due to the non-cooperation of the Vice-Presidents and it is also due to Government officials. The Presidents need not worry. They may authorize the other Ward Members of their Panchayat to sign the documents. He referred to the Northern States like Madhya Pradesh, and Bihar where the 33.3 per cent reservation has not yet been provided for women in local self-governance. They did not have the power to sit in front of the males or to hoist the flags, but Tamil Nadu has given the opportunity for 33.3 per cent reservation for women in the political arena. He urged the EWRs to work confidently and try to work with creativity and become role models. A children's park with the name of the President of India was established in his Panchayat, he stated.

The SC Union Chairperson of Mailam Union of Cuddalore District shared the following ideas: (a) All activities should be implemented with people's participation; (b) All forms of oppression against women under the patriarchal society should be prevented; and (c) Leadership and capacity-building training should be provided at the initial stage to the elected representatives of local self-governance.

Ms. Stella Ruby, a President hailing from Kanyakumari District, stated that the EWRs of each district should share their experiences and raise their voice against the district administration. She referred the G.O. issued by the Government regarding the interface with the district higher officials. She requested the Government to take several measures for improving women's participation in the political arena. She said that there was lack of cooperation between the Block officials and the Presidents. The EWRs who were members of the association should organize periodical meetings.

Ms. Chandrika Sarvesan, President of Siruthondanallore Panchayat of Tuticorin District, talked about her challenges. The Union Councillor of her Union always interfered in her Panchayat activities and spread scandals against her. He urged the Government to take severe action against her under Section 205. As a result most of her time was spent in providing press notes against such scandals. The Union Office did not provide information regarding the Drought Prone Area Programme and never respected the Presidents. The followers and the supporters of the politicians never analyse issues but handle the issues in favour of the politicians, whether they are correct or not. She urged the association members to fight against such hurdles.

Mr. Arockia Raj of Cuddalore District suggested that the representatives of local self-governance need not be worried during critical situations. They can boldly face the issues with the help of legal advisers. Necessary action may be taken if any charges framed against them. He said that his village created a Water Committee which was managed by the women groups. They never bothered about the MLA's or the MP's interference. They strictly followed the procedures and courageously cut the illegal water connections. So, he urged the representatives to become people-friendly and to build up good relationship with officials and the police department.

Thiru. Ilavarasan, the *Dalit* Panchayat President of Shenbgaramannallore of Tirunelveli District, explained that the MLA/MP never inform the Panchayat Presidents before undertaking any work within the Panchayat area. The Government officials also implement public projects without informing the Panchayat and so the benefits do not reach the intended community. For that he has continuously faced the challenges and solved them with the help of the police and the legal departments. He suggested the following: (a) All developmental activities have to be carried out with the approval of the Gram Sabha; (b) SHGs should be motivated to participate in the Gram Sabha and involve themselves in the development activities; and (c) The Panchayat should not allow Government officials to organize any programme without the knowledge of the President.

The President of Karisalpatty Panchayat of Dindigul District stated the following: (a) the Panchayat has to plan for developmental activities; (b) each Panchayat has to prepare all the basic details;

(c) the Panchayat has to approach several departments based on the problems; and (d) the Panchayat need not bother about politicians.

The officials are afraid that the Panchayat Presidents will attain more power than themselves. So they try to dominate the Presidents, he said. He stated that the Presidents all over the State have to raise their voice against the lack of funds from the State Government, particularly against the funds meant for Panchayats being used for electricity bills.

Ms. Bhavani Ilango, the President of Merpanaikadu Panchayat of Pudukkottai District, suggested the following: (a) the Government should provide free electricity to Panchayats and it may collect a fixed amount per year, or at least the prevailing rates should be reduced; (b) the Government should take up the responsibility for paying the balance amount which has not been paid by the previous Presidents; and (c) like MPs and MLAs, the President must be provided an honorarium.

The cheque power was curtailed when the President of Thiruvasi, Trichy District, raised his voice against the sand theft from the river bed within the Panchayat area. He stated that the politicians interfered in this case and the Government officials were the supporters of the politicians. The Public Welfare Department interfered and recommended to the Government to take action against the President under Section 205. The President, along with the people, put the Government officials in the school and locked them up and urged the Government to stop the sand theft. From the MLA/MP fund, he got Rs. 30 lakhs and utilized it for several Panchayat activities. He insisted that the representatives of local self-governance should fight against the atrocities perpetrated against them. He urged the representatives to work hard for their own Panchayats. If any challenges or critical situations arise because of the clerk. The Panchayat Presidents have the responsibility to answer, but not the clerks, he added.

The Chukkampatti President of Dindigul District stressed that the representatives should work for the elimination of caste discrimination, because people's participation has been reduced due to communal hostility. The President should work without discrimination and prepare development plans with the participation of the people of the entire village.

Gender discrimination should be avoided because, at present, more women role models are available, more women groups talk about global issues and are aware of their rights. Women are the prime movers towards sustainable development, said the President of Nallukkottai Panchayat of Sivagangai District, Mr. Ramanathan. He stressed the importance of people's cooperation and urged them to approach several Government departments. A special fund was needed in the name of the Panchayat to face natural calamities, he added.

Special Meet with His Holiness Sri Sri Ravi Shankar

> *"We identify ourselves as somebody. I belong to this religion, this culture, this tradition—but we forget the basic identity that we are human beings. When that stands first and foremost, all other identities follow behind that. Then, I think, that we can achieve what we are really looking for."*
>
> **—Sri Sri Ravi Shankar**

In the afternoon, His Holiness Sri Sri Ravi Shankar, founder of the Art of Living and the International Association for Human Values decided to share his precious spiritual global phenomenon of caring, sharing and service. His Holiness's life and work have been dedicated to reviving human values and bringing about world peace and development through an individual commitment to joyful living, selfless service and self-awareness. He brings together the pristine wisdom of ancient India, the knowledge of breathing techniques, meditation and the importance of doing selfless service and offers them as tools to humanity to recover joyous peaceful living.

His Holiness Sri Sri Ravi Shankar travels to over 40 countries every year to reinforce the message that all religions and the great spiritual traditions share common goals and values. His simple message of love, practical wisdom and service encourages harmony and teaches everyone to follow their chosen religious or spiritual path while honouring the paths of others.

Sustainable Rural Development

Art of Living started its development work in 1982 and initially focused on the provision of primary education to poor children and vocational training to rural women in India. In 1997, the foundation expanded its activities to encompass rural communities for addressing the needs of the poor and the disadvantaged in a holistic manner. Today, the organization's work in rural areas ranges from comprehensive rural development to education, tribal welfare, organic farming, micro-financing, vocational training and emergency relief.

Art of Living organized various workshops and training courses for the children and adults of rural areas. The programmes blossom the individual's full potential with its emphasis on conscious holistic living and personal self-development. These courses promote a better quality of life, increased happiness and peace. Youth empowerment seminars focus on the arduous education system, rising competition, increasing parental pressures, common teenage issues, tough careers and large expectations from the young minds. The Breath, Water Sound course has been extremely effective in increasing overall health and mental well-being, eliminating stress, reducing alcoholism and drug abuse, and domestic violence.

Based on the activities, His Holiness has identified the Village Panchayats which have devolved power to the grassroots and have a good rapport with the people. He decided that the Village Panchayats can combine love, wisdom, harmony, selfless service with joyous, peaceful living. Hence His Holiness wanted to orient the Panchayat Presidents on the above concepts. The Elected Women Representatives from Thiruvarur District and the Panchayat Assistants who were staying Gandhigram Rural Institute for attending capacity building training, both men and women Panchayat Presidents from all over Tamil Nadu participated in the meet. Nearly 300 people, including Panchayat Presidents, Assistants, Faculty of Gandhigram Rural Institute and students of Gandhigram Rural Institute attended this special meet.

Dr. G. Palanithurai welcomed the gathering and spoke about the work carried out by His Holiness and asked the Panchayat Presidents to clarify their doubts. White sheets were supplied to the Panchayat Presidents to put down their questions to Sri Sri Ravi Shankar and all the questions were collected and answered by him. The following issues were discussed: (a) Maintenance of rural sanitation; (b) Involvement and active participation of youth groups in Panchayat activities; (c) Seeking supportive financial contribution for village development activities; (d) Organizing Art of Living courses in rural areas; (e) Prevention of alcoholism and other vices; and (f) Way of establishing communal harmony

Suggestions were provided by Sri Sri Ravi Shankar regarding the above issues. Dr. G. Palanithurai also added his ideas and clarified the Panchayat Presidents' doubts on behalf of His Holiness.

Highlights

The participants suggested the following issues and sought necessary measures to overcome certain hurdles: (a) Legal measures for the compulsory construction of individual household toilets. Family cards might be distributed on this condition; (b) The EB charges should be reduced or free electricity supply should be provided by the Government; (c) The MLA/MP fund activities undertaken or implemented within the Panchayat area should be informed to the Panchayat in advance and they are to be approved by the Gram Sabha in advance; (d) Like the MLA/MP, the Panchayat President should be provided with a salary; (e) Funds from the Central Government should reach the Panchayat directly; (f) Training for eradication of proxy politics leadership is necessary for Panchayat Presidents; (g) More involvement of SHGs in Panchayat activities; and (h) Frequent information dissemination by Government departments.

1. More importance should be given to sanitation through appointment of more sanitary workers.

Observation

During the experience sharing the male elected representatives talked about their performance like provision of roads, drinking water supply, street lights, transportation facilities, the tactics for mobilizing financial resources, etc. But the EWRs talked about Panchayat issues like hike in electricity charges, cooperation needed from Government departments, education for girl children, health hazards due to open defacation, etc. The EWRs have more confidence in group participation. They believe that all problems can be tackled up through groups. A mass of women's will surely overcome any kind of obstacle or hurdle. This was the tendency that appeared among the EWRs.

Extended Scope of the Federation

During the Parliamentary elections, the Federation put forth its demands to various political parties and insisted upon their being included in their party manifestoes, but only a few parties obliged. Even though the Central Government announced various rural development plans and schemes and allocated funds for rural development, the funds did not reach the rural areas directly, but reached them insufficiently through the State Government. So each and every Panchayat faced a severe financial crisis. The Panchayats were not provided with the funds under the SFC and the amount for electricity charges was taken from the SFC grant directly by the Government without informing the Panchayat Presidents. Likewise, the Panchayats' share of income from various sources was not properly handed over to the Panchayats. To overcome such types of financial crises, the EWRs wanted to raise their voice against such artificial crises to the Government through various sources like the DRD, the Minister and the leaders of the opposition.

At this juncture, the Legislative Assembly started its budget session. The Federation decided to discuss their State level demands and planned to draft a resolution for compelling the political parties to speak in favour of the Panchayati Raj System in the matter of the demands. For this State level discussion, the Federation President invited district level representation to discuss and to share the volley of problems faced by them. For this, they expected facilitation from Gandhigram Rural Institute, to invite the EWRs from each district to this State level meet and to help in meeting the Minister concerned and the opposition leaders. In this context, the Rajiv Gandhi Chair for Panchayati Raj Studies, with the support of the Singamma Seenivasan Foundation, Bangalore, organized a one-day State level meet at ICSA, Chennai on 5th March 2005. 30 EWRs from 13 districts like Trichy, Nagapattinam, Erode, Pudukkottai, Ramnad, Coimbatore, Dindigul, Cuddalore and Villupuram participated.

Objectives

The main objectives of the State level meet were:

- to share the district level crises for policy advocacy.

- to insist on various political parties presenting the several crises in Panchayati Raj Institutions during Legislative Assembly sessions.
- to highlight major critical issues through the media for the Government's consideration.
- to seek the DRD's response to the resolutions.
- to identify several ways and means for strengthening the Federation.
- to find out the implications and challenges faced in the course of Federation activities.

Experience Sharing

The programme was chaired by Ms. Ponni Kailasam, the President of the Tamil Nadu Elected Women Representatives Associatiòn. Ms. Jesumary, the Vice-President of the Association, Ms. Papa, the State Planning Committee Member, Ms. Salma, Association Member, Ms. Rani Sathappan, Assistant General Secretary of the Association and Ms. Suganya participated. Ms. Ponni Kailasam welcomed the district representatives, listed the reasons for the gathering and explained the major issues to be discussed. Then she suggested that the EWRs should work cooperatively for achieving the task, which is not only to fulfil the demands of the EWRs but also to provide sustainable development to all the Panchayats of Tamil Nadu. The issues projected by her were receiving powers over the scheduled 29 subjects, reducing or removing electricity charges for Panchayats, demanding the unpaid SFC grant for the year 2002-2003, removing Section 205 against the Panchayat Presidents, retrieving encroachments, fund allocation on population basis, Panchayat share of cable TV charges, etc. She motivated the EWRs to fight full-fledgedly for getting several rights to the Panchayats. She asked the EWRs to share their experiences.

Ms. Bhavani Elango, President of Merpanaikadu Panchayat of Pudukkottai District, narrated her bitter experience over the payment of electricity charges. Her Panchayat paid a lot of money to the Government as interest for the unpaid electricity charges. The Government asked them to take or adjust the amount from other accounts, or else they said that the President was responsible for paying the amount. She said that the MPs and MLAs were also elected by the people, but they led a luxurious life and did not meet the people frequently. They expected some financial contribution from the people for fulfilling any kind of demands put forth by the people. But in the case of the Presidents they rendered services to the people and also faced the wrath of the opposing persons and the people whose demands were not fulfilled. This hurt/affected the Presidents who work hard, sincerely, transparently and truthfully. She stated that it might be the last meeting to insist on this because she was frustrated by insisting on this in every meeting. She had decided to demonstrate and fight against the Government directly. She pointed the problem of noting improper electricity consumption readings by the officials without any proof and taking the amount from the SFC without the knowledge of the concerned Panchayat President.

The Presidents never interfered in or cross checked the grant allocated to the Union Councillor but the Union Councillor criticized each and every work carried by the Presidents. She shared one instance which took place in her Panchayat. The Union selected four good Panchayats. One among them was her Village Panchayat. An amount of Rs. 35,000 was given to her Panchayat as subsidy for its good performance. With this amount, the Panchayat decided to repair the street pipes. The estimated work order was accepted by the AD Panchayat and he passed the bill. Usually, under the first account, if the amount involved is more than ten thousand, the work has to be tendered. This was pointed out by the Deputy BDO. Then the work was sanctioned and the bill was passed. But the Union Councillor published a news item in the papers saying that the President did not do the work, but took the amount for herself. The officials also said that the President did not report anything and that they did not know anything. This created a false impression among the people regarding the President's honesty. She worried a lot. The association members convinced her not to worry, because she had had the evidence with her. So they asked her to take necessary steps by consulting a legal expert and face them through the court. They motivated her not to bother about such type of criticism and to solve any kind of problem and assured her that the Federation would support her all the time.

Ms. Suganya, the President of Vellimallaipattinam of Coimbatore District, stressed the importance of the reduction of the EB charges and narrated her woes. The District Collector transferred the stamp duty amount allocated for her Panchayat to another Union. The officials stated that it would surely lead to audit objection because they hadn't got the permission from the Panchayat. Another problem was under the Jawahar Rozgar Yojana Scheme. The amount left over after the implementation of the scheme was taken away by the Government. Even though the President planned to utilize this balance amount for another Panchayat work, the amount was taken away by the officials, she added. This same problem was experienced by Ms. Murshidabeevi, the President of Srimoolakarai Panchayat of Tuticorin District.

All EWRs should work together and fight against the problems unitedly. Cordial relationship with others will ensure the achievement of their goal and vision. This was stated by Ms. Jesumary, the President of Micahel Pattinam Panchayat of Ramnathapuram District. She added that women should not be confined to the home but come out to the outside world where they have to learn a lot. She insisted that courageous attitude, efforts and experience would enable them to cope with any kind of threat. She advised the EWRs that this type of attitude made the officials render positive action in favour of them and that no one should be afraid of action under section 205 because nobody has the power to dissolve the Panchayat President's post. Everyone should maintain the vouchers perfectly and meet the officials along with the evidences, she added. She also stressed the reduction of EB charges and finally urged the association to take follow up action on the demands/resolutions put forth to the Government. This was also insisted on by Ms. Salma, the President of Thuvarankurichi Panchayat of Trichy District.

Ms. Mainmekalai, the President of Keeranor Panchayat of Erode District, felt proud of Ms. Jesumary for her effective interface with Government higher officials and for her trip to New York for the implementation of rainwater harvesting. She felt guilty for not having a meeting exclusively for the EWRs of Erode District. The higher authorities never treat EWRs with respect and never disseminate proper information to them. She insisted that the District Collector should meet all the EWRs once a month or else he should meet the EWRs union-wise. Then only he will be able to create a cordial relationship between the EWRs and the officials.

Ms. Rani Sathappan, the President of K.Rayavaram Panchayat of Pudukkottai District, said that the EWRs should approach the

Government officials for getting schemes and projects for their Panchayats. They should not miss any opportunities. With regard to the Government's withdrawal of the balance scheme fund pointed out by Ms. Suganya, she revealed that, when an EWR has explained the details with evidence, like the proposals designed for village development activities, the officials would surely take them into consideration. She shared one instance wherein she got tree saplings from the unutilized balance scheme fund from the Government office and planted a large number of trees in her Panchayat area.

Most of the EWRs said that an amount of Rs. 6,000 was insisted upon to allot money for the maintenance of the sanitary complex, but the SFC grant was not regularly provided to the Panchayats. The SHGs collected a charge from the user group for the maintenance of the sanitary complex. They insisted that the Panchayat should be provided with direct funds from the Central Government.

After the experience sharing, the major demands which needed immediate solutions were drafted by the EWRs, so as to put forth these demands to the political parties, to the higher officials of the Rural Development Department and to the media. The personnel from the print and visual media not only covered the programme but also interacted with a few EWRs regarding their crises.

Resolutions

The Association pleads with all the political party leaders and members of the Legislative Assembly to voice their appeals and resolutions in the budget session of the Tamil Nadu Assembly. While the State political parties raise their voice against the Central Government not to take action on the States using Article 356, they should also tell the State Government not to remove the Panchayat Presidents using Act Section 205 of the Tamil Nadu Panchayat Act because the Panchayats are the third dimension of governance. The Association strongly condemns the removal of a number of women Panchayat Presidents by using Section 205 in Thiruvallur District. The cost of 1 unit of electricity, which was Rs. 1.60 during the previous regime, has been raised to Rs. 3.40 during the present government. Keeping this in mind the Government may pay the electricity bill for public activities like drinking water and street lights (as does the Karnataka Government). For the first time in India, the rotation system for women representatives has been extended to 10 years in Tamil Nadu. The Federation pleads with the honourable Chief Minister to extend this again for one more term of five years. The Constitution of India and the 1994 Panchayat Act provide powers to the Panchayat with regard to the 29 subjects. But, in Tamil Nadu, not even a single department has taken steps to empower the Panchayat. Eight per cent of the total income of the State is being provided to the local body institutions. The Federation requests the Government to announce the quantum of funds allocated and released during the past 3 years, namely, 2001-02, 2002-03 and 2003-04. The financial allocation for nine months during the year 2001-02 has not been released till today. The Federation requests the Government to release the balance amount immediately. The Federation requests the Government to release the subsidy on cremations for the last 3 years. The Federation requests the members of the State Legislative Assembly to take steps for the immediate release of local cess for the year 2003-04. The Federation requests the Government to release the State Finance Commission grant which has not been released for the period from 1.9.2003 to 1.1.2004. Just like the MP Area Development Fund and the MLA Constituency Development Fund, the Panchayat President also should be given some funds for area development.

While selecting Panchayats for awards of the Nirmal Gram Puraskar, only those Panchayats with minimum population which have completed the total sanitation programme are selected. But there are Panchayats with huge populations which could not complete the Total Rural Sanitation Programme (TRSP) and these are neglected. But the Federation requests the Government to select Panchayats keeping in mind the population and the proportion of the activities carried out.

From the last year onwards, the right of auctioning sand has been taken over by the Government. But the rights over mines and quarries are vested with the Panchayat. Keeping this in mind the Government may release the share from the sale of the sand to the Panchayat immediately. In Tanjore, Nagai and Thiruvarur Districts the majority of the irrigation tanks are under the control of the earlier Panchayat Presidents, their relatives and other traditional Panchayat leaders. The Government has not taken any steps to take back this power. It was stated that, in 1996, as soon as the Panchayat Council assumed powers, all the Panchayat properties should be handed over to the Panchayats. But the Revenue Department was not supportive of the Panchayats in taking possession of the properties. The Federation requests the Government and the MLAs of these 3 districts to take immediate steps to recover and resolve these properties to the Panchayats.

Now, the duties and responsibilities of the Panchayat have been extended. Women and Scheduled Caste members have been elected to all the positions. As a result of the reservation, about 4000 women have assumed positions as Panchayat Presidents. Keeping this in mind, the Government should come forward to provide honorarium to these Panchayat Presidents. The Government should issue appropriate orders to provide Rs. 5,000 per month to the Gram Panchayat Presidents, Rs. 7,000 per month to the Block Panchayat Presidents and Rs. 10,000 per month to the District Panchayat Presidents.

The developmental activities and the infrastructural developmental activities which are carried out with the help of the 12th Finance Commission have to be selected only by the Gram Sabha of the concerned Panchayat. The district administration should not interfere in this. The Federation requests the Central Government to allocate funds for Social Forestry in Panchayat areas and for the maintenance of roads. To make the Government Orders which are related to the Panchayati Raj Act very effective and to learn about the powers of the Panchayats, the District Panchayat should publish a Newsletter regarding the district issues. The State Government should allocate funds to Panchayats as per the 2001 census. But the Government has followed the 1991 census in prescribing the financial criteria for Panchayats. This has handicapped the Panchayats in fulfilling the basic needs of the public. Hence, the State Government should raise the funds to the Panchayats.

The State Finance Commission allocated 8 per cent from the State revenue (1997-98) for the Panchayats. It was recommended that the State Government should raise it 1 per cent more every subsequent year. Based on this, for the financial year 2004-04, it should be raised to 15 per cent and allocated to the Panchayats. At present, the District Collector has the power to dissolve the Panchayat administration and to suspend the Panchayat President. Dissolving a Government elected by the people and suspending a President are objectionable under the democratic philosophy. Hence, the Federation requests the Government to rescind Section 205 of the Tamil Nadu Panchayati Raj Act. The Tamil Nadu Panchayati Raj Act exists only in writing, but is not practically realized. The employees for the 29 subjects should be brought under the Panchayats.

Some important departments under the 29 subjects are funded by the Central Government, particularly departments like Education, Sanitation, SC Welfare, Agriculture, Animal Husbandry, Fishery, BC and MBC Welfare, Nutrition, and Women Welfare. The Federation requests the State Government to take necessary steps for implementing these departments' activities under the Gram Panchayat administration. Still the Village Panchayat has not been provided with the cable TV tax for the past two years. The Government might take 5 per cent as collection charges and the balance 95 per cent should be handed over to the Panchayats.

The Federation condemned the Revenue, Public Welfare and Forest Departments for cutting down valuable trees in Panchayat areas without informing the Panchayats. The State Government should take necessary action to give preference to the Panchayats in auctioning. The share of the auction amount has not been handed over to the Panchayats for years. Under the Panchayati Raj Act, the auctioning amount should be given to the Panchayats. Based on this Act, from the share the Government should give 65 per cent of the auction amount to the Panchayats.

The State Government ordered the Revenue Department and the Police Department to support the Panchayats during the removal of encroachments by individuals, especially of poramboke lands which are to be turned into housing patta lands (the Government officials should be supportive in the selection of lands for housing, especially, in the tsunami affected areas). But these departments are indifferent. The funds allocated by the Central Government for the development of women are utilized in rural areas by non-governmental organizations. This should be avoided and the Government should take necessary steps to hand over the funds to the Panchayats and the implementation of activities by NGOs should be through Panchayats. Panchayats are equivalent to Central and State Governments. Taking this into account, the funds allocated by the Central Government should be directly sent to the Panchayat account.

The pension for old-age women and widows and birth and death certificates should be issued through Panchayats. For this the Government should take necessary action. The concerned sectoral departments should take up responsibility to implement the schemes which are resolved upon in the Gram Sabha. The Government should issue Government Orders in this regard. A law should be enacted to make the Tamil Nadu Revenue Department and the Police Department adhere to the resolutions of the Panchayat Council. In the Kerala Panchayat Act, Rule 252 states that the police have to adhere to the resolutions of the Panchayat Council and also that any police official who ignores those resolutions will be punished.

Interaction with Role Models

Thiru.Ilango, the President of Kuthambakkam Panchayat, shared his experiences with the EWRs and suggested various Panchayat management techniques and solutions to overcome various crises in Panchayat administration. He appreciated the Women Panchayat Presidents for making the Government design plans for rural development and provide opportunities for the officials to visit other countries. He appreciated them for discussing the Panchayat issues which are common to both men and women. He highlighted the following ideas: (a) The EWRs should frequently visit the Government departments. This will change the mindset of the bureaucrats and develop a cordial relationship between them and the EWRs; (b) For every unsolved problems, they have to write letters to the officials and ask for relevant explanation and keep the evidence properly; (c) He quoted several experienced role models in handling Panchayat administration successfully even amidst the interference of the various political parties and other hostile groups; (d) The EWRs should not worry about the false news flashed in papers and anonymous letters from some disgruntled parties. They should consult legal experts, former experienced, pro-Panchayat members and take necessary action according to the nature of the problem; (e) They have to work along with Ward Members, who are the supporters of the Presidents; (f) The rotation system has its impact on *Dalit* communities. Hence the EWRs have to create a good relationship among the people, without communal rivalry; (g) Social transformation can create economic development which will be achieved through co-operation. Supportive institutions should be drawn closer for collaborative work; (h) The EWRs should fight against social evils individually or as a group; (i) They may provide counseling to the AIDS affected persons and can create income genrating development activities for them; (j) They should create a movement of 'Friends of Panchayat', along with pro-Panchayat institutions and officials for its development; and (k) The EWRs can follow many excellent role models for developing not only the Panchayat management but also their capacity.

As a whole the Panchayat Presidents should not depend on the Government. They have the capacity to plan for village development and have the creativity to make use of the local resources and provide a good Panchayat administration, despite getting insufficient fund. The Panchayat has the capacity to adopt several techniques like saving on electricity, provision of pure drinking water, low cost technology for different types of houses, implementation of projection non-conventional energy sources, etc. He urged the EWRs to face any kind of challenge without fear.

Implications Felt by the EWRs about Federation

The EWRs discussed/shared among themselves, what changes occurred due to the formation of the Federation and they were: (a) It built up the concept of mass participation; (b) It helped to identify various EWRs from other districts; (c) It created courage to face any kind of problem; (d) It developed the personality from good experiences like meeting higher officials, Prime Minister and President of India; (e) It created a platform such as Gandhigram Rural Institute, which provided them training, experience sharing, interface with role models, other state experiences, etc; (f) It gained popularity through the media; (g) It provided opportunity to contest for MLA/ MP seats; (h) It created collaborative links with Panchayat-supportive NGOs; (i) It created supportive pro-Panchayat officials; and (j) It gave them more power to raise their voice against atrocities not only against Panchayat administration but also against women.

Meeting with Shri Suriya Kanta Mishra

Experience sharing is a thought-provoking process, which facilitates exchange of thoughts, valuable information, solutions to crises, ideas for creativity, wider dissemination of information, etc. Within the State of Tamil Nadu experience sharing between block level and district level Elected Women Representatives is rare. They become familiar with other Elected Women Representatives during several meetings organized for them. Hence, with the assistance of SSF, exposure visits were arranged for the Elected Women Representatives to enrich their administrative skills, capacity to perform within the poor financial aids, utilization of available resources for increasing the Panchayat revenue, and to make them role models for others, especially to reduce gender discrimination. Many of the Elected Women Representatives stated frequently that the Panchayati Raj System in Tamil Nadu is rigid and that they were not able to work independently. But, as per the information disseminated through various mass media, West Bengal has fair traditional grassroots governance and the best example for proper Panchayati Raj structure.

Fortunately, the West Bengal Minister of Panchayati Raj, Dr. Suriya Kanta Mishra visited Tamil Nadu and, Dr. G. Palanithurai, the Coordinator of SSF, created an opportunity for the Elected Women Representatives of Tamil Nadu to meet him by inviting the Hon'ble West Bengal Minister to Gandhigram Rural Institute. He accepted the invitation and delivered his lecture on "Panchayati Raj and Poverty Reduction: The West Bengal Experience".

The Rajiv Gandhi Chair for Panchayati Raj Studies, with the support of the Singamma Sreenivasan Foundation Project, Bangalore, organized a one-day regional workshop for the Elected Women Representatives on 22nd May 2005 at Gandhigram Rural Institute. The Elected Women Representatives from all the districts of Tamil Nadu participated in the programme.

Objectives

- To spell out the crises encountered by the Elected Women Representatives during their Panchayati Raj administration.
- To find out the solutions for their crises.

- To discuss topics like Governance of Education, Governance of Health, Governance of Environment and Governance of Weaker sections.

Hon'ble Minister's Speech

The Hon'ble West Bengal Minister, Dr. Suriya Kanta Mishra, delivering his lecture on "Panchayati Raj and Poverty Reduction: The West Bengal Experience," gave a general overview of the three-tier Panchayat system in West Bengal. He explained that West Bengal has had a long tradition of rural local self-government institutions and spoke elaborately on the origin of the Panchayati Raj System during the British era and the maintenance of law and order under colonial rule. The radical changes after independence, now approval of Panchayats in the Indian Constitution, the Directive Principles of State Policy, formation of several committees and election methods were also referred to by him.

He said that several surveys were conducted on class composition of the Panchayats elected in successive elections and also to find out whether their class character has changed over the years. The survey pointed out that most of the Panchayat representatives were small and marginal farmers and a few are landless labourers, teachers and social workers. Simultaneously, he explained the areas of research studies conducted by West Bengal. Some of them are:

- Increase in people's participation.
- Breaking of dominance vested in rural Bengal by direct elections.
- The influence of caste system has declined.
- The presence of more SC/ST members without reservation.
- The political organization of the disadvantaged classes has succeeded in ushering in a significant change in the balance of political power.
- Criticisms against the Left Front.
- Conflicts with traditionally dominant village leadership.
- Recognition of women in Panchayats.
- Land reforms and political will.
- Gender and caste composition.

- Formation of programmes for women and children.
- Functions assigned to Panchayati Raj Institutions.
- Finances and functionaries.
- Democratic functioning.
- Achievements—growth with equity.

Finally, he concluded that in West Bengal the people have learned from their own experience. It was from their experience of participation in socio-economic development, development of class and mass struggles to demolish all limitations imposed by the existing order that people turned to revolutionary changes.

Area for Discussion

The following subjects were elaborately discussed among the Elected Women Representatives and they were framed by the Project Facilitators. They were:

Drinking Water

1. *Protection of drinking water sources*

- desiltation,
- prevention of sewage water contaminating drinking water sources,
- maintenance of purity.

2. *Importance of Saving Water*

- prevention of wastage of water,
- proper water supply to all,

3. *Need for Protected Pure Water*

- awareness
- various unprotective measures
- handling water management

Sanitation and Health

1. *Public Sanitation and Health*

- prevention of open defecation
- construction of toilet facilities
- removal of sewage water
- disposal of wastes
- prohibition of liquor

2. *Women's Health*

- teenage girls
- reproductive mothers
- mothers

3. *Children's Health*

- preventive medical aids
- provision of nutritive food

Education

1. *School Enrolment*

- children from 5 years of age enrolled in schools
- dropouts

2. *Basic Infrastructural Facilities*

- drinking water
- toilets
- buildings
- study materials
- teachers

3. *Students' Health*

- Parents and Teachers Associations

- Medical camps
- Awareness on sanitation
- Maintenance of clean environment

Environment

1. Maintenance of CPR

- gathering information
- removal of encroachments
- secure
- creation of income generation

2. Protection of Natural Resources

- water
- land
- air

In the afternoon session the participants were divided into four groups and they discussed the above themes.

Panchayat Governance and Weaker Sections

Initially, the group identified the various levels of weaker sections lists. The BPL list prepared by the Government is not relevant. Many ultra poor people's name are not included, but wealthy people are added. Hence, the BPL list should be prepared through people's participation with the supervision of the Gram Panchayat. The group members stressed that the available list should not be considered by the Government for further implementation.

Then the group listed the various types of welfare schemes and also the several sectoral departments which were involved in the implementation process. They were the following:

- Social Welfare
- Revenue
- Rehabilitation of Physically Challenged
- Adi Dravidar Welfare

- Education
- Family Welfare
- Public Distribution
- Employment Exchange

The above said Government department officials have not realized the mindset of weaker sections. The follow-up action on the demands are delayed but no reasons are given in this regard. Some of them expect contributions and also dismiss petitions by quoting several Government rules. They haven't pointed out any reason for the delay but have made the leaders walk for days. They have not given the replies to the petitions submitted but have asked the leaders to submit fresh ones. The rules and norms are not specifically given during the submission of petitions, but afterwords they reject the same. The weaker sections have no money. Hence the leaders themselves spend their own money for the weaker sections.

Panchayat Governance—Implementation Process

1. The Panchayats suggested that the list of weaker sections, the gathered census survey details, the release of the total report by the Government should be got approved by the Panchayats for implementation.
2. The Panchayats tried to insist that the appropriate reasonable demands should not be rejected under rules but the rigidity be somewhat relaxed.
3. Physically and mentally challenged should be not only provided with pension but also extended some socio-economic support.
4. The Panchayats should conduct a survey and established special schools for the physically challenged children.
5. Provided employment opportunities for the weaker sections under food for work scheme and planned various ways for getting funds allotment from the Government.
6. Awareness programmes were organized for the prohibition of liquor.
7. Conducted surveys for the identification of the poor and they were linked to the SHG groups.

8. Tied up the weaker sections with the sectoral departments which are working for the welfare of the weaker sections.
9. Housing schemes were properly allocated for the weaker sections.
10. Identification of wasteland and several arrangements were made for providing these lands to the people below poverty line.
11. Implementation of several available welfare schemes for children belonging to the weaker sections.

Recommendations

1. The fund allocated for the welfare schemes of the poor should be increased.
2. The sectoral departments should link with the Village Panchayats for the effective implementation of the welfare schemes.
3. The rigid norms and rules laid for the widow remarriage scheme fund would be relaxed.
4. Loan scholarship might be granted for the higher education of the poor family's children.
5. The Government should take necessary action against officials who work against justice during the implementation of welfare schemes.
6. House pattas should be given to the poor.
7. Free Registration of will should be done for the poor house owners during partition among family members.
8. Family counselling centres should be formed for the poor.
9. Poor youth should be provided with income generating activities through vocational training

Role of Gram Panchayat in Sanitation

— The water sources like canals, ponds and tanks should be protected from garbage.
— The above sources should be frequently desilted.
— The encroachments should be removed.
— The Village Health Nurse should stay in every Panchayat and the Government. Hospital should recognize the patients who are identified by the VHN.

— Every Health Centre should be provided with technological inputs like ECG, Scan, X-ray etc. and should be protected with clean environment.
— The ration shops should supply hygienic protein rich food.
— The separate sanitary complex should be maintained properly.
— A sanitary complex for men should be established.
— Both the Central and the State Governments should raise the funds allocated for the construction of individual household toilets.
— The Health Committee should be structured systematically and should organize meetings periodically
— The Government should recognize the physically challenged persons' list which was passed through the Gram Sabha.

Governance of Education

— All the infrastructural facilities were provided to schools
— *Pucca* school buildings were constructed with the support of the SSA.
— Schools were provided with regular protected drinking water supply.
— Ensured the enrolment of children above 5 years.
— There was no cordial relationship between the teachers and the Panchayat Presidents in a few Panchayats.
— In some Panchayats, the Presidents are not invited to PTA meetings.
— The Panchayats contributed wastebaskets and separate toilets for girls, boys and teachers.
— One of the Panchayat Presidents from Trichy District, who was a graduate, was taking special classes for students.
— Ensure education of all children below 14 years.
— In many Panchayats child labourers are engaged in the Gem Cutting and food processing units of other States. This was identified by the EWRs through door-to-door survey. They brought them to their native places and sent them to schools.
— A few EWRs tried to establish Balwadis.
— The EWRs appointed the unemployed youths from their own Panchayats, where sufficient teachers are not available.

— Planted trees around the compound walls.
— The essential items like badges, clothes, tics, nail-cutters, books and other study items were collected by the EWRs from donors and distributed to the school students.
— Children below poverty line were enrolled in the schools which were run by NGOs.
— During School Annual Day celebrations prizes were distributed to the students, emphasizing the importance of children's education among parents.
— Gypsies' children were enrolled in schools and now they have completed their graduation.
— Two Panchayat Presidents conducted special classes on subjects like Indian Culture and Tradition and they brought about desirable changes in the students.
— In some management schools, the poor students who failed to pay the fees were ordered to stand outside of the classes for the entire day and they also appoint poor in experienced teachers.

They Suggested the Following Ideas

— Improvement of education.
— No discrimination among the students.
— No difference according to their economic status.
— Cable TV should be disconnected by the parents.
— Regular PTA meetings every month.
— Non-expectation of community certificate.
— Teachers should not be included in the Census report collecting process.
— The Private schools should be under the control of the Gram Panchayat to ensure educational quality.
— Educational institutions must be monitored by the Panchayats.
— Local residents should not be appointed teachers in local schools.
— Regular sports items must be provided to schools.
— Teachers should not collect money from the students.

Governance of Environment

— Removal of encroachments from ponds, Panchayat poramboke lands.
— Income generation created from natural manure.
— Toilets for schools, Anganwadis and communities were constructed to avoid open air defecation.
— Trees were planted on road sides, near Panchayat offices, river banks and schools to prevent soil erosion.
— Cancel the approval of pollution causing industries.
— Construction of drainage canals for the control of spreading sewage water.
— Maintenance of water supply by SHGs.
— Applied solid waste management system.
— Periodical checkups of chlorinated water.
— Goat rearing was controlled through Gram Sabha for the maintenance of trees which were planted by the Panchayats.

Outcome

— Preparation of vulnerable families' list through Gram Sabha.
— Understood the processes of vulnerability reduction.
— How to maintain close rapport with the people.
— Understanding governance properly.
— Priority to Health and Education Governance.
— Attending to Land and Water issues in the community.
— Enrolment of students, reduction of dropouts and abolition of child labourers, improvement of educational inputs, enriching the school environment and regular committee meetings.

These meetings helped the EWRs to share their views on governance, problems faced by them and also helped them raise their voice collectively. Further, it helped them meet various personalities and seek their guidance. They have found out and forum to project their demands collectively and act collectively. This gives them strength and provides them with a source of inspiration.

8

Annual Meet

The First Annual Mela

The Elected Women Representatives' Federation meets annually in Gandhigram Rural University with the support of Rajiv Gandhi Chair for Panchayati Raj Studies. So for they have conducted four such Annual Melas in which several persons like Panchayat Presidents, State level officials, academicians, researchers participated and discussed the progress, challenges and difficulties faced by the EWRs.

Dr. G. Palanithurai, Coordinator of the project while explaining the significance of the mela, recollected the services rendered by the founders of Gandhigram Rural Institute, who were the disciples of Mahatma Gandhi. The ultimate aim of the founders of Gandhigram Rural Institute is centered around women's empowerment. The efforts of Dr. Soundaram Amma are further strengthened by the institute through empowering Women Panchayat Presidents, Dr. G. Palanithurai added. The Rajiv Gandhi Chair has established a close contact with the elected women representatives for the past five years and carried out several programmes including capacity-building. But ever since the 73rd Amendment to the Constitution of India was enacted, Gandhigram Rural Institute understood its importance and implications and created awareness among the rural masses since 1992. Dr. G. Palanithurai added that 33 per cent reservation of seats were filled up in the midst of obstacles in the social set-up where women have been suppressed and humiliated. It was the general expectation that the critical mass created through the reservation would bring the needed transformation in the society in many aspects. It is a general question: how can women representatives respond to the challenges in the context of increasing violence against women?

Inspite of hurdles and obstacles, the women presidents at the grass-roots institutions have achieved a lot. It is now necessary to take a close look and understand the processes of devolution of powers and how these powers are being used and people who supported them and the factors that instill confidence in them to face the challenges. So far, a section of women presidents (negligible in number) failed to prove their capacity and independent action. In future, they have to fill the 33 per cent of seats in Local Bodies independently without the influence of their male members.

The State level Federation is a forum of the elected women leaders in the Local Bodies. The role of Gandhigram Rural Institute is only that of facilitation and it encourages women presidents to think over their problems and take decisions independently. Gandhigram Rural Institute would not influence the decisions of the Federation and it would only guide and counsel them. The elected women representatives have to face the problems and they could not escape from the reality. Hence, they have to equip themselves to tackle these problems. Others could help them by providing necessary information and training.

Dr. G. Palanithurai observed that inspite of stiff opposition women representatives have functioned independently and as a result increasing number aspirants would be ready to contest. From among 4000 and odd Women Gram Panchayat Presidents, more than 1000 are *Dalits.* Among them only a very few were in trouble and the rest have overcome the obstacles. And a lot of them have proved their work by achieving many things silently. However, about 98 women presidents have been affected by the Rule 205 of Tamil Nadu Panchayat Act. From the field experience, we came across a number of achievers who performed their duties well inspite of obstacles and problems.

We have analysed and documented the problems pertaining to the women leaders of the local bodies. The women leaders themselves knew about all the problems as they are in the field. The development achieved in the villages are the achievements made by the local bodies. Even though the fund might be allocated by the State Government, the local leaders by their hard work and voluntary spirit have been completing the works. All these things would not be known to everybody. Instead of facilitating the presidents, the officials in general refer to the rules and regulations of the Act and discourage the leaders when they take up innovative works. The State Government does not seriously take into cognizance of the Rule 243(G) of 73rd Amendment to the Constitution of India which assures the status of self-governance to the local bodies. As per the claim of the State Government, it has entrusted 760 powers to the three-tiers of the Panchayats which are in general, namely, supervisory, monitoring and advisory in nature, not the power of decision-making.

Dr. G. Palanithurai pointed out that from the history one could understand the fact that powers are not given by any one but they must be taken. He pointed out that the village presidents initiated a number of activities for which necessary powers have not been conferred upon them yet, they assumed powers and performed. He recalled that the failure of the strike organised by the Government staff in the local body offices was due to the continuous performance of the Presidents of the Panchayati Institutions. Dr. G. Palanithurai referred to the mentality of the higher officials who did not show any interest in the programmes in which women presidents were participants. The women presidents would raise questions and express their views fearlessly. Further, he informed that the Gandhigram Rural Institute has always properly oriented the officials with regard to gender equality.

Women presidents give priority to the issues like sanitation, education and public distribution as they realise such problems are so vital for the community and more particularly to the women folk. They overcome obstacles at various levels right from the family, community, the officials, and the co-members. We should not compare them with men presidents. It is our duty to remove the obstacles and facilitate the women presidents to make Panchayati Raj, a movement. Dr. G. Palanithurai explained that the officials do not interact with the women presidents. They encouraged the proxies. But later, the officials have realized the fact that women presidents have potentials. The officials have changed their perception and do recognise the women leaders.

When pointing out the necessity for the formation of a Federation exclusively for women presidents Dr. G. Palanithurai informed that the opportunity was denied to most of the women leaders in the organisations and associations run by the local body leaders both men and women. He watned to challenge those issues. Gandhigram Rural Institute understood the dynamics of the issues and decided to facilitate the women leaders to address their issues on their own. Some of the leaders might think that the conference—'Mela' is convened very late and, of course, it is organised during the fag end of their tenure with a specific reason that we have to furnish facts and figures about the issues and to list out the practical problems of the elected women representatives. We could get all the details about the problem and with this assumption we have convened their meet now. Further, Gandhigram Rural Institute would not independently initiate the process of consolidating women unless a demand was put forth by the women presidents, Dr. G. Palanithurai noted. He appealed to the elected women representatives to ponder over the problems faced by the elected women representatives and the problems of women in general. He further appealed to the elected women representatives to stand on their own and suggested that for this a strategy has to be worked out.

Presidential Address by Mrs. Ponni Kailasam

In her presidential address, Mrs. Ponni Kailasam reminded the proverb "The day is not dawned by Hen's cry" but the women presidents proved that they could also perform excellently. As an example, she cited the successful action of a women president in tackling the illegal mining of silicon sand in the Vedaranyam block of Nagapattinam district, inspite of threats to her life. Mrs. Ponni Kailasam, noted that the revenue department officials failed to properly bring out the field realities to the knowledge of the higher officials. As a result the women leader had to suffer a lot.

She explained that all the felt-needs of the people are fulfilled by the Panchayats. She informed that when the PWD did not attend to the maintenance works (inlet and outlet sub-channels), by the initiative of the Panchayat, these works were completed with the contributions from the farmers. And the farmers organised a felicitation meeting to honour the women president. Unable to bear the recognition given to the Panchayat President, the cadres of local unit of political parties made a false complaint against the woman president in this regard in the PWD office. The women president successfully faced these issues.

After facing such problems, she felt that an association is very much essential to protect the women presidents from the attack of the mafia. When the demand for the winding up of the District Panchayat was raised by the politicians, the women representatives association promptly retorted and wanted an effective District Panchayat with adequate powers, she mentioned. Further, she informed that the autonomous status of the Village Panchayats should be preserved along with the representations in the upper tiers. She suggested that the existing system of fund allocation should have to be reframed. In the allocation made to the sectoral departments, there should be a nominal fund earmarked to the Panchayats for maintenance works, she suggested. The Panchayat could easily execute the works with a lesser estimate, she added.

She compared the perception of people belonging to the urban local bodies and the rural areas about the local bodies. In the beginning people did not give due recognition to Women Panchayat Presidents and later they extended support to all the good works undertaken by the Village Panchayats. People in the nearby towns demanded her services as she achieved a lot in the Village Panchayat. She explained that through this association, lobbying was carried out to influence the Government to keep the existing reservation for women for one more period and the request was accepted by the Government. This showed the success of united efforts, Mrs. Ponni Kailasam told. Education, health, protection of girl-children, prevention of female infanticide are the major social issues prioritized by women presidents whenever they are given opportunity to perform. If more grant is earmarked for them, a lot of work could be carried out by women presidents, she informed. Concluding her speech, Mrs. Ponni Kailasam called the fellow presidents to strengthen the unity and cooperation among the women presidents and urged the association to make an impact at national level. She further demanded that documentation of the sacrifices made by the various local body leaders should be undertaken. They are really the crusaders of the Panchayat movement and women empowerment.

Mr. Mythili Sivaraman, in her inaugural address informed that she herself considered this event as an opportunity to learn much about the problems of the women leaders from the women presidents themselves. She dwelt at length on the context in which women's political empowerment was emerging. The women folk who used to keep themselves in the kitchen, came out and even participated in the freedom struggle. She cited the example of courageous action of an adolescent girl named Kalpana Dutt to whom the capital punishment was imposed during the freedom struggle. Women have the political orientation but how are they going to establish themselves at local level, she questioned.

Reservation means not merely increasing the number of seats. It has deeper meaning and implications. It should be properly understood and acted upon accordingly. Otherwise, the whole purpose will be defeated. Elected women representatives have to be careful in this exercise. There is a misconception prevailing that women could not function well as representatives of the people at the local level. These doubts could be dispelled only by the successful performance at the local level by women leaders, Mrs. Mythili Sivaraman opined. She further informed that inspite of male chauvinism, poverty, illiteracy and economic inequality and oppression, the women leaders have emerged as successful leaders. She outlined the happenings in North India where women leaders struggled hard against their own husbands as they themselves kept the official rubber stamps and not allowed the women to use them. She reminded that the ratio between male and female population showed a decreasing trend in the total number of girl children among the 1 to 6 years age-group.

Mrs. Mythili Sivaraman recollected a poster she had seen in USA in which a lean women is equated to five men. "Hard work and sacrifice are the qualities associated with women", she added. Women have dual responsibility. *Dalit* women are not respected and caste Hindus are unable to tolerate the emergence of *Dalit* women; they have successfully divided the *Dalit* community by using various tricks. Against this backdrop, how a woman leader could manage the issues single handedly?—Mrs. Mythili questioned.

Further, she listed out the leaders who worked on the ideology of social causes. Smt. Leelavathi, the councillor of Madurai Corporation was a poor weaver and she was not ready to bend her straight forwardness. She took up the cause of the poor in providing basic entitlements of water and for which she fought against the mafia. In the struggle against the local rowdyism, she was murdered. Sri Murugesan, the *Dalit* president of Melavalavu was murdered by caste

Hindus as he questioned the misuse of common properties by some traditional leaders. Ms. Menaka has sacrificed her life in the hands of anti-social elements in Orappakkam. She vehemently opposed the illegal activities of some individuals with vested interest who tried to sell common properties belonging to the Panchayats. Ms. Menaka was a sincere President. She constructed a common graveyard but some communities boycotted the common graveyard.

Ms. Menaka had won in the general constituency. When Anna Marumalrchi Thittam was not sanctioned for her Panchayat, she met the Chief Minister and threatened to commit self-immolation in front of the Chief Minister's office. While responding to the Panchayat President, the Chief Minister appreciated the boldness of the women leader. But ultimately, in the process she lost her life. All these incidents showed that the majority of the local body leaders possesses the required leadership qualities, she observed. In order to overcome the atrocities of the upper strata of the society, people should constructively participate in the Village Panchayat activities, she opined. She outlined the method of functioning of the Panchayat system in Kerala which people are considered important. In Kerala, land legislation was successfully carried out about 30 years back. And now to ensure good participation in the socio-economic development activities of the Panchayat, the village people are oriented in planning. 15,000 volunteers, 25,000 officials and 75,000 village volunteers were trained in micro-level development planning. The subject "women development" was one of the aspects in the training, Mrs. Mythili referred.

She further outlined the strategy of organising the people in Kerala. Neighbourhood meetings are successful in which the villagers casually comment upon the activities of the Village Panchayat. The provision of housing to the poor especially *Dalits* is prompt and quick due to the Village Panchayats in Kerala. In Tamil Nadu, the people do not get adequate information. There is a right to transparency in theory but not in practice. In Kerala, the distribution of water is handled by the public themselves. The SHG women are politically empowered and they are well versed with political happenings with their various dimensions. In Tamil Nadu, it is a different story. When the two women members of a SHG in Tiruvallur District were murdered by hooligans, the SHG women organised a demonstration.

The Collector declared that the SHG supported by the Government would not participate in the demonstration. The Collector considered that the participation of SHG in the demonstration is illegal, though the issue was related to women. But on the next day, all SHG women members participated in the demonstration in front of the Collector's office regardless of Collector's threat. Moreover, it is essential that at the village level, the women have to prove their leadership, intelligence, courage and worthiness. The new role played by rural women leaders would be a lesson to the next generation. She read out a poem from the magazine "Mahazhir Chinthanai" in which the women are called to shut down their traditional outlook and prepare themselves for the changing socio-political scenario.

Dr. G. Palanithurai recollected the experiences of women presidents who have been taken to Kerala for an exposure. The women presidents after visiting Kerala Panchayat described Tamil Nadu Panchayat system as 'administrative raj' in the hands of the officials whereas in Kerala it is "people's raj in the hands of the people".

Mr. Kottathur Ramaraj, the President of All India District Panchayats Association appreciated the need for guiding the women presidents to have good governance. He criticised the mind set of State Government with regard to the application of clause 205 of Tamil Nadu Panchayat Act when it opposes the imposition of the Rule 356 in the Constitution of India. While explaining the power of Panchayati Raj, he requested the women leaders to mobilise people to take any action against the bureaucrats. He recalled the earlier meetings in which women presidents kept silence when they were requested to openly share their administrative problems. Now, even in the men's meetings, women presidents shared fully and fearlessly their administrative problems with the higher officials. In India and its neighbouring countries, women leadership has been acknowledged by the people, pointed out Mr. Ramaraj. It is a guiding principle to all nations in the aspect of women empowerment. He opined that the election to the local bodies would not be delayed for any reasons. He felt sorry to note that in Bihar the Chief Minister was accompanied by her husband and her husband gave orders to the officials in lieu of the Chief Minister. He was happy to see the trend in Tamil Nadu where the majority of women presidents function independently. He expressed his hope that the next generation of the women leadership would get recognition and respect. Women presidents' good work will definitely bring good name to women in general Mr. Ramaraj observed.

Dr. G. Palanithurai recalled the earlier events in which the women presidents were accompanied by their husbands while attending the training. Now the situation has improved a lot, he added.

Mrs. Sujaya, Advisor to Singamma Sreenivasan Foundation, Bangalore, in her felicitation address observed that women think of themselves as members of a family but not as leaders, although women possess many qualities of leadership. She equated the family with Panchayat and informed that financial management, human relationship and cooperative efforts are featured in both.

While listing out a number of leadership qualities of women, Mrs. Sujaya pointed out that opportunity was not given to women to prove their worthiness. Corruption is due to the selfishness and the greediness of men and the leadership of women is an antidote negating such practices. Otherwise, there will be no respect for women leaders. Moreover, to achieve progress in our socio-economic front, the qualities exhibited by men leaders such as corruption misappropriation and non-transparent administration have to be done away with. "It is very difficult to perform the dual responsibility by women", Mrs. Sujaya observed. She expected that there should be a change in the attitude and functioning of men in families. Men have to share the family responsibilities voluntarily as the legislations alone could not make any attitudinal change among menfolk. 'Young women should bring transformation' Mrs. Sujaya expressed her hope.

Mrs. Vasantha Periyasamy, the President of Marumpattur Village Panchayat shared her feelings that the State Government does not properly plan the training programmes to the presidents and the Government orders are not properly circulated to them. Inspite of their handicaps, women presidents sustain their spirit and serve. She narrated the practical problems experienced in the maintenance of street lights, public taps and motor pumps. She told that in the next tenure, these obstacles should not stand in the way of the Panchayat administration. She questioned the meaning of Gram Sabha when the fund allocation was not in order. She expressed her hope that if proper guidance is available, all women presidents would be successful practitioners.

Selvi. G. Uma proposed a vote of thanks. The sharing sessions, however, continued.

Sharing Session I

Dr. Suriakanthi presided over the session.

Dr. Lalitha served as rapporteur

In her address Mrs. C.Manimekalai claimed that the women are educated and they achieve a lot. Women leaders challenge the activities which belittle women. She explained her untiring efforts to acquire the declared award conferred on her by the Central Government for her outstanding performance. She informed that due to political interference, the officials of the State Government failed to provide necessary details even after informing her of the award. She disclosed that she met the National Women's Commission in New Delhi. Because of her determination to fight against the injustice meted out to her, she was able to get the award. She informed that with the support of women, the sale of illicit liquor was stopped. She referred to the sufferings of Sita and Kannaki. She instilled confidence in the minds of the participants by singing the songs of Bharati and asked them to strengthen the association.

Smt. G. Navamani of Kanyakumari district asked the participants to have a self-evaluation whether the women presidents executed the responsibilities entrusted to them. She narrated her experiences with rowdy elements in the village. She reminded that the women president should not expect help from the husbands or other male members of their families and they should seek the support of the other women leaders. She explained how her husband allowed her to function independently as the president. Smt. Vasantha Rajendran of Thanjavur district shared her concern that when other women presidents were asked to attend the State Meet, they did not show any interest. She expressed her happiness that her participation in a State Meet was an experience to remember.

She accused that the real powers were not given to the Panchayats in accordance with the responsibilities listed under the 11th Schedule. She claimed that a lot of innovations and improvements are made in the sectors like education, health and public distribution system by the intervention of the Panchayat. She disclosed that the enthusiasm of the public in participating in the Gram Sabha meeting was declining and to satisfy the Government even the non members are made to sit for photographs as a proof of the conduct of Gram Sabha. She expressed that meeting four times in a year is not a good arrangement. She accused that the Vice-Presidents are a burden as they do not cooperate with the Presidents and expect commission or a share for signing the cheques. But the Presidents are helping the public to get certificates from the revenue department without getting any bribe, she explained.

As a *Dalit* woman, Mrs. Kaliammal explained how she was not given due recognition nor did she receive any help from any quarters when challenging issues were taken up. She informed that the community gave undue importance to the traditional leaders during village festivals but the woman president is neglected due to gender discrimination. Mrs. Kaliammal accused that partiality in the name of caste existed even among the village elders. She said that she experienced no threat from the side of the people or officials to her administration but only from the traditional leaders when the necessary basic amenities are provided to all in her village.

Smt. Ellammal, the leader of Mathar Sangam from Kancheepuram sang songs on women liberation. She narrated how she became a literate and a woman leader, and had an opportunity to go abroad, to South Africa. She explained that the women can do even a most difficult task very easily. She questioned the logic of male supremacy and called upon the participants to fight for their rights.

Mrs. Selvamani, the Panchayat ward member from Karur District gave details of the women's federation activities in the name of 'SWATI'. She revealed that only in a women's sangam problems related to women especially *Dalit* women could be properly analysed. She called upon the women leaders to develop a vision and action framework. Environmental degradation is a real issue which affects women first. She narrated the issue of transporting sand illegally in her area. In this activity, young women are sexually exploited, she added. Further, as the cultivable land was getting degraded due to exhaustive mining of sand, the women fought against the anti-social elements and got a stay from the Supreme Court. She informed that her leadership was discouraged by her close relatives themselves. She told that in order to honour the feelings and expectations of fellow members of the 'SWATI' movement, she contested the Panchayat election even though her in-laws opposed her decision. She disclosed that the women sangam took up the social issues as a basis to contest in the election whereas menfolk estimated the work of a candidate on the basis of caste and poverty.

Mrs. Reeta of Kanyakumari who was awarded 'The Best Panchayat Award', shared her concern as to how she witnessed the harassment meted out to a young woman by her family members. She felt sorry to inform how her husband dissuaded her from doing the relief work to the victims. She told that the youngsters who are supposed to do services courageously are now addicted to liquor and drugs. She informed that no one was ready to come forward to give witness against the male members who ill-treated women. She told that she developed courage in her in the process and she was appreciated as a "Courageous lady" by one and all.

She further told that to do better service she was asked by the public to contest in the election whereas her husband did not support her decision. Inspite of his opposition, she contested and won the election. Ms. Reeta informed that her husband does not prevent her but always cautioned her that anti-social elements would take revenge on her. She declared that she had faith in God. She narrated how the Government was irresponsible to Panchayats' genuine demands in maintaining public sanitation. When the septic tank in the toilet of a private building was filled and overflowing, the president tried to take necessary action. But due to political interference, the efforts were thwarted by the officials. She added that a false case was registered against her by the owner of the building. When she was taken by the police for interrogation, people gathered and prevented the officials, she informed. She warned the participants that if any compromise was made with the wrong-doers for the sake of personal benefit, the leadership of women would be ridiculed by the public. She voiced that determination, courage and faith in God are the essential qualities of the women leaders.

Smt. Kala of Dindigul District narrated her efforts in providing the drinking water facilities to a *Dalit* community. She shared her personal experiences that she was not able to sit in a chair in the Government office in front of the officer as the chair was not offered to her. She complained that the staff in the Village Panchayat were paid a meagre salary. She told how she successfully managed the Panchayats despite the presence of undue influence from political bigwigs. Further, when she took an issue to the women's court, the accused was taken to the police station, but with the intervention of the public he was let free, she added.

Mrs. Uthami of Sivagangai district shared her experiences with the participants. She told that a politically empowered family tried to prevent her from contesting as they proposed their woman as a candidate. She further told that the public disowned the political patronage but supported her as she worked for them. Reservation for women is the right step. Otherwise women will not enter politics, she said. She explained how an encroachment of a land for 33 years was removed successfully at last by the intervention of the Chief Minister's office. She had to suffer a lot because of this initiative. MLAs and MPs are getting alarmed as the public are getting the help and guidance of the local body leaders for the redressal of their grievances, Mrs. Uthami informed. She told that another encroachment of a VIP was yet to be removed, inspite of all efforts taken by the council. She criticised the Government officials for they expect a commission when any welfare measure was sanctioned. She opined that if one is honest, they are need not fear.

Dr. Suriakanthi in her remarks at the end of the sharing session observed that one has to see all kinds of achievements even inspite of poor devolution of powers. She appealed to the participants to equip themselves especially in decision-making. She commented that inspite of enacting the Panchayati Raj Legislation, the practical application of the same was a difficult one if the problems of women leaders are not properly understood. Dr. Suriakanthi suggested that an association at Union level was necessary along with the State level organisation as most of the issues needed immediate attention. For higher level advocacy or judicial remedy, the State organisation could be approached, she opined. Further, they should know which model of operation could be effective and successful to tackle the issues of women leaders, Dr. A. Suriakanthi pointed out. She called upon the participants to create their own history as there is opportunity to do so today.

Sharing Session II

The Chairman of Kallal Panchayat Union of Sivagangai district Mrs. Victoria Mary presided over the session. In her address, she recalled her experiences in the first Union Council meeting. In order to get guidance in conducting and managing the council meeting, she met the then Collector. The District Collector encouraged her to take up responsibilities and powers as the Union Chairperson. With this encouragement and counselling from experts like Dr. G. Palanithurai and Dr. Regina Pappa, she is able to get the credit of heading the best union, she informed.

By frequent visits and sustained spirit she met various officials of the sectoral departments in connection with union activities. She informed that with the support of NGO, she mobilised the public and organised non-violent struggles in fulfilling the demands of the community. She felt sorry for the mindset of the officials and the Government as her service was assessed on the basis of her political agitation. She appealed to the women presidents to take into account the strength of public support in tackling any threat to their leadership.

Mrs. Margaret Mary, Chairperson of Athur Panchayat Union in Dindigul district was happy to observe that women leaders are awakened. But the women leadership is yet to get due recognition in the political parties, she commented. She condemned those women who failed to acknowledge the leadership of women. Women leaders too have the perception as men leaders in tackling the issue of discrimination on the basis of caste. They have to come out from this mindset she added. She urged the participants to sustain tolerance as the women leaders have to face problems every day in all directions. She pointed out that the absence of organic linkage in the three-tier system was a handicap. She suggested to strengthen the self-help groups and encourage the participation of women members to achieve women empowerment. She referred to her experiences with the officialdom where the officials felt hurt when the chairperson occupied the front seat in the jeep. She appealed to the participants to contest again or to encourage the newcomers. Smt. Karliarasi from Sivagangai district informed about the contribution of SHGs. She emphasised the importance and implications of the works done by the SHG in the rural areas. She appealed to the participants to have collaboration with the SHG leaders and members and by which a lot could be done to empower women.

Smt. Vani, Vice-President expressed her feelings to the remarks on the performance of Vice-Presidents. She told that the corrupted Vice-Presidents could be easily handled if all ward members of the concerned Panchayat were informed properly by the President. She informed that as the Vice-President was very serious, the fund was properly spent. Smt. Sakunthala told that men presidents could manage several issues whereas even convening of Gram Sabha was a problem to women presidents. She revealed that husbands did not permit them to function independently by making reference to so many things that are not known to women.

Smt. Kaliammal accused the officials as they expected that women presidents had to obey what the official told. She informed that a number of welfare facilities were not provided to her village even though her Panchayat was poor. This could be achieved only through a sustained and prolonged struggle against the officialdom. She informed that she was interested in organising more number of SHGs. She said that SHG is a supportive factor for the women Panchayat leaders.

Smt. Sivakami, who is the Vice-Chairman informed that she helped her ward members and people without expecting any commission in executing union works. She complained that political interference was increasing in PRI administration.

Smt. Amutha of Cuddalore district told that majority of women did not face the danger that Smt. Menaka, the President of Orappakkam who was murdered. She told that all common properties must be physically handed over to the panchayats as per the records. The State Government must help the panchayats in this regard.

Smt. Subbulakshmi shared her experience in small savings campaign. Out of 220 families who joined the small savings scheme only 60 families completed the five year duration due to frequent reminders by her. She told that this was the mentality of rural women who need continuous prompting. Further, she narrated that she paid more attention to children and the Noon Meal Centre. It functioned outstandingly and received the best award. She informed that encouragement and guidance were received from her family members who lived together as a joint family. She told that her Vice-President's hamlet was a very old one. As there was no protected drinking water in the hamlet, with much efforts, the facility for potable water was provided. She informed that the people of the same village requested to help them to construct a temple as there was no temple. This demand was also fulfilled with the help of donors and now people compel her to contest again for the presidentship.

Mrs. Thaiyalnayaki of Pudukkottai felt that women are the sufferers. From womb to tomb, women are suffering a lot. She told that the women are against traditional leadership. She felt sorry to share that when her husband expired in the meantime and the powerful traditional leadership tried to oust her. She told that she was threatened several times. On such occasions, she recalled Gandhiji's principle of service as a guidance in her life. She explained that her opponents had a game plan to put her into jail by false complaints that she was instigating caste violence. She managed these issues with the help of the MLA. She told that women leaders should not give up but must keep their steps always ahead.

Smt. Malarvizhi of Trichy district narrated her courageous act in removing an encroachment. She told that when her opponents expressed their doubts about her future, she confidently replied to them that she could become an MLA or MP despite their opposition.

Mrs. Mani, a ward member informed that when an encroachment was removed they accused and abused the women members. She told that they lodged a complaint to police against the culprits and thus the problem was solved. Smt. Lalitha, of Dharmapuri district told that the present day women leadership would be the role models to the newcomers. She told that as unemployment was a continuous problem, necessary training had to be arranged to acquire new skills and techniques. She told that women would successfully execute their responsibilities both in the family and society. Dr. Celine Rani served as a rapporteur and presented the key points of the presentations of the elected women representatives.

While concluding the proceedings, Dr. G. Palanithurai observed the following points: The dignitaries who addressed the conference are the field based personalities and hence the mela is not a celebration but it should be treated as a task force meet. When persons in the field meet, a practical plan is devised. The sangam would do wonders if and when the State level association becomes consolidated. It could make its impact at the national level. The various dimensions of women's issues can be analysed through the sangam. Women leaders need not follow the model presented by men politicians of the present. They need not borrow men's ideas and values. Women leaders have their own agenda. They have to pursue the agenda of their own. They need not follow the agenda of men leaders and the officials. They have to maintain their identity. They should keep their selves. Men in different forms make the women leaders and orient the women leaders to think as they do. Consciously the women leaders take necessary steps to maintain their self identity.

Dr. Regina Pappa taking the clue from the observation of Dr. G. Palanithurai cautioned the participants and requested them to develop perspective in their own domain. She indicated that it would take time. She pleaded with them to keep the association intact and integrate it with various other associations to strengthen the women base and their activities.

Smt. Pankajam the President of the Federation of the elected women representatives explained that the institution like HRF facilitated women leaders to handle situations like the one in which the President of Orappakkam was murdered. Only because of media influence, a case was registered and the culprits were put into prison. State level Federation was very much helpful to meet and lobby with the police official and higher-ups in the Government. The Federation has started its work now. It has to be consolidated and strengthened further. Organisations like Rajiv Gandhi Chair for Panchayati Raj Studies have to help in this regard. She appreciated the steps taken by Gandhigram Rural Institute to empower the women through the panchayati institutions.

Ms. Juliana said that that Panchayat was very close to her heart as the new culture of governance had to be generalised in India only by women. Gender equity must be a work of the Panchayats for good governance, she felt. Apart from providing basic amenities, the women presidents had to initiate other activities with a vision to transform the existing male chauvinistic society, she suggested. She informed that as the reservation was given to women in local bodies and the rest of the world looked at India with great expectations. Against this backdrop, the women leaders have to sustain their struggle with the help of their supporters and well wishers.

Dr. Nata Duvury finally made an observation that the critical mass formed in the Local bodies due to the reservation of seats for women has started working in the society for meaningful social transformation. Yet, the process is difficult with full of obstacles and problems. These obstacles and problems would be tackled collectively and for which this kind of the Federation would be of immense use.

Dr. G. Pankajam, Vice-Chancellor in her valedictory address expressed her solidarity and support to the Federation of the elected women representatives of local bodies in Tamil Nadu for all its meaningful activities in the years to come as they are also engaged in the activities that are carried out by this institute as per the wishes of the founders of Gandhigram Rural Institute. Rajiv Gandhi Chair for Panchayati Raj Studies would function as a resource centre for the Panchayati leaders. These leaders have to make use this opportunity to discharge their responsibility to the maximum satisfaction of the public. Ms. Uma read out the resolutions passed in the meet and the participants expressed their acceptance whole heartedly.

The Second Annual Mela

The mela started with a prayer, after which Dr. V.Ragupathy welcomed the gathering. In his address, he recollected the very objective of the Gandhigram Rural Institute when it was inaugurated in the year 1947. He stated that the founders of Gandhigram Rural Institute and the disciples of Mahatma Gandhi, Dr. G. Ramachandran and Dr. R. Soundaram joined with Dr. Muthulakshmi Reddy from Chennai on the advise of Gandhiji to work for the betterment of rural women. Thus, the Gandhigram Rural Institute from the beginning keeps on working for the development of the poor in general and women in particular.

Dr. G. Palanithurai, Coordinator of the project and the programme gave a brief introduction on the purpose of the meeting. In his speech, he articulated that for the past 10 years, Gandhigram Rural Institute has been successfully working for strengthening the Panchayati Institution and Rajiv Gandhi Chair, in particular is empowering women through strengthening Women Panchayat Presidents, for the last 5 years. He also acknowledged the NGOs contribution in the networking of these institutions to achieve economic development. When pointing out that Tamil Nadu stands third, next to Kerala and Punjab in terms of development he said that it is not only the Chief Minister's aim to make Tamil Nadu the best State in the country in every sphere, but also the desire of every one in the State.

Dr. G. Palanithurai specified that the women should first realise that power is not something to be given by any one from the above, but to be acquired by themselves. They should realise the fact that times have changed and that women are marching forward to take the power in their hands to work for their well-being. The Women Panchayat Presidents should realise that they are representatives of their community and that they should strongly feel that only women's development would pave the way for the development of rural community, and the country as a whole.

He also observed that the honourable Minister for Rural Development, Shri. M. Venkiah Naidu in his inaugural address at the Women Panchayat Leaders meet on 20th of February, held at Gandhigram Rural Institute wished that the decisions taken at the Lok Sabha, would lead to real Gram Swaraj. He also insisted that the decision should not become a dream but a reality. It will become a reality only when people use their power appropriately.

Dr. G. Palanithurai also remarked that the Panchayati Raj Institutions and the Rural Development Departments are not two separate departments, but they are one and the same as it is obvious to note that the rural development activities are carried out only through Panchayati Raj. Thus, it is a joint venture. So, it is clear that Women Panchayat Leaders should realise that the development of their community, villages and the country lies in their hands. To work effectively, they should increase their knowledge on Panchayati Raj System, the duties assigned to them, and the powers acquired by them. They should understand that educational institutions, like Gandhigram Rural Institute, academicians and experts are ready to educate, train, motivate and train them in the management of the Panchayati Institutions. So, they should readily approach the specialists in this regard.

Tamil Nadu is the first State in India

(i) to have agreed upon to keep the rotation of reserved seats for women for every ten years on the basis of the pressure from the elected women representatives association to continue with their work and prove their ability;

(ii) to have declared 33.3 per cent reservation for women in all statutory committees, which is an initiation to break the evil implications of male chauvinism; and

(iii) to introduce 33.3 per cent reservation of seats for women in the cooperatives also.

So, women leaders should rise and show their willingness and strength to work towards greater possibilities.

Dr. G. Palanithurai also advised the Women Panchayat Leaders to form an association or a council of administrators, academis and NGOs to have insight into the problems, to overcome the hurdles and also to firmly put forth their ideas as members of the council. They should also persuade the political party leaders, and experts to join the council which would strengthen the base of the Panchayat System.

Panchayat leaders have appealed to the Collector to call a meeting of the Panchayat Presidents once in a month to know their problems, needs and the difficulties. He added that it is a good beginning and a sign towards development. He motivated the women leaders to continue and take the chance as a challenge and set an example to other States.

Through proper implementation of the 15 points programme introduced by our Chief Minister, Ms. J. Jayalalithaa covering all aspects of development, Tamil Nadu can be brought to No.1 position in India. The significant parts of the programme is under the purview of 29 subjects. So, it should be felt by the panchayat leaders that if they function effectively, there would be no doubt in bringing Tamil Nadu to No.1 position in India.

Prof. G. Palanithurai emphasised that power devolution is a part of the empowerment process of the community itself. Panchayati Raj System has to bring progress in our villages through the involvement of the community so that it could achieve what sofar has not been achieved by the Federal and Union Governments. In the place of Lok Sabha, Gram Sabha is referred to as it ensures the change of mind set among the rural populace that the progress of the nation depends on their contribution. Power to Panchayati Raj Institution meant power to the community, he added. Dr. Palanithurai appreciated the efforts of the Federation in influencing the State Government to extend the reservation of seats to women and *Dalits* for a period of one more tenure in the same constituency without rotating every term. He informed that similar efforts were made in other States and the Governments in those States had excuses in this regard by pointing out lack of adequate provision in the Act to extend the reservation. He appealed to the participants to make use of this second time opportunity for further consolidation of women empowerment process by delivering good governance to the rural community. He cited that reservation to women was recognised and now it is proposed to be implemented in the cooperatives also.

Prof. G. Palanithurai appealed to the participants to prepare themselves to prove their leadership potentials as an yet another opportunity is now available. In this regard he referred to the 15 point programme announced by the Chief Minister of Tamil Nadu to take the State as number one in India. It could be achieved if people participate in the developmental initiatives. Moreover, the activities to attain growth and progress must be streamlined properly at the micro-level which means, it must be through the local governance system. He criticized the supply-driven approach of the Government machinery and target oriented system of administration. He told that the leaders of the local bodies could be well versed in reflecting the real felt needs of the community. He pointed out the laucane in the district planning system. A data base is to be created to identify the sectoral backwardness of a district whereas there is no systematic efforts to collect necessary data at the village level. Social development indicators like IMR, BR, Nutritional Status of Children, Educational Status, Delivery of Social Security schemes etc. have not yet been properly disseminated to all concerned. He opined that women leaders could easily comprehend the concept and details of the 15-point programme and he appealed that they have to equip themselves to play their role in the implementation of the 15-point programme. He related the sequence of their role performance with the strengthening of the Federation and *vice versa.*

Panchayat presidents should always concentrate on fulfilling the basic needs of the people. So, they should discuss with the people in moving towards development. Statistical data of a Panchayat is a must to plan for its progress.

Dr. G. Palanithurai narrated the success story of the village 'Karisalpatty' in Dindigul district, which stands second in the State in terms of development. He stated that the Panchayat has built a public toilet and made it a pay-and-use toilet, through which the Panchayat earns and pays the EB bill of the Panchayat and also pays for the salary of the Panchayat staff. They do not wait for Government's money. Likewise, they also auction the products of the common properties and earn an income for the Panchayat. He said that all the Panchayat Presidents likewise should create a source of income for their Panchayat on their own and carry out the development activities and not to wait for Government's money.

Dr. G. Palanithurai observed that it is sad to notice that 35 per cent of infants born in Tamil Nadu are underweight, and 35 per cent of children under the age of 5 are malnourished. This is the health status of Tamil Nadu today. So, he requested the Women Panchayat Presidents to take steps to improve the health condition of their villages. Whether male or female, only people who have taken up the problems in hand have found solutions, solved and have attained success, he observed. So, it is the duty of the Panchayat Presidents to bring the problems to limelight and find solutions to overcome the problems with courage.

He concluded his remarks by requesting the elected women representatives to focus on the objectives of the meeting listed out in the agenda. Thereby, all those issues could be discussed in the meeting and details would be worked out in the meeting to be held on 9th May, 2002 with the officials and the report might be sent to the Government as recommendation for further clearance.

With those introductory remarks, the occasion was started by lighting a 'Kuthuvilakku' by the chief guest Shri. S. Ayyar, I.A.S., along with Dr. G. Pankajam, Ms. Ponni Kailasam, Ms. Pushpaleela, Ms. Kavitha, Ms. Venkateshwari and Dr. P. Senthil Kumar, I.A.S.

In her presidential address, Dr. G. Pankajam asserted that it is a surprise to see so many old friends back to the Second Annual Meet. It is happy to know that these familiar faces of the elected women representatives have been re-elected for the second term, she added. The achievements of the women representatives have brought them to the chair again. They set an example to all. New leaders should realise that true work always rewards and makes people speak of it and honour it.

Leadership ability is neither a bed of roses nor bed of thorns to be accepted easily, she stated. Ms. Ponni Kailasam, is a leader and a model to be followed. Every Panchayat President should comprehend that they have not come to rule the people but have come to work for the welfare of the people, she added. Needs and expectations differ between male and female. Our country has given an opportunity to women to work for their own betterment. So, the Panchayat Presidents should keep it in their minds, concentrate and work for the good of all.

Dr. G. Pankajam added that six years back, when we were meeting here, requesting women to contest in the elections, no one was ready to contest. Even when requested to come to the stage and speak a word or two, no one dared to come to the stage. But today times have changed and the whole socialisation process has changed the women and to-day the stage is filled with women and women alone. Society has given a chance to the women to come to the forefront and challenge men in terms of serving people.

It is a known fact that only women in the house come to know about what is needed and how it could be achieved, be it rice, groceries, kerosene or children lacking in health. Women only come to know about it first, as they are the ones who run the family. When women can manage a home so elegantly with so much deficits, she can very well take the responsibility of developing her own community, she added.

Women should contribute to the country's progress by serving their community, their village, and so on. Government's money is nothing but people's revenue. So, it is fair only to go back to the people. So, Women Panchayat Leaders must act as a catalyst to return the revenue to the people in different modes. They should stand up boldly, approach the respective officials and get the needed help from them, as they are the public servants.

She concluded her speech by saying that women leaders should always keep in their minds that the people have elected them only to work for their good. And if they worked effectively and efficiently, they would be praised and honoured by all.

In her address, Ms. Ponni Kailasam, Chairperson of the Federation asserted firmly that women representatives are working only for the welfare of the people and that the people have started recognising it. She also stated that they have demanded power only to serve the people. She also quoted the statement made by I.A.S. officer, Mr. Vasudeva Iyer in the training programme. He stated that a work to be done by the local body institutions within 5 lakh rupees is being completed by PWD by 8 lakh rupees. This shows Government's ineffective handling of works.

To make the 15-point programme a success, officials should cooperate with the women presidents, she requested. She also said that more than politicians, the officials gave more trouble to the presidents. She also appealed to remove Article 205 of Tamil Nadu Panchayat Act of removing Panchayat leaders from position by the Collector as it violates the principle of representative democracy.

She concluded her speech by thanking the Chief Minister, Ms. J.Jayalalithaa for having accepted their request of keeping the reserved seats for women for two terms, and abolishing the cheap liquor shops in the rural areas of Tamil Nadu.

Ms. Pushpaleela, the Sivagangai District Chairman felt that the women presidents should thank the great leaders and great men who had struggled to reserve seats for women in the local bodies. All women leaders should have Chief Minister, Ms. J.Jayalalithaa as their role model and develop courage and confidence to work for the welfare of their village people the State and the Country as a whole.

Ms. Kavitha articulated that power should not hurt the people but should provide warmth to the people. Woman is the one who manages a home. Having it in mind, women have been entrusted with the responsibility of developing the community. They should realise their value. They should not act as proxies to male members of their families and should use their power and not allow men to have it and use it.

Women presidents, chairman and members are not aware of their duties or powers properly. So, she requested the officials to train them in such areas, which would help them to work efficiently, without any obstacles. She also stated that programmes should be evolved by the people only, as they are the beneficiaries. If they are introduced by the Government, the people should be well-informed about it.

Ms. Venkateshwari, Gandhigram Panchayat President expressed that Gandhigram Rural Institute always takes a stand in empowering Women Panchayat Leaders. It is a great motivation for the women leaders. She opined that the 15-point programme is a good programme which would living in development, provided the full information/ details of the programme be well-informed to the Panchayat leaders and the people to make maximum utilisation of it. She also advised the Government to invite the women Panchayat leaders to be on the Dias of the local functions, conducted by the Government.

Dr. P. Senthil Kumar, Dindigul Collector declared that the women leaders' participation in local body institutions is significant and is growing day by day, which is a good sign towards the development of our country. He stated that the annual meet should serve as a base for effective functioning of the 15-point programme and devolution of powers.

Shri. S. Ayyar, Director Rural Development, Government of Tamil Nadu in his inaugural address said that the Government is taking all steps to make the Panchayats Institutions of self-governance. He also added that officials are paid servants to train the Panchayat Presidents to serve the people effectively, just as a mother trains and motivates her child to walk. Soon, as the presidents gain expert knowledge, the officials are to disassociate themselves from the presidents and not to interfere in their decision-making process. Women are good finance ministers, as they have good knowledge in managing their houses. That is why they have been awarded with 33.3 per cent reservation of seats. Thus, they should show their intelligence, effectiveness in their work and claim for 50 per cent reservation of seats in the local bodies and Parliament, he added.

Government is interested in making women the owners, instead of making them mere beneficiaries. Thus more opportunities are given for the Self-Help Groups to develop. He mentioned about the Government's proposed plans and programmes of the year towards women's development. State Government would set up information centres at an estimated cost of Rs. 30 crores in 10 Districts beneficial to 6,000 Self-Help Groups. The sophisticated information centres along with the internet facility would be maintained by self-help groups in 10 districts. People can also get application forms from the centre and petitions can be sent through E-mail from their village to the Collector. Action taken by officials too can be known from this centre.

It is proposed to construct buildings for every Panchayat to conduct Self-Help Groups meeting. Besides, commercial complexes are to be constructed for each district for the use of Self-Help Groups to display and market their products. These centres would also serve as information service centres to sell their products. A massive programme is proposed to train 5 lakh women entrepreneurs. Two lakh worth integrated sanitary complex for women in each Panchayat is to be constructed. It would include toilets, bathrooms and place to wash clothes.

Thus, he added that this Government is concentrating on women's development in all spheres, social, economic, health and education. So it is the responsibility of the women to realise it and make proper use of it. He concluded his speech, saying that women have expert knowledge, ability, strength, talent and competence to work effectively. There are academicians, officials to support and guide them properly.

Session I

Topic: Discussion on the 15-point programme and the Powers Conferred upon the Panchayats

Dr. Suriakanthi chaired the session
Ms. Kanmani served as a rapporteur.

Dr. Suriakanthi stated that it is understood from the meeting that Women Panchayat Leaders have dedicated their lives to serve the people, she briefed the Women Panchayat Leaders on the 15-point programme. She said that the programme encompasses all the 29 subjects given under Article 243(G) of Tamil Nadu Panchayat Act. So, it could be noted that the programme has been introduced to make Tamil Nadu the best State in the country in every sphere. Such a result can only be accomplished by hard work.

She briefed on the programme.

Evergreen Revolution

Raising farm productivity for prosperity; saving every drop of rain; more crop per drop.

Food Security

Providing balanced diets to every man, woman and child.

Livestock Security

Upgradation of livestock, providing better veterinary care; supplementing farm income; improving fish diversity and increasing fish density.

Water Security

Providing safe drinking water and adequate water for agriculture, industry and ecosystem maintenance.

Health Security

Controlling preventable diseases, preventable blindness and eradicating diseases for which effective vaccines are available; reduction of Infant Mortality Rate, Maternal Mortality Rate and incidence of low birth weight children; fight against HIV/AIDS; special attention to physically and mentally handicapped children, women and men.

Livelihood Security

"Work for all" and transition from unskilled to skilled work; a new deal to the self-employed through technology, training, techno-infrastructure and domestic trade.

Shelter Security

Promotion of housing activities designed to harvest sun and rain so that solar energy capture and rainwater harvesting become everybody's business.

Ecological Security

Conservation of land, water, forests and ocean; recycling of solid and liquid wastes and composting of all organic wastes; safe disposal of hospital wastes; bio-environmental control of material.

Energy Security

Energy self-sufficiency for the farm, industrial and domestic sectors.

Infrastructure for Development

Provision of basic amenities in rural and urban areas; bridging the rural-urban divide.

Literacy and Technicality

Attention to quality improvement in education ranging from the pre-school to university; special attention to the technological and skill empowerment of illiterate or semi-literate women and men; eradication of child labour.

Folk, Classical, Modern Arts and Culture and Drama

Generation of awareness and appreciation of the cultural heritage of Tamil Nadu and revitalisation of cultural traditions, including the street theatre.

Gender Equity

Removal of gender bias, elimination of adverse sen ration, and support services to working women, taking into account the multiple burdens on a woman's day-to-day life.

New Deal for Oppressed Classes

Educational and economic empowerment of the Adi-Dravidas, Scheduled Tribes, Backward Classes, Most Backward Classes and Denotified Tribes.

Technological Leapfrogging

Promotion of research and development in frontier areas of science and technology like biotechnology and information technology launching a movement for fostering greater public understanding of science and promoting a new social contract between scientists and society.

Ms. Sukany said that if officials cooperate well with the Women Panchayat Leaders, they would fufil all the programmes successfully. She also pointed out that Panchayat can earn as income by planting mango and tamarind saplings in 'Porambokku' lands, which would lead to increased income of the Panchayats. Check dams can be built for water conservation. Women Panchayat Leaders can intensively work on the 15 programmes provided needed power is given to them.

All 7 committees referred in Panchayat Act should be formed and should function together, to make the 15 point programme, a success, she continued. People who agitate or who are against the presidents should be invited and important responsibilities should be given to them and should be made to involve in decision-making which would carry out the work smoothly, she said.

Ms. Rani Sathappan gave some suggestions to the women Panchayat Leaders to work out the 15-point programmes. Census should be taken and people should be alarmed about it and population should be checked. This will be more related in raising farm productivity. Presidents should check PDS and supervise proper weighing of ration items supplied in the rationshops. Better veterinary care should be given to the livestock. Presidents should try to afford safe drinking water to the people; desilting and deepening of ponds should be done and more importantly, encroachment of ponds should be removed with the powers given to the Panchayats. Presidents should advise women to make use of the integrated sanitary complex. Developing entrepreneurial skills in women, thereby, providing economic opportunities and thus, increasing their income. Women presidents should be the priority role is to identify appropriate people for providing houses. Saying 'no' to plastic bags, and planting as many trees as possible by Panchayats. Producing Bio-gas by using human wastes as used in Maharashtra. Providing basic amenities for people for development. To train students in technical education and technological skills. To motivate rural artists to improve traditional folk arts. Socialising and sensitizing men and women to treat girls at par with boys. Treating the marginalysed with dignity and ensuring them their entitlements and that could be done by Panchayats.

Helping rural people to use computers and with these suggestions, she thanked Rajiv Gandhi Chair associates for their initiatives in training, motivating and guiding the Women Panchayat Presidents for their work. She declared that she has been re-elected for the second term based on her performance.

Ms. Maruthambal, felt that when they had taken leadership the first time, she felt like a black cat left in a dark room. She stressed that only Gandhigram Rural Institute educated, trained and motivated her in her work and that they had also arranged trips to Kerala to observe the effective functioning of the Panchayats there, and thereby, increasing the performance of the Women Panchayat Presidents. She then gave some suggestions to the Women Panchayat Presidents on how to take up the issues related to the 15 point programme in the Panchayats.

Women presidents should supervise PDS in issuing ration items by weighing correctly. People should be initiated to give proper veterinary care to the livestock and motivate the people to take the diseased cattle to the veterinary hospitals. Insisting people, especially women to make use of the integrated sanitary complexes. Saying 'no' to plastic bags, by making people aware of the dangerous ill-effects of using them through street plays, dramas, etc. Producing Bio-gas by using animal wastes like cow dung and vegetable wastes, like perished cabbage, etc, and using them. Compelling the parents to send their children to go to balwadis and schools. Inviting great personalities like Dr. Vijayalakshmi and Mr. Pusphavanam Kuppusamy to disseminate knowledge on folk arts and motivate people to encourage traditional arts.

Gandhigram introduced bio-gas at Panchampatti and there are nearly 25-50 bio-gas plants functioning at Panchampatti. It is of great help to the people there, she said and also advised the women presidents to take the help of Gandhigram Rural Institute to introduce Bio-gas plants in their villages also. She then pointed out that when she met Mr. Thirumal Valavan, DPI President, he argued that he has appealed to introduce a law to penalise women presidents who take their husbands, as proxies. She insisted that presidents should work independently.

Ms. Vasantha, former Panchayat President stressed that women presidents should go to the Collectorate and Union Offices individually or in groups to know about the policies and programmes, so that they can escape from criticism. She also added saying that officials are also interested in educating them, when approached.

Ms. Ruby Parvathalingam reminded the proverb 'Behind every man, there is a woman' and added that it also works *vice-versa.* She thus stressed that the women presidents should respect the men, in the family and society, that they would definitely encourage the presidents to do their duties freely without any obstacles.

Dr. Suriakanthi while concluding the session said that women leaders have had a chance to know about the 15 point programmes clearly, in this meeting and wanted the participants to start working on the implementation of these programmes.

Session II

Topic: Discussion on Strengthening the Tamil Nadu Council for Elected Women Representatives

Dr. G. Palanithurai opined that he had found a significant difference between the first and second annual meet. In the first meeting, there were complaints on the Women Panchayat Presidents using men as proxies to them. But there were no such complaints about proxies or rather nobody spoke of it in the second meeting.

It should be noted that Government is concentrating on empowering women through self-help groups, and as a result everybody speaks of 'Micro-Finance' and 'Micro-Enterprise', rather of loans, he added. Even if the finance comes from the World Bank, it should only be handed over to the Panchayats. This is the condition of the State now and the reasons behind it is that everyone believes that women will not mishandle the opportunities given to them, rather they will make use of them.

Women presidents should form associations and strengthen them, through which they can overcome the problems and solve them. Today, Tamil Nadu has issued an order to enable the women to continue in the same position for the second term. Except CPM and CPI leaders, no body supported it or rather no body thought of it, that it would happen. But today it has happened and has become a reality. This credit goes only to the Women Panchayat President's association.

Women should take Dr. G. Pankajam as their role model he asserted. He narrated her life history by saying that Dr. G. Pankajam studied in the school in Gandhigram and then in Gandhigram Rural Institute. She studied in the some college after which she became the secretary of the Gandhigram Trust. She then served as the Principal in Lakshmi College of Education and at last has become the Vice-Chancellor of the University, where she had studied. So, he asked the women leaders to act boldly and confidently.

He also suggested that the association can take the help of NGOs and Universities who are ready to help them. There are also experts and specialists likè retired I.A.S. officers, higher officials, doctors and Vice-Chancellors of the Universities, who are ready to work as honorary members in any council to support the Federation. The association can take their help, which would doubly strengthen them and which would be a great support to them, he added. He also advised the women leaders not to act egoistically. He asked them to respect to accept the decisions, recommendations made by their subordinates too. This would as well as make the association function smoothly. He concluded by advising the Women Presidents to extend and strengthen their associations, to make them work independently and perform efficiently.

Ms. Manimegalai suggested that the associations should invite the officials and give due respect to them, who would inturn fulfil the demands put forth by the association. She also suggested that like Kerala, Tamil Nadu should also give permission to conduct Gram Sabha meetings in the late evenings to the convenience of working women, which would enable more women to participate in the meetings. Likewise, officials from the various departments should participate in the Gram Sabha meetings, which would make the people get their doubts cleared, if any or to get information, if any from the different department officials. This would also increase the strength of the common people.

Ms. Chandrika Sarvesan said that she was a housewife and the role of the Panchayat President was totally new to her. She was compelled by her village people to contest in the elections, as she was educated, she said. Inspite of performing a new role, she still managed the Panchayat well, as she also concentrates on solving even minor disputes among the people and by making all the people involved in decision-making. She declared said that this was the reason for her success. Ms. Samruth Beevi asserted that the women presidents try to fulfil the basic needs of the people, they would always support the presidents in all their work. She then explained the troubles that she went through and how she overcame them, while working for the welfare of the people.

Ms. Senthamizh Selvi reminded of Gandhiji's words—"A country's progress depends on the development of its villages". She then added that Gandhiji's words have come true today that there is much development in the villages and that to sustain it, woman have to come to the forefront to work for the welfare of the people.

Ms. Ponnikailasam spoke on how to strengthen the association. She asked all the women presidents to join the association. She also requested Gandhigram to help the association to use the IT-enabled services. She also urged the women to come in mass to attend the association meeting, which would demonstrate their strength to the nation. Dr. G. Palanithurai concluded the session by saying that the association would function properly, if the suggestions given above are given due attention.

Valedictory Function

Ms. G.Uma welcomed chief guest Dr. Kousalya Devi and the participants. Ms. Kanmani and Ms. Kala Murugan, the rapporteurs of the two sessions, gave the main points of the deliberations of the two sharing sessions respectively.

Dr. Kousalya Devi in her special address referred to the questions "What can women do"? which was the question raised by men five years back. But "Women can achieve anything" is the phrase heard everywhere now, said Dr. Kousalya Devi. She congratulated the Gandhigram Rural Institute for its achievements in empowering women by gathering a mass of women with so much motivation and enthusiasm. She also advised women to act independently without using proxies to them and asked them to demand 50 per cent or more reservation of seats.

Women presidents should not act on prejudice in Panchayat administration, which would spoil their whole notion of developing the weaker sections. Efficient presidents would treat everybody equally. They should set an example to everybody. Men in future should accept that women are the best leaders, she said. She also gave a few suggestions to women in accepting help from the VHNs who would provide better health care to women. Marriage ceremonies should be conducted in a simple manner and spending extravagantly as such is a waste and should be stopped, she said.

Highlights of the Annual Meet

By comparing the transactions and discussions of the II Annual meet of the Elected Women Representatives with the I meet held in the previous year, one would find a quality change in the discussions. In the previous year, they were discussing their own problems individually. They could not find out the common barriers which preventing them in their march towards empowerment. Further they could not move much into the domain of the social development issues. They were not adequately oriented on the gender issues and as a result many of the problems faced by women were not adequately highlighted.

But this year, they moved into the issues of social development. They are sensitise towards gender issues. They have gone to the extent of criticising the schemes of the Government. They have come to the level of addressing the issues and commenting on the policy matters from their perspective. Sometimes even the political parties won't make such statements and observations about the policies and decisions of the Government. The new Government has issued a new 15-point programme to make Tamil Nadu first in the whole of the Country in social development. The EWRs have responded to the Government by making a declaration that they would carry out all the fifteen programmes as they all come under the purview of the Panchayat System. They worked out the details of the activities to be carried out at the grassroots and they have presented a charter of works.

In the previous years they talked about powers. But this time they talked much about the issues and problems that are common in nature. Now they have started working on strategizing for achieving their goals. The Elected Women Representatives have adequate clarity on the points that on what ground we have to support the Government and on what ground that they have to oppose the Government. Slowly, they are establishing their grip over the issues. They have drawn the attention of the media and the intellectuals. By their actions, they have drawn the attention of many NGOs. Now they are coming closer to form a Federation of women leaders.

For the past five years, they have articulated their problems coherently when they meet the officials. But now they give suggestions and solutions to the problems. It is very clear from their presentations and statements that they are on the side of solutions and not on the side of the problems.

Now they have started moving with variety of institutions and organisations. They have realised the importance of capacity-building and as a result they are demanding capacity-building exercises from the training institutions and NGOs. They have indicated what type of training they need. They have learnt the art of managing the association. Now they are in a consolidation process. At present the Federation leaders are able to directly negotiate with higher level officials on certain matters and bring positive results. This created enthusiasm among the members and it acts an instrument for strengthening the Federation of women leaders.

Another striking feature is that the presidents act with sagacity and experience which yields some good results which give motivation to the newly elected women representatives. It is unique in Tamil Nadu as the period of rotation has been fixed for every ten years.

Still more advantage the elected women leaders association has this time as a large number of Self-Help Group women leaders have entered the domain of the Panchayat especially at the Gram Panchayat level with the support of NGOs in Tamil Nadu. The Self-Help Group members had been already oriented towards social development issues and hence their entry would help the association to strengthen further.

The elected women leaders have realised the value of the media and they use to express their opinions freely. Media have been properly cultivated and the women leaders are using the media and thereby they have brought out several issues to the public for open debate. They are gaining voice. Their voice is being heard and respected.

The Third Annual Mela

The State level annual mela cum conference of the Gram Panchayats Women President Federation was held on 15-5-2005 at Gandhigram Rural Institute. The morning programme was started with a silent prayer. About 100-150 women Presidents who are the office bearers of the district unit of the Federation participated.

Dr. G. Palanithurai after welcoming the participants delivered the introductory speech. In his address Dr. G. Palanithurai reviewed the overall performance of the Panchayati Raj Institutions in India and shared his concern over the plight of stagnation in the functions of Panchayati Raj Institutions. A decade has been gone but the perception and understanding on Panchayati Raj Institutions is yet to be improved among the stakeholders. He emphasized that the mindset of grassroots leaders in Panchayati Raj Institutions should be improved in accordance with the expected role expected by the New Panchayati Raj System. Dr. G. Palanithurai observed that the real potentiality i.e., the power and authority of local governance has not been properly perceived by the stakeholders. But, one could see an overall positive trend in the activities of the Panchayati Raj Institutions in Tamil Nadu, as the Village Panchayat Presidents in Tamil Nadu were able to perceive and perform their roles and responsibilities, Dr. G. Palanithurai remarked.

Dr. G. Palanithurai when reviewing the Tamil Nadu scenario, observed that there was a slackness of will on the part of State Government in devolving of power to Panchayati Raj Institutions in letter and spirit. But the Village Panchayat Presidents of Tamil Nadu have proved their leadership and bagged twelve awards out of thirty nine awards declared by the Government of India in connection with the maintenance of environmental sanitation and cleanliness in villages, which indicated the strength of Gram Panchayat Presidents in Tamil Nadu who did not wait for the devolution of powers but exercised their powers and authority as they themselves perceived, Dr. G. Palanithurai pointed out.

Dr. G. Palanithurai was emphatic on the capability of leadership in Village Panchayat administration, and referred to one Village Panchayat President of the tsunami affected villages in Nagapattinam District, who was able to play a significant role in the activities of relief and rehabilitation. The President of Prathamaramapuram Village Panchayat did not wait for any order directing him to involve in the tsunami relief. He ensured his leadership by assuming himself the responsibility of accountability and transparency. When a few families were found cheated the authorities by stating that they were the sufferers in tsunami and enjoyed the fruits of benefits illegally, the Village Panchayat President was able to exercise his power over them and made them return the relief packages to the concerned authority. Dr. G. Palanithurai appealed to the participants to cultivate the leadership qualities by undertaking activities voluntarily. Dr. G. Palanithurai appreciated the capacity of women leaders who met together and discussed role of Village Panchayats when the Government declared the 15-points programmes aiming at the sustainable livelihood in rural areas.

The system of local governance should be a self-governance. The system is not to carryout the orders given by somebody situated somewhere else, whereas it has to function locally, involving local people and resources, Dr. G. Palanithurai observed.

Dr. G. Palanithurai declared that inspite of the various hurdles encountering the performance of the presidents, there are pathfinders who overcome hurdles and face the issues efficiently, in the State of Tamil Nadu, to the expectation of various bodies. Dr. G. Palanithurai cited an example the President of India, Dr. Abdul Kalam during his scheduled visit to Annamalai University, first visited the Village Panchayat 'Keerapalayam' and spent sufficient time to interact with the villagers. Dr. G. Palanithurai appealed to the office bearers of the Federation to workout the strategies for strengthening the functions of elected women Presidents.

Dr. G. Palanithurai acknowledged the role of media in empowering Panchayati Raj and the functioning of women Presidents. He explained that in the task of democratization of our rural community, each and every one of us has a role to play, and requested the elected Women Presidents to work more closely even with those who have misunderstanding. Dr. G. Palanithurai shared his experiences of participating in the Gram Sabha meet held at Thiruvasi Village Panchayat. One member of the SHG marked her participation in the deliberations more meaningfully and democratically. Dr. G. Palanithurai appealed to the elected women Presidents to perceive the climate that existed in Tamil Nadu and to equip themselves to meet the challenges in self-governance.

Sri A.K. Venkatasubramanian in his inaugural address explained the wish of Gandhiji that it was only through Panchayati Raj Institutions that the voice of the people could be heard. Gandhiji emphasized that more power should be given to the Panchayati Raj Institutions so that they could function independently. Sri A.K. Venkatasubramanian when tracing out the stages in the process of power devolution in the State of Tamil Nadu, criticized the imperfection in the perception of Government irrespective of the political orientation.

A.K. Venkatasubramanian further explained the hurdles in the implementation of Panchayati Raj System. The legal provisions are there but the society is yet to be prepared to take off.

A.K. Venkatasubramanian referred to the issues of Pappapatti and Keeripatti Village Panchayats where the President position were reserved to SC but the local community did not allow the leaders belonging to SC to be elected and to hold position's. The power of the legislation could be ensured i.e. only people give recognition to it and respect it. It is by the performance of the Village Panchayat Presidents, the expectation on the Panchayati Raj Institutions is improved, A.K. Venkatasubramanian observed. The rights of the local bodies should be protected and all the stakeholders of Panchayati Raj System must raise their voice when any attempt was made to be little the respect and value of the Panchayati Raj Institutions. A.K. Venkatasubramanian cited an example when the devolution of power to Panchayati Raj Institutions with regard the various sectoral developmental activities was denied, the Government instead of protecting the cause of legally constituted Panchayati Raj Institutions, the then Chief Minister expressed his fear over the protest of the teachers who were not willing to be with the local government. In this context, there should be public voice against the suppression of legal powers entrusted with the Panchayati Raj Institutions.

The leadership of Village Panchayat is different from the other tiers' leadership as the leaders of the Village Panchayat are standing on their own image and performance whereas leaders of upper tiers are taking shelter under the political parties. Hence, the leadership of the Village Panchayats need not fear over any factors and must come together to protest against the suppression of rights of the local bodies. It is proposed to establish a body consisting of activists, NGOs, leading Presidents and other institutions who are supporting the cause of the Panchayati Raj System to generate further alliances so that any attempt to suppress the rights of Panchayati Raj Institutions could be challenged in solidarity, A.K. Venkatasubramanian remarked. The scope of good governance is in the strength and performance of local governance. In this context the role of civil society was significant, he added.

A.K. Venkatasubramanian appealed to the Women Presidents to plan for the socio-economic development, especially, to eradicate illiteracy and child labour system, to give care to the welfare of the marginalized sections of the community and in economic activities for self-help group members. A.K. Venkatasubramanian further explained that there were volunteers among the retired Government Officials whose services could be utilized in these activities. A.K. Venkatasubramanian appreciated the role of Gandhigram Rural Institute in facilitating the elected women representatives consistently.

In his valedictory address, Dr. T. Karunakaran, the Vice-Chancellor of Gandhigram Rural Institute, shared his experience of interface with one village community in Rajasthan where the social issues like child marriage, *sati* etc., were in practice. Dr. T. Karunakaran explained that the rural community of Rajasthan is not ready to discard the age-old traditional beliefs and practices but in Tamil Nadu the rural community was a progressive one. He felt sorry for the incident of showing disrespect to the Women Presidents in some places. He appealed to the members of the Federation to unite together and enable the affected Women Presidents to overcome the hurdles. The proxy system in Tamil Nadu should not be allowed to exist, he emphasized.

Dr. T. Karunakaran suggested nine directions through which the empowerment of women leaders could be attempted: (a) sensitization of Women Presidents with regard to the delivery of services in the department of education, health and Public Distribution System; (b) sustaining the progress of womenfolk by adhering to small family norm by eradicating alcoholism, by promoting thrift and saving and social control on unwarranted expenditure; (c) ensuring development: through watershed activities, encouraging SHG activities and skill orientation to all; (d) ensuring the liberty and rights of *Dalits* Women Presidents; (e) taking a Vow to step in during the time of any atrocity against womenfolk; (f) encouraging them becoming models/innovators/pathfinders; (g) establishing consultancy services; (h) communicating news and views through regular newsletters; (i) constant encouragement and motivation.

He appealed to the elected women Presidents that initiatives of the Gandhigram Rural Institute, especially, the Rajiv Gandhi Chair for Panchayati Raj Studies and the effective leadership of Dr. G. Palanithurai should be fully utilized for their improvement. Gandhigram Rural Institute is ready to assist in the transmission of rural technologies and managerial skills to the Women Presidents.

Director of Rural Development gave reply to all the questions raised in the meeting. They are: (a) the representatives of the

Federation could submit their recommendations with regard to the devolution of finance, to the 3rd State Finance Commission which was recently constituted; (b) those Village Panchayats where the micro level planning exercise was carried out and a development plan was drafted, the Government would ensure that the works prioritized by the Village Panchayats would be taken up for implementation; (c) in the case of payment of pension to the really needy individuals among the aged and widows, the merit of the cases could be considered by the Government, inspite of the condition of non-eligibility as per the existing rules. Village Panchayats could facilitate this process; (d) the issue in releasing of Funeral Grant, meant for SC would be sorted out very soon. The issue was taken up with the finance department; (e) The delay in distribution of SFC installment during 2005-2006 will be regulated very soon; (f) the Village Panchayat Presidents should come forward to do innovations in many areas where adequate fund is available in schemes like housing loan to SHG members, construction of kutcha houses, establishment of gasifier/biogas plants, etc; (g) there are guidelines pertaining to those Panchayats which attract tourists or pilgrims, by partnership with Corporates in improving the cleanliness and environmental sanitation in those villages.

9

Interface with Institutions

In order to know about the functioning of Panchayati Raj Institutions which may stimulate for their better performances, the members of EWRs Association were taken to other States such as Kerala and West Bengal by the Rajiv Gandhi Chair for Panchayati Raj Studies. Kerala and West Bengal are serving as the best models for democratic decentralization in India. Moreover, people's participation is high in these States. To sensitize EWRs of Tamil Nadu, they were taken to these States. Moreover, within Tamil Nadu itself certain Panchayats like Odanthurai, Semmipalayam, Devipattinam, Michealpalayam, Sakkarakkottai, and Thamaraikulam are performing amazingly among the few. So they were taken to these Panchayats with the hope that EWRs can be motivated and they may replicate the same in their Panchayats.

Interface with Kerala Panchayat

Objectives of the Programme: (a) to concientise the Elected Women Represenatives (EWR) on the ideas and setup of the Village Panchayat and its functions; (b) to make them understand the qualities of leadership as Panchayat Women Presidents; (c) to identify the differences between Tamil Nadu Panchayats and Kerala Panchayats; (d) to get the needed information and Government orders pertinent to the welfare of Panchayats; (e) to analyse the situations which are problematic in the villages and to overcome such situations by evolving some solutions immediately; (f) to acquaint them with the powers, functions and responsibilities of elected representatives in the Village Panchayats; (g) to familiarise them with the structure, rules, procedures, regulations of Panchayats; (h) to familiarise them with the various programmes available for development activities of the Panchayats; (i) to motivate them to take up activities in the area of economic planning, social development and social justice; (j) to build leadership quality among them and to train them to function independently, (k) to motivate them to work along with SHGs and CBOs and NGOs working at grassroots; (l) to sensitise them on the need for networking of women elected representatives from grassroots.

With these objectives the EWRs were taken to Ahathathera Gram Panchayat.

Visit to Ahathathera Gram Panchayat

The Panchayat President of Ahathathera, Ms. V. Lakshmi Devi, explained the setup of Ahathathera Panchayat and its functions. She is a graduate administering her Panchayat very effectively. She is politically influenced by the Communist Party of India. She is also a member of the People's Plan Campaign. There is a neighbourhood group under the Gram Sabha. There are 12 ward members in Ahathathera Panchayat. They belong to CPI, CPM and Congress. However, there is no party-based approach in decision-making.

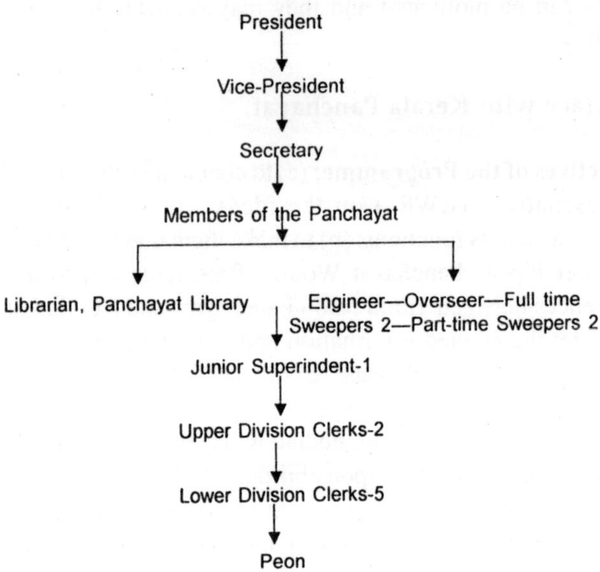

Fig. 9.1: Administrative Setup of Ahathathera Gram Panchayat

Basic Details of Ahathathera Panchayat

Ahathathera Panchayat is a special grade Panchayat. It has got 24,000 population and for each ward they have 2000 population with the area of 23 sq km.

The following institutions/organisations are functioning in the Panchayat area:

PHC	1
Sub-centre	3 (Doctors, Staff, Health Inspector)
Upper Primary Schools	2
High School	1
Kendriya Vidayalaya	1
NSS Team	1
Management Schools	2
Agricultural Office	Krishi Bhawan
Veterinary Hospital	1
Ayurveda Dispensary	1
Anganwadi (ICDS)	1
Engineering College	1 (The Vice-President is working as a clerk in the Private engineering college)

Government originally managed the following institutions: (a) PHC, (b) Sub Centres, (c) High school, (d) Agricultural Office, (e) Veterinary Hospital, and (f) Ayurveda Dispensary. Now they are under the control of the Panchayat. The Panchayat takes decisions on the menu to be given to the children in the Anganwadi. Kanji (wheat) and pulses are given now for lunch. Wheat uppuma (dry pudding) is provided at 3.00 pm every day. There are totally six Anganwadies constructed on the Panchayat's own land.

The Panchayat itself has constructed 119 houses and it has a plan to provide houses to all. From the year 1996-97 to 2000-2001, 119 houses have been constructed through the People's Plan Campaign in Ahathathera Panchayat and 350 toilets have been constructed—almost one in every house.

Fund flow has been reduced by the new State Government based on political considerations. The needy people get a total amount of Rs. 35,000 for constructing a house. Beneficiaries are able to get the amount in 3 instalments. The beneficiaries are selected by the Gram Sabha by fixing a few criteria based on marks given to them considering the degree of poverty, educational standard, and number of female children in the family. The list of the beneficiaries is put up on the notice boards of the Panchayat Office. Complaints can be filed if any change is needed. Based on the complaints the list will be checked again and the final list will be displayed.

There is a cordial relationship between the President and the Vice-President. Legal advice is given by the Secretary of the Panchayat. Resolutions are passed with the cooperation of all the members in the Panchayat. The income of Ahathathera Panchayat is:

• Building Tax	11 lakhs/year
• Professional Tax	9 lakhs/year
Total	20 lakhs/year

During E.K. Nayanar's (Government) period, the 73rd Amendment was passed and it resulted in a people's movement in Kerala. The people started struggling to get the rights and powers due to them. That is the reason how the Panchayat has got all the powers to achieve socio-economic development. Millions of people are involved in the people's movement. The Communist Government bravely took decisions to involve the people in governance. Hence, they succeeded in their attempts. The officials were against this movement. The people said that swimming could be learnt only by swimming in the pool not by learning through books. So the Government gave power to the Panchayat to proceed with its activities. The people's movement gained momentum as well as strength by involving the people.

Schools are guided and supervised by the Panchayat. Village Committee, i.e., Education Standing Committee, has been formed to run lower primary schools effectively. The members of the Education Standing Committee are: (a) Headmaster; (b)Staff of the schools; (c) Panchayat President; (d) Vice-President; (e) Ward Members; (f) Educated Persons; and (g) Retired Officials.

Plan fund can be distributed for the modification and development of buildings of the school, and the laboratory. The Teacher's Association is a powerful body in Kerala. The Panchayat has the power to take any step or action on the teachers of the school and can make suggestions to the Government. But there is a cordial relationship between the Panchayat President and the teachers in Kerala. The Panchayat facilitates a few activities of the school. Funds for the schools are distributed only through Panchayats. Officials are involved in every action of the Panchayat.

People who have less than Rs. 24,000 year as income are regarded as deserving beneficiaries to be benefited by the schemes implemented by the Government. The MP's fund is not directly spent by the MP. The fund is received by the Collector. The Presidents of Panchayat will discuss with the Collector the needed activities in the areas of the Panchayats. Based on the needs, funds are provided through the Collector.

Visit to SHGs

There are totally 34 SHGs in Ahathathera Panchayat. There is a Village Extension Officer who facilitates the SHGs' activities. The SHGs' activities are considered a service to the Gram Panchayat. SHGs have been formed in 216 Panchayats of Kerala. Each SHG consists of 15 to 20 members. One group is having a savings of around Rs. 11 lakhs. They are functioning on their own with their own funds. The Panchayat has given Rs. 10,000 only for self-employment programmes. Through the activities of SHGs women are getting employment opportunities and are earning on an average Rs. 800 to Rs. 2,000 per month. Their important activities for generating income are: (a) Mushroom cultivation; (b) Pickle making; (c) Soap making; (d) Yujala making; and (e) Vathal making.

An SHG in Ahathathera panchayat has bagged the Kerala State award for 2001 and also participated in National Level Exhibition-2001 in Delhi. The leader of the SHG Ms. Ammini is a Diploma holder in Civil Engineering and also a CPI member as well as the district secretary of SHGs. She wants to construct a building for the SHGs. Their products are sold in civil stations or shops directly. They are directly connected in touch with the Collectorate. So it is easy for them to contact the officials for any help.

Visit to Anganwadi at Ahathathera Panchayat

There are 15 children who come regularly to the Anganwadi run by ICDS (Integrated Child Development Services). There is an *Aaya* to take care of all the children. There is a teacher to teach songs and to feed the children properly. There is a weighing machine to weigh the children periodically. Special care is taken of pregnant women. The Anganwadi has received a prize from the Panchayat. The centre is clean and the children are healthy. Panchayat leaders visit the Anganwadi regularly. The menu of the Anganwadi is decided by the Panchayat. Nutritive, food in sufficient quantity is provided.

Visit to PHC (Primary Health Centre)

A new Primary Health Centre has been constructed at a cost of Rs. 6 lakhs. There is a lady Health Inspector, a Junior Health Assistant and staff to assist the doctor in the PHC. There are mother-child care charts on pre- and post-natal care and immunization to create awareness on health, nutrition and child care among pregnant and lactating women. A water tank worth Rs. 66 lakhs is being constructed near the Primary Health Centre.

Discussion with the Elected Representatives

The participants met Mr. Sumesh, a ward member of Ahathathera Panchayat and Ms. P. Padmini, Secretary of Panchayat. Mr. Sumesh is an I.T.I, diploma holder doing business. Periodical meetings are held as per rules and decisions are taken after considering the needs and activities of each ward. For each sitting, each ward member is paid Rs. 32. There are two meetings in a month. The Secretary is the adviser to the Panchayat President in carrying out all Panchayat activities. There is always a cordial relationship and mutual understanding among all the staff in the Panchayats. This is one of the main reasons for the success of the Panchayats. Since all are educated and well informed the Panchayat functions effectively.

The participants found the interface programme in Kerala very educative and useful. The number of staff members in Kerala Panchayats is large and the work is shared by all. So it is easy for them to carry out the functions and satisfy the needs of the people quickly. Some of the observations made by the elected leaders on their interface programme in Kerala are listed below:

(a) In Kerala, a favourable social base has been built up over the years to facilitate the process of women empowerment; (b) the State Government of Kerala is favourable towards decentralization and encourages the Panchayats to govern well and deliver quality services;

(c) the fund flow to Panchayats in Kerala is better than it is in Tamil Nadu; (d) the social development in Kerala has made the responsibilities of Panchayats much easier; (e) the Gram Sabha meetings in Kerala are held at ward level and this has enabled the people to participate in the discussions; (f) in addition, the neighbourhood committees, SHGs, and CBOs are also supporting the Panchayats; (g) the size of the Panchayats has made the system viable and more staff could be employed by the Panchayats; (h) officials—Non-officials relationship in Kerala is good and well-coordinated; (i) as the elected leaders get honorarium, they are able to concentrate on Panchayat activities; and (j) in general, the Panchayats in Kerala are found to be powerful, resourceful, effective, transparent and honest.

Interface with West Bengal Panchayati Raj Institutions

Fifteen Gram Panchayat Presidents of Tamil Nadu visited West Bengal on the invitation of Hon'ble Minister of Panchayati Raj and Rural Development Dr. Suriya Kant Mishra. They were accompanied by the staff members of Rajiv Gandhi Chair for Panchayati Raj Studies in Gandhigram Rural Institute. The interface programme was hosted by SIPRD of West Bengal situated in Kalyani of Nadia District and sponsored by Singamma Srinivasan Foundation and Department of Political Science and Development Administration, Gandhigram. The team reached SIPRD on 4th July, and their programme started on that day itself with the welcome by the Director of SIPRD Mr. Alok Kumar Mukhopadhyay, I.A.S., Mr. Dhilipkumar Gosh, facilitated the programme. On the first day, the first session was devoted to explain the history of Panchayati Raj System in West Bengal. Mr. Utpal Chakravarthy explained how the Institution of local governance and local self-governance came into existence right from the beginning of pre-vedic and vedic period. He also said about the stages of decentralization from the Bengal Village Chaukidar Act of 1870, where there was a provision for the nomination of members for a local institution to look after and settle local disputes. Second important change brought by the Britishers was the revolution of Lord Rippon where the provision of tax collection was entrusted with the institution to perform municipal function. In between these two phases, there was a significant change, the nominated persons from the role of watchman and informer to the Britishers where entrusted with certain responsibilities to look after the local bodies. Moreover, it lessens the burden of the British Government in providing civil amenities and also resulted in savings. Further, the District Boards were created through Bengal Local Self Government Act, 1885. But the power centre was the landlords who were supposed to be the supporters of the Britishers. Subsequent changes were brought about through Montague-Chelmsford Reform till the Constituent Assembly. Especially, he said about the discussion held in the Constituent Assembly on the Panchayats. Briefing the steps taken in Nehruian era, he said about the provision of West Bengal Panchayat Act, 1957 where two tier system was introduced at Gram Panchayat and Anjal Panchayat. Another Act was enacted in 1963, abolishing Gram Panchayat and creating District Panchayat and Block Panchayat. In 1973, the Congress Government in West Bengal enacted new Act to create a three tier system but only the Communist front Government conducted elections. Till February 2005 that Act had been amended twenty four times to favour the decentralization process.

He dwelt on explained the functions entrusted with the Gram Panchayat like generation of revenue, infrastructure building and also about the roles and responsibilities of standing the committees constituted in the Gram Panchayat in order to look after (i) Finance and Planning, (ii) Agriculture and Allied business, (iii) Industry and Infrastructure, (iv) Education and Health, and (v) Women and Social Development. To ensure people's participation and to enrich social capital 'Gram Unan Samiti' is constituted. Unlike in Tamil Nadu, the office of the Gram Panchayat is manned with a secretary, Sahayog and Executive Assistant who are all Government servants, appointed to assist the functioning of Gram Panchayat. Panchayat President is the drawing and disbursing officer and executive assistant will be the joint signatory of the check.

After briefly explaining about the system of Panchayati Raj in West Bengal, the participants were taken to the Sugandha Gram Panchayat in Hoogli District headed by Ms. Shamoli Bhavin. She explained about the functioning Panchayats. When the participants enquired about the selection of beneficiaries for various schemes, she said that her Gram Panchayat has constituted a Beneficiary Committee which looks into the whole operation from selection to the completion of the project with the participation of the beneficiaries. On seeing the brick-kiln in this area, the participants asked the President to explain about the problem of child labour and the President replied that several people with their family members from Bihar and Uttaranchal used to migrate to this region and will get back to their natives during the rainy season and so they find it difficult to eliminate the problem of child labour and to educate those children. Since this is a rain-fed area, they don't face any water shortage but there is no household drinking water connection and people collect water from the common taps. When she talked about the problem of gender issues, she said women suffer problems due to the consumption of liquor by their spouses and wife beating is common and they try to solve this by giving counselling through Ward Members and other volunteers. When asked about SHG's, it is found that West Bengal is in the initial stage and totally 1 lakh 50 thousand SHGs have formed and they are trying to make it as a movement through SGSY. And with these SHGs, the Government is trying to create awareness on immunization, women issues, health and education.

Participants were then taken to Hoogli District Panchayat office to meet its Chairperson Ms. Krishna Banerjee whose status is equivalent to the Minister of State. She spoke a few words with the participants explaining their linkage with the Gram Panchayat and told about her achievements in the following area: (a) Mid-day meal scheme; (b) Sanitation; (c) Health; (d) SHGs; and (e) Education.

Since she involved herself with the mass movement and maintained a close collaboration with the people she has achieved this much.

On day two Ms. Gayathiri Basu, Senior Faculty Member of SIPRD whose specialization is on public health, shared her time with the participants. She discussed the following issues with the participants: (a) Organic linkage of 3-tier Panchayat system in West Bengal; (b) Party politics in Local Governance; (c) Sanitation movement; (d) Standing committees roles and responsibilities; (e) BPL list preparation; and (f) Audit system in West Bengal.

They also discussed the plan document prepared in West Bengal Gram Panchayat which includes: (a) Agriculture; (b) Health; (c) Education; (d) Women and Children; (e) Social Development; (f) Infrastructure; and (g) Small and Cottage Industries.

They further talked about the following scenario in West Bengal and Tamil Nadu: (a) Mortality of Mothers; (b) Infant Mortality; (c) Trained *Dais;* (d) Institutional Delivery; and (e) Family Planning.

Next, they were taken to the Pandua Panchayat Samiti situated in Hoogli District and met Mrs. Shukla Mukherjee who heads the Panchayat Samiti. She is a leader of grassroots movement and now she concentrates her attention on mid-day meal scheme and SSA. Next, the team went to Jamna Gram Panchayat which collects more revenue than other and has a shopping complex on it's own which has increased their income. They had discussion about the Sanitation, mid-day meal and IAY houses. Participants were taken to look at a IAY house entrusted by one beneficiary.

On the final day, Ms. Subarna Ganguly discussed women issues with the participants. They are: (a) Girl child education; (b) Family planning; (c) Marriage; (d) Dowry; and (e) Alcohol consumption and so on.

She led the participants to the women SHG members and those women were shy and they hesitate to show even their faces and are reluctant to speaks. Their facilitator said that they have joined the group to earn and save money and most of them are destitute women. Their situation is pathetic and the participants felt sorry for them. With these meetings the programme came to an end.

Elected Women Representative's Observations

The Elected Women Representatives asked to share their observations about the Panchayati Raj Institutions of West Bengal. Some of their observations were the following: (1) More people's participation; (2) Innumerable water resources; (3) Greenish unpolluted environment; (4) Formulation of various committees; (5) Organic support within the three-tier system; (6) Gram Sabha held in each hamlets; (7) Birth and death certificates issued by the Panchayats; (8) Systematic land and house approval system was followed; (9) Fine collected from the people; (10) The opposition party leaders are the members of several village development committee was appreciable; (11) Government employees like teachers contest in the Panchayat elections; (12) Industries and pollution; (13) Traditional agricultural methods; (14) The involvement of former Panchayat

Presidents to enrich Panchayat development activities; (15) Greater importance given to agricultural activities; (16) Preparation of village development plan with the people; (17) District Panchayat (Zilla Parishad) with more powers; (18) Provision of salary for Panchayat Assistants and honorarium for elected representatives; (19) SHGs are involved in the preparation of the list of physically challenged children; (20) Formation of more number of cooperative societies; (21) Importance given to education, mid-day meal scheme and health; (22) Elected representatives were vested with more powers; (23) Panchayat income generated through shopping complexes; (24) Panchayat office campus is enormous, which has provided with meeting hall, health centre, and telephone facilities; (25) Vice-President post is provided with reservation; (26) Elected representatives belong to political parties; (27) Controlled by the Panchayat Assistant who was recruited by the Government; (28) Poor sanitation—IAY houses are constructed without toilets and the villages have no public toilets; (29) SHG women have overcome taboos and are motivated to wipe out ignorance; (30) Child labourers are more due to frequent migrations for seasonal occupations; (31) Roads are highly damaged and no proper roads have been constructed; (32) Women are neither involved in Panchayat activities nor participated in the Gram Sabha; (33) No *pucca* construction of IAY houses and the amount allotted for the beneficiaries are very low; (34) The Pandua Block Panchayat office is full of wastes and is verty dirty; (35) Non-conventional energy sources were not introduced; (36) No proper drainage system; (37) Less importance given to social development issues; (38) Low standard of living; (39) Women are highly dominated by the patriarchal society; (40) No Gender sensitization; and (41) No proper income generating activities for SHG.

The Elected Women Representatives of Tamil Nadu utilized the favourable situations found in Panchayats in Tamil Nadu. They have decided to disseminate the information as they have learnt from West Bengal with other Elected Women Representatives, who have no faith in the Panchayat administration. And they wanted to concentrate more on social development issues. They were felt proud that if the Tamil Nadu Panchayat has vested with power like West Bengal, they would contribute more. Further, they have decided to disseminate their learning through the media. They have invited the Elected Women Representatives of West Bengal to their Gram Panchayats under interface programmes.

Key Observations

1. In West Bengal, the Gram Panchayat has been vested with more powers but the Elected Women Representatives are controlled by the party leaders and Panchayat Secretaries.
2. There was a link among the three tier system and District Panchayat Chairperson has more powers like a Collector and his position is equal to that of a Minister of State.
3. The Panchayat activities are implemented with people's participation.
4. They have financial crises but they try to create income sources by the construction of shopping complexes, lands, house plans approvals, etc.
5. But they are not able to change the mindset of the people regarding sanitation. They have neither individual latrines, nor public latrines and they do not think about how manage the solid waste.
6. Women are highly dominated by the patriarchal society and recently the Government tried to bring them to the public spaces by the formation of Self-Help Groups.
7. Due to seasonal migration all the children are not properly enrolled in schools.
8. The enormous Panchayat office with all administrative facilities has one health centre. The nurse from this health centre takes care of mothers, teenage girls and children by providing several immunization and other medicinal helps under the ICDS programme.
9. The formation of various Village Development Committees like Standing Committee, Beneficiary Selection Committee, etc., has played its significant role, which planned its activity along with the Ward Members, Former Panchayat Presidents and other experienced pro-Panchayat leaders. It was appreciable that the opposition party members are also action in all developmental Committees.

10. Birth and Death Certificates are issued by the Gram Panchayat and several sectoral departments are supportive in the Panchayat activities.

Exposure Visit to Odanthurai and Semmipalayam Panchayats—Coimbatore District

The Rajiv Gandhi Chair for Panchayati Raj Studies has trained innumerable women functionaries of local governance and provided valuable guidance to all the Panchayat Presidents of Tamil Nadu through its various research projects. It has conducted many capacity building exercises, pathfinders' meet, media workshops, and many other activities to enrich the Presidents so that they could emerge as transformative leaders. It has not only built up the capacity of women leaders, but has also facilitated the flow of information to quench the thirst of researchers and scholars from within and outside the country. It has also laid a base to draft policies from its rich experience. These activities have motivated and impressed the elected women representatives to form an association and act appropriately thanks to the Singamma Sreenivasan Foundation Project.

To convert the federation into a pressure group, the project enables EWRs to strengthen the Federation, concentrate on Gender and Social Development issues and transform the federation into a mass movement by contacting media persons, meeting higher officials and approaching national leaders and supportive agencies.

Objectives

The interface programme had the following objectives:

- to create an opportunity to share their experiences with other EWRs within their district for strengthening the association activities,
- to learn about the functions and functionaries of model Panchayats,
- to identify the differences between their district and the other districts,
- to learn about the needed leadership qualities for EWRs,

- to discuss problematic situations and solutions to overcome such crises,
- to find out the strength of the administrative linkages between Government officials and Panchayat Presidents,
- to motivate the EWRs to work along with SHGs, NGOs and other community supportive institutions working at the grassroots,
- to build confidence among them to perform independently,
- to urge them to take up activities in the area of economic planning, social development and social justice.

Earlier most of the exposure visits were held in other States like Kerala and West Bengal. The federated members felt that it was a good experience but the entire PRI setup was entirely different when compared to Tamil Nadu and hence they preferred to visit successful model Panchayats of Tamil Nadu. The EWRs were brought to Odanthurai and Semmipalayam Panchayats which are situated in Coimbatore District. Both Panchayats were awarded prizes for their performance. The EWRs from southern districts were invited for the exposure visit to 12 Blocks. Totally thirty five EWRs participated in the interface programme as per the decision of the block level representatives of the Federation.

Odanthurai Panchayat Activities

1. Installation of Solar lamps,
2. Construction of a Biomas plant,
3. Electricity through Gasifier plant,
4. Bacteria-free drinking water supply (under National Drinking Water Mission),
5. *Pucca* Group Houses for STs and all other communities,
6. Gobar Gas to the kitchens of IAY Houses,
7. Construction of proper drainage system along with rain water harvesting setup,
8. Provision of economic/income generating activities of SHGs and youth.

EWRs Interaction with Odanthurai President

The EWRs get clarified their doubts about how the President was able to collect 100 per cent house tax, that too with a moderate increase in the tax. The President asserted that if people were united and basic amenities were made available to them anything could be done with the people's support. EWRs were wonder-struck when they say the facilities available in the Panchayat office and they felt that due to the presence of technologies like computers with internet link, facsimile and telephone facilities, information dissemination would be much easier. Another pertinent question raised by the EWRs was about the tenders for work. The EWRs felt that the work done by the contractors was not satisfactory but they could not find any other way of doing the work. Mr. Shanmugam replied that most of the work in his Panchayat was carried out well. He would give the work to a person who is reliable and trustworthy. He advised them to avoid contractors and try to seek alternative sources or the EWRs themselves can take up these works and contribute by purchasing high quality materials for getting impressive results. He again stated that high quality materials will surely prevent repairing/service charges and save the Panchayat finance.

The EWRs tried to find out whether the auditors sought any bribe during account closing and if he resisted threatened to take severe action against the President by refusing to affix his signature. The President exhorted/the EWRs not to worry about threats. He stated that a transparent administration would never land the President into trouble. The EWRs asked the President about the people's participation in the Gram Sabha and how he invites all the people to attend the Gram Sabha. The President replied that due to the fulfillment of the needs, all the village people attended the Gram Sabha. The last Gram Sabha meeting was attended by the District Collector, he declared with pride. The EWRs, after visiting the biogas plant, voiced a serious doubt. Among the ST Group Houses only 15 houses were provided with biogas supply and the others were not. So the EWRs asked the President if the households which were not provided with gas supply might express their resentment to the President. The President stated that due to the sincere care taken by the President for fulfilling their needs, they never expressed any opposition, because they are satisfied with the other amenities provided.

The EWRs wanted to know whether any work was assigned under the MLA/MP constituency fund, the President replied that he never sought for such type of funds. The EWRs put a question regarding the relationship between the President and the Government officials. The President answered that the Secretary for Rural Development, the Project Officer, the District Collector and other officials were very supportive in all activities. They visited the village frequently and recovered his name for the programmes organised for the Panchayats. The Police department was also people-friendly.

Since he has abiding faith in and is supportive of SHGs, the EWRs asked the President what type of economic activities were undertaken by the SHGs. He listed out the activities undertaken by the SHGs. There are nearly 45 SHG members who belong to the STs. Each member was provided with a milch cow and they have established a milk production cooperative society for themselves. Doormats and *chappals* are also manufactured by these groups. He plants to establish a mineral water plant for these SHGs. The EWRs asked about the activities undertaken under the SSA and the enrollment of students in schools. The President replied that a pucca building was constructed under the SSA, a lot of trees have been planted around the school campus and the students enrollment is quite high.

The EWRs wished to know about the youth's participation in Panchayat activities. The youth group from the Nehru Yuva Kendra participated in public activities, the President stated.

Regarding alliance building with NGOs, the EWRs asked, whether any NGO is involved in community development activities. The NGOs organised income generating training programmes for the SHG members, but did not guide them in marketing the products. Now they have no link with the SHGs. So there is no collaborative activity going on with the NGOs. But many NGOs have contacted him for organizing community development programmes, the President replied. Rainwater harvesting and environmental protection through total sanitation programme are the recent steps taken by every Panchayat. The EWRs asked about these two programmes. The President said that 100 per cent rainwater harvesting has been completed and the group houses are constructed with pre-planned setup for rainwater harvesting. The rainwater is planned to be saved in the Bhavani river itself. Under the sanitation programme, a sanitary complex has been constructed and is being utilized by the community and maintained by a SHG. Individual toilets have been constructed outside the IAY houses where the biogas plant has been set up. The people use the toilets and know the importance of the biogas plant as a non-conventional energy source.

Regarding the gasifier plant, many EWRs posed many questions to the President. How does it reduce the electricity charges? How did he plan to setup this gasifier plant. The President answered the questions posed by the EWRs about the gasifier which produces electricity. At present the electricity charges for getting water from the river has been reduced 3 times from Rs. 16000 to Rs. 4000 and the people are assured of bacteria-free water supply. The idea for establishing this gasifier plant was created when he visited Gujarat where a gasifier plant had been installed. The President got details from the exposure visit and some more information from the Ministry of Non-Conventional Energy Sources like subsidy, the capacity of the gasifier, raw materials, etc. Then he planned to set up this plant under the need-based schemes.

In future, he plans to setup wind/solar energy systems for getting electricity through wind/sunlight. He finally advised the EWRs to concentrate on non-conventional energy sources and try to conserve the financial resources and generate income through the available local resources. He again and again stressed that the EWRs must plan every activity as per the needs of the people.

Semmipalayam Panchayat Activities

1. Drinking water supply under the Rajiv Gandhi Drinking Water Mission.
2. Installation of a Gasifier plant.
3. Biogas supply to houses and noon meal centre.
4. Solid waste management.
5. Construction of toilets/sanitary complexes with proper drainage.
6. Economic income generating activities for SHGs.

7. Educational development through anganwadi, middle and Government High School.
8. Wind pump for frequent water supply.
9. Roadside park.
10. Planned construction of pucca group house.

The EWRs visited the various places along with the President, the Vice-President and two Ward Members.

Participants Observation

The participants were interested to implement the schemes of non-conventional energy sources and solar energy. They were impressed by the activities performed by these two Presidents. Due to hike in electricity charges they wanted to install a gasifier plant to save on electricity expenditure. Not only that, they have a large number of trees available in their area which can be utilized for the gasifier plant. The process adopted by the Presidents to avoid wastage of water also impressed the EWRs to implement the scheme in their Panchayats.

The wind-water pump also attracted the attention of the participants, because Tuticorin District is located in the coastal area where wind is readily available in plenty. They also wanted to install biogas plants, which are environmental protective and provide biogas to kitchens. Installation of solar lamps, which reduce the consumption of electricity, made the participants ask more questions. The participants decided to create a park for children in their Panchayats.

Participants Suggestions

- The Government should make arrangements for reducing the cost of non-conventional energy source plants, which would be useful to the Panchayats having insufficient funds.
- Visit by the model Panchayat Presidents to their area would be helpful to them to implement such novel schemes.
- The Ministry of Non-Conventional Energy Sources should provide an orientation to EWRs about its activities and provide information on the various types of energy plants.

General Observations

The Panchayat Presidents got the support of the people and ensured their participation since the President has met the basic requirements of the people satisfactorily:

1. In every work, people's contribution finds a place as the major resource and so care and importance is given to that work.
2. The Ward Members, the Vice-President, the Clerk and Government officials extended their cooperation.
3. Due to the provision of basic amenities, there was no problem in the collection of taxes and implementation of various schemes.
4. SHGs are supportive in all Panchayat activities, especially income generating activities, e.g., animal husbandry, vermin compost, fertilizer preparation, etc.
5. Alliance building with the NGOs in the solid waste management process keeps the Panchayat environmentally protected. The NGO also provides self-employment training and organises awareness campaigns.
6. Most of the Panchayat fund is saved due to the less consumption of electricity, thanks to the alternative sources of non-conventional and solar energy.
7. Their goal in Panchayat administration is justice, transparency, quality maintenance, honesty, fearlessness, confidence and planning for financial resources management.
8. There is free flow of Panchayat funds due to efficient CPR management and installation of non-conventional energy plants.
9. More care is given to children's education, sanitation, women's development and the development of people below poverty line.
10. The Presidents have visited various States, attended many programmes to gather more information regarding non-conventional energy sources like the gasifier plant, various types of solar energy materials, wind pump, etc. Further, they have contacted the Ministry of Non-Conventional Energy

Sources for getting the information needed regarding schemes.

11. The installation of the gasifier plant highlighted the importance of the prevention of deforestation and soil erosion.
12. The biomass plant provided smokeless gas to kitchens and stressed the importance of utilizing public and individual toilets and getting manure for agriculture.
13. The process of solid waste management not only raised the income but also educated the people about the maintenance of a clean environment.
14. The construction of a sanitary complex with appropriate technology like proper drainage system, optimal usage of water, biogas plant, waste water for the preparation of manure shows the Presidents' tendency to avoid wastage, creating wealth from waste and encouraging income-generating activities of the SHGs.
15. The establishment of a park not only amuses the visitors, but also motivates them to think about the importance of tree planting/afforestation. The nursery garden, which has a collection of castor saplings, helps the farmers to get saplings from the park. It also generates income for the Panchayat and individuals.
16. The desiltation of the five ponds and construction of check dams show the Presidents' enthusiasms and fore-sightedness for rainwater harvesting.
17. The installation of high quality (TATA company) solar lamps has eliminated repairing charges. The amount allotted for the same might be utilized for other essential work. The electric street lights need service charges and high consumption entails more electricity charges.
18. Through the wind pump, 24 hour water supply is given to both the middle and the higher secondary schools.
19. The gasifier plant ensures 24 hour water supply by producing electricity from burning wood. Wood from thorn trees is utilized for two purposes, removal of thorny trees and saving the underground water. Innumerable trees have been transformed into an income source.

20. *Pucca* well planned group houses for ST, SC and other communities have several facilities like water supply, biogas supply and a proper drainage system.

The participants enjoyed the trip and felt that the programme was very informative and useful. Both Odanthurai and Semmipalayam Panchayats gave much importance to community welfare measures and the community also reposed faith in their Panchayat leaders. They said that they never had the idea of living in their own houses because of their poverty, but their President made it a reality by providing own houses to everyone. The Vice-President, Ward Members, Government officials, and others cooperatively work together. Both Panchayats have the favour of good economic resources and enormous sources of income. This was made possible due to the strenuous efforts taken by the Presidents. Hence, it is easy for them to discharge their duties satisfy the needs of the people.

The participants requested the organizers of the training programme to arrange for similar programmes in order to equip themselves better for the Panchayat activities. Further, they decided to organize periodical meetings under the Federation to discuss the innovations to be carried out in the Panchayats.

Exposure Visit to Michaelpattinam, Thamaraikulam, Devipattinam, and Sakkarakottai Panchayats—Ramanathapuram District

The EWRs Association organises periodical meetings to exchange their ideas and experience and try to workout strategies to tackle their problems, which they face in the day-to-day administration. With the support of various pro-Panchayat programmes, the EWRs have innovatively equipped themselves to extend their activities from the fulfillment of basic needs to the Governance of social development issues. From the experiences shared by the successful EWRs, they are interested to learn about the strategies for the discharge of duties and responsibilities along with people's participation. The process of experience sharing along with exposure visits may enhance the leader's qualities of EWRs. The field experience induces and motivates the EWRs to become people-centric and paves the way for effective administration.

EWRs from various districts like Dindigul, Madurai, Trichy, Theni, Tirunelveli, Madurai, Tuticorin, Pudukottai and Salem were selected for the exposure visit. These EWRs were taken to four Panchayats of Ramanad District like Michelpattinam, Devipattinam, Sakkarakottai and Thamaraikulam.

Objectives

- To facilitate the sharing of experiences among EWRs not only within the district but also within the State.
- To interact with the active empowered women role models and pathfinders of other districts.
- To urge the EWRs to concentrate on the governance of Health, Environment, Sanitation, Education and Weaker Sections etc.
- To stress the significance of alliance building with SHGs, NGOs, Youths and pro-Panchayat institutions.
- To share the experience of EWRs on Gender and social development issues.
- To impress upon the significance of people's participation in Panchayat activities
- To discuss their future plans of action for strengthening the EWRs' association

The facilitators orient the EWRs on the purpose of the visit, important activities undertaken in the selected model Panchayats and asked about their expectations from the exposure visit. The EWRs want to know about peoples' participation in Panchayat activities, role of SHGs, works under TRSP, innovative rainwater harvesting system, reasons for the possibility of communal harmony women's participation in Gram Sabha, the possibility of solid waste management system with the participation of the NGO, maintenance of common property resources, status of marginalized sector, women and children and teenage girls. They want to find out the governance of education, sanitation, environment, health and weaker section.

Michealpattinam

Ms. Jesumery, President of Michealpattinam Panchayat of Ramanathapuram District is very active and has performed her

Panchayat activities with the support of the district administration. She has received many awards for the cent per cent fulfillment of rainwater harvesting and sanitation under TRSP. She was awarded by the Chief Minister of Tamil Nadu and visited United States with the support of the World Bank for the successful implementation of rainwater harvesting. She has performed the Panchayat activities with the support of the people, ward members, traditional Panchayat leaders, women SHGs and weaker sections. She solved the problems of the oppressed persons of her Panchayat by fulfilling their prime demands. The activities undertaken in her Panchayat are the following:

1. She has constructed low cost public toilets for men and women, which were made up of asbestos sheets and tin sheets. They have no separate water connection; the people fetch water from the public tap with the help of buckets and mugs provided by the Panchayat. The toilets are helpful for the agricultural labourers.
2. She has recovered 3 acres Panchayat land from the community leaders and the land is now cultivated with Jetropa plants with the help of SHGs, youths and the community. An amount of Rs. 24000 was received under SGRY scheme and an amount of Rs. 15000 was spent for the purchase of 300 seedlings and a balance amount of Rs. 9000 was not enough for the preparation of fertile land. Hence, the thorns and bushes were removed with the help of people's participation; especially the youths played a major role by channelising the water for the growth of the plants. The weeds are periodically removed and maintained by the SHGs.
3. The rainwater from the old Panchayat building and the sanitary complex is channelised towards the sanitary complex borewell. This converts the salt water from the borewell into soft water and this soft water is utilised for the irrigation purpose of Jetropha plants. One acre of the Panchayat land situated near the sanitary complex has been given to the SHGs and the SHGs have planned to grow vegetables like snake guard, pumpkin bitter guard, beans etc. The waste water from the sanitary complex is utilised for the vegetable garden. The decomposed solid waste is used as natural manure. She has decided to arrange a pit for vermin composed manure.

4. Most of the available ground water is salty. The people of this area utilised the pond water for drinking purpose and they have realised the importance of rainwater. Hence, all the houses are provided with *pucca* rainwater-harvesting system and the collection of underground rainwater is channalised with PVC pipes, filtered and sent to the drinking water pond.
5. The rainwater collected from the school building is stored in a 10 feet tank and a bore is made at the centre of the tank. The drinking water from this borewell is taken with the help of a hand pump.
6. There is no separate tap connection made for the separate toilets constructed for the teachers and girls and boys in the school campus. The water is fetched from the nearby pond. The school situated here is under the control of the Christian Management, hence, the Panchayat has no provision for giving water tap connection and borewell. Realising the significance of education, the Panchayat President supports this institution.
7. Various awareness campaigns organised have been for the people with the support of the students towards sanitation and personal hygiene. Many competitions were conducted for the students by stressing the importance of clean village and the women are given prizes by the Panchayat President. Separate dustbins for the collection of decomposable and polythene papers are provided to each classroom and the students are trained to keep the school campus clean. The students have developed the habits of collecting the wastes from the campus and put them into the bins.
8. The Panchayat President rehabilitated a number of physically and mentally challenged destitute women. She facilitated them by getting the available State Government welfare schemes and she fulfills their basic needs, by the provision of clothes and some financial aids. She counsels them whenever they face problems. She provided her monthly TA (from the Panchayat fund) to these women. A mentally disordered women from the SC colony was not able to utilize the money for her livelihood, hence, the President provides grocery for her from her TA amount.

Thamaraikulam

Mr. S. Sivalingam is the President of Thamaraikulam Panchayat, Mandapam Panchayat Union in Ramanathapuram. He belongs to Nadar Community and the major caste group in this Panchayat is Nadars. The community leaders have come from his family (traditional leaders). Both before and after the 73rd Amendment he has been the President of this Panchayat. He has also served as the Chairperson of the District Cooperative Bank and helped the poor people by providing loans for cattle, miltch cows, house loans, household gas connection loans, etc. Being the District Secretary of Nadar Mahajana Sangam, he has donated his own land for the construction of ITI in his Panchayat. This helps the youths of his Panchayat to undergo technical education. These technically educated youths have migrated to foreign countries for their employment. The people accept the Panchayat President's decision and he gets the support of the people and easily mobilises the people. Hence, he can easily form women SHGs, Village Development Committee, and able to maintain the village clean with people's participation and support. He has also created a cordial relationship with the district administration, Panchayat Union, MLAs, MPs etc. So he able to get all Government schemes and development funds. Hence he was awarded with Nirmal Gram Puraskar by the President of India, and was also awarded by the District Collector under TRSP.

EWRs Interaction with President

The EWRs shared the experience of Thamaraikulam Panchayat President Mr. S. Sivalingam, the interaction covered on the following activities and the Panchayat President responded to the question.

- About his educational qualifications,
- How he started his career,
- How he managed to carry out Panchayat activities,
- His family members support,
- How people cooperate for the implementation of TRSP,
- What is the contribution he made for widows, old age persons, daughters of widows, physically and mentally challenged people etc.,

- Whether he has fulfilled the needs of the ultra poor,
- How many houses have been constructed under IAY scheme,
- Education for the school dropouts,
- The self-employment opportunities for the SHGs and whether they started their self-employment with local resources,
- The income sources of the Panchayats,
- His approach towards government officials and political party,
- The status of *Dalit* women,
- How to solve the Panchayat problems,
- Crime and violence against women,
- His own political party affilitation and contribution,
- Intervention from the opposition party,
- The age at marriage of teenage girls, health care for teenage girls, female feoticide, female infanticide, maternal mortality and infant mortality,
- Implementation and utilisation of non-conventional energy sources,
- Meetings organised by SHGs and their contribution to the Panchayat,
- The ward members and Vice-president cooperation,
- Tree planting,
- Activation of village development committee,
- Education for girl children,
- Encroachment of evictions, and
- Management of the water sources.

The EWRs appreciated the achievements of the Thamaraikulam Panchayat President and realized the significance of people's participation. They felt that:

1. The Panchayat streets are kept clean.
2. Ponds are clean without wastes or garbage.
3. Drainage water is utilized for the maintenance of house garden.
4. Each street has been provided with a wastebin, the people of the village put the wastes into the dustbins. Nobody dropped the wastes into the streets. Even the visitors automatically throw the wastes in the bins. This habit is created through

IEC with the support of TRSP (Total Rural Sanitation Programme) by the President.

5. The students properly cut the nails, utilize the toilets, wear *chappals* and keep the school campus clean. They force their parents to make use of the toilets. The entrance of each classroom is kept with a bucket full of water and soap. The students are training to clean their hands before taking food and after the use of toilets. The teachers and Headmistress are women and they teach the students regarding personal hygiene through songs.
6. The Women and Children Sanitary Complex is maintained by SHGs, the beneficiaries of this complex pay an amount of Rs. 10 towards its maintenance charges. The SHG members collect this amount and a separate account has opened for this purpose.
7. The sweepers collect the wastes and bring them to the Solid Wasteshed where the decomposed and plastic wastes are separated. From the decomposed waste, the SHGs prepare vermi composed manure and sell it for the agricultural labourers at Rs. 15 per kg.
8. Various welfare schemes have been implemented by the Tamil Nadu Government. They are displayed on the walls of the Panchayat buildings like library, school, Panchayat office, SHG building, Vertinary Centre, PHC, etc.
9. To save the saplings from cattle, the Panchayat has purchased well-grown tree saplings (middle growth) and planted them in the Panchayat areas.

The EWRs like to implement these activities in their Panchayats with people's participation.

Devipattinam

Due to some unavoidable situation, the Devipattinam Panchayat President Ms. Jamruth Beevi could not meet the EWRs. She requested the ward members and the Panchayat Assistant to explain the activities undertaken in the Panchayat.

The EWRs appreciated the Panchayat President for the construction of a retain wall on the banks of the bath tank. The wall was constructed for the sake of women, because the women wanted this.

The provision of solar lamp, fencing for the cremation ground which is useful for the entire community are the achievements of the president.

Desiltation of Poovodai River with the help of the people enabled the Panchayat to save rainwater. If increased the ground water level helped the irrigation.

Sakkarakottai

EWRs Interaction with President

The EWRs discussed the following issues with the Sakkarakottai Panchayat President Mr. Noor Mohamad;

- Increase in house tax with people's cooperation.
- Creation of communal harmony between Muslims, Hindus and Christians.
- Ponds are desiltated and utilised for fishery. Income generation through fish auction.
- Convincing the opposition party and fulfil their demands.
- People-friendly attitude creates a cordial relationship among the people communities and religions.
- Family support leads to success.
- Inter-caste and inter-religious marriages are conducted between Muslims and *Dalits.*
- Problems of women are solved through SHGs and also by the Panchayat President.
- The Community Hall is utilised for Muslim women's worship.
- Group Houses, Formation of SHGs, Education for the children, construction of temples, welfare schemes, rice for the poor are the activities implemented for *Dalits.*
- 22 women SHGs have been formed and a few groups are involved in making palm products and cloth dolls.
- Gram Sabha meetings are organised in all the hamlets in order to ensure the participation of STs.

After interacting with the President, the EWRs were requested by the President to visit their Panchayat to witness for the participation of Muslim women in the Gram Sabha and SHGs. They enquired more about the functioning of the solid waste management system with the support of the NGO and they wanted to prepare natural manure from the solid waste. They appreciated the cleanliness, discipline of the students maintained with the support of the teachers. The EWRs were interested in creating communal harmony in their own Panchayats, especially for the participation of Muslim women in the SHGs.

EWRs Interaction with Jamath Members

Mr. Noor Mohamad arranged for a discussion with the Jamath members in the Arabic Education Centre of Sakkarakottai Panchayat. The EWRs asked questions regarding the status of Muslim women, girls and SHGs. The EWRs wanted to know about the education of Muslim girls, and their enrolment in schools after puberty. They said that in Tuticorin and Kayalpattinam, the Muslim girls are not allowed to go to school after puberty. The Jamath replied that all Muslim students go to schools and have higher education. When they enquired about the Hindu, Muslim relationship i.e. how a Muslim is able to construct or renovate a temple with the Hindu's support. The Jamath spoke in praise of the communal harmony and stated that both the Hindus and Muslims are living like a family and have created a cordial relationship among them.

They asked the members about their experience in the formation of SHGs among the Muslim women. Regarding this they replied that now the President motivated the Muslim women and formed 3 SHGs and tried to inculcate the saving habits and to provide training for getting self-employment opportunities. Regarding the acceptance of inter-caste marriage, the members stated that the bride or spouse who belonged to Hindu religion was converted to Muslim after their marriage. The EWRs requested the Panchayat President to visit their areas for motivating the Muslim women to join in SHGs. When they enquired about women's participation in the Gram Sabha, the members said that they have not restricted their participation in the

Gram Sabha, but only a few women were participating. Hence, they have formed SHGs among the Muslim women, they added.

Then they enquired about the Jamath's participation and cooperation in Panchayat activities. The reply to this question was that the Jamath was not able to function better and fulfil the needs of their own community. The President's efforts to fulfil the demands was appreciated and the Jamath has been providing some financial contributions for the development of the Panchayat.

Suggestion provided by the EWRs to model Panchayat Leaders

- Ms. Jesu Mary, President of Michelpattinam Panchayat, stressed and suggested the President of Sakkarakottai Panchayat to ask the Collector regarding the establishment of a shed for the decomposing wastes, because the Panchayat is waiting for the completion of rainy season and the work was pending. She again suggested that a separate shed for the preparation of vermi-composed manure should be established.
- Ms. Jesu Mary, suggested that the President of Thamaraikulam Panchayat to concentrate more on women issues, as per the plan framed by Namathu Gramam Scheme for social development Ms. Pappa, President of Athankaraipatti Panchayat enquired about the status of women in the Panchayat, violence against women, welfare activities for *Dalit* women, destitutes, widow and self-employment opportunities for women SHGs.
- They suggested that the Thamaraikulam Panchayat President should establish a biogas plant and bio-gasifier, which they have seen during the exposure visit to Semmipalayam and Odanthurai Panchayats.
- The EWRs motivated the SHGs in the SC colony of Sakkarakottai Panchayat for getting several self-employment opportunities for the improvement of their economy with guidance of the Panchayat President.

Observation

The following observations have been made by the project facilitators of the SSF project:

1. The EWRs appreciated the cooperation of the people and their participation in Panchayat activities.
2. The EWRs suggested that their ideas for the model Panchayat leaders to enrich the Panchayat development activities, especially, for the provision of hygienic drinking water. In Michelpattinam Panchayat, the pond water is purified with some seeds.
3. The experienced women supportive EWRs asked the model Panchayats to concentrate on the issues on women like violence against women, maternal mortality, infant mortality, female infanticide, widows, destitute women, age at marriage, teenage girls, etc.
4. A few EWRs who worked with SHGs tried to enquire about the activities undertaken by the SHGs for self-employment.
5. Some of them asked about the income sources of the Panchayat.
6. They were appreciative of the cooperation among the Hindus and Muslims. They tried to learn about the status of Muslim women.
7. They felt sad for the non-cooperation of Government officials and the intervention of political party leaders.
8. The *Dalit* women representatives working for the welfare of the *Dalits,* enquired elaborately about the conditions of *Dalit* women.
9. The method adopted for the preparation of natural manure and vermi compost was keenly observed by the EWRs, a few bought samples of manure packets for their gardens.
10. The discipline of the students of the Panchayat schools highly impressed the EWRs.
11. The mentally disabled and physically challenged women are supported by the Panchayat President of Michelpattinam Panchayat. It was highly appreciated by the EWRs and it

motivated them to take steps to provide livelyhood security for these weaker sections.

12. The EWRs enquired about the family members' cooperation for the Panchayat Presidents and asked about the decision-making process.
13. The EWRs decided to motivate the SHGs for the creation of vegetable gardens in the Panchayat lands and a few EWRs decided to insist on the people to form kitchen gardens in their houses.

Decisions for Future Action: Outcome of the Visits

The EWRs realized that the proper implementation of rainwater harvesting system is essential.

They have decided to develop the habit of sanitation among the students, advised the parents to use toilets. They want to keep the school campus clean. They are interested in student's discipline, creation of gardens and tree planting.

The involvement of women SHGs in solid waste management system, maintenance of Sanitary Complex highly motivated them to collect resources for the maintenance of toilets.

The importance of people's participation was highly realised by them.

They felt that the low cost technology adopted for the construction of toilets highly impressed them and they want to promote the utilisation of toilets by the people.

They want to ensure the participation of women in Panchayat activities and SHGs, especially, they want to improve the Muslim women's participation in social activities.

They want to replicate the methods adopted for the solid waste management system.

Programme Highlights

The EWRs frequently ask questions and try to get more information on the following:

- They suggested parameters for the role model Panchayat President on the governance of social development issues.
- They remembered and referred to the activities undertaken by the Semmipalayam and Odanthurai Panchayat Presidents in the implementation of non-conventional energy sources like bio-gas plant, aerojet pump and bio-gasfier plants.
- They have also referred to their own Panchayat activities and techniques adopted for sanitation, environment, education and drinking water.
- They felt that the successful women Panchayat Presidents should concentrate more on women and children issues than the problems of the male members.
- They wanted the successful Panchayat Presidents to documenting their activities and publish them with the support of the media.

10

Interface with Officials

Women leaders gain self-confidence and start realizing their responsibilities, performing their roles and becoming role models provided they are trained and oriented properly. To prove the above the elected women representatives, as a pressure group, on behalf of all other women Presidents, planned to arrange an interface with the officials of the Rural Development Department periodically. The Tamil Nadu Association of Women Presidents of Panchayat's sought an appointment with the Director of Rural Development, Government of Tamil Nadu, on several occasions and the elected women representatives put forth some demands and discussed their issues at length with the Director of Rural Development. The following are the demands:

1. Due to hike in electricity charges, Panchayats are facing a severe financial crisis, especially, the Panchayats which are economically unsound. According to the G.O., the electricity charges is to be met from the SFC grant itself. Most of the Panchayats pay a huge amount as electricity charges and have no money for maintenance. In order to overcome this situation, Panchayats being equivalent to State and Central Governments, the Government should allot them sufficient monthly grants for paying the electricity charges.
2. The Government should immediately withdraw the hike in electricity charges (electricity charges have been increased from Rs. 1.60 to Rs. 3.40) and pass an order to restore to the charges to the earlier levied.
3. The Tamil Nadu Panchayat Act 1994, Section 10, empowers the officials to take action against the elected representatives. This Section should be removed from the Act. District

Collectors can remove the Panchayat Presidents under the Tamil Nadu Panchayat Act, Section 205. This Section should also be removed immediately from the Act. On many occasions procedures are not also followed and in many cases, this provision is used to victimize individuals for political reasons.

The Government should give an untied grant of Rs. 10 lakhs to each Gram Panchayat as has been given to MPs and MLAs to develop their constituency. An assurance is to be given that this money could be spent on social development sectors that too on the software side and not on the hardware side.

4. To ease the severe the financial strain, the Government should release house tax matching grant as it was in vogue earlier.
5. The unpaid 2002-2003 quarterly grants for the past 9 months should be given to the Panchayats immediately.
6. The monthly grant for the financial year 2003-04 should be given to the Panchayats.
7. The power to disconnect the EB power supply for unpaid cable TV charges should be given to the Panchayats.
8. MLA and MP funds could be spent in the Panchayat area on the works identified by the respective Gram Sabhas.
9. The auctioning rights for the trees within the Panchayat area (belonging to Department of Highways, Public Welfare Department and Revenue Department) should be handed over to the Panchayats.
10. Panchayat trees should not be cut without getting permission from the Panchayats.
11. The Government should give instructions to the Departments of Police and Revenue to be Panchayat-friendly during removal of encroachments.
12. The Government departments which are working in Panchayat areas (like constructing dams, deepening channels, constructing small bridges) should consult the Panchayats before starting their work.
13. To perform Panchayat activities effectively the clerk should be appointed as a full time regular worker.

14. The forest development fund should be handed over to the Panchayats.
15. According to a High Court order, sand quarrying is banned (river bed, irrigated lake area and coastal area) and Gram Panchayats have the right to take action against illegal sand quarrying. The Government of Tamil Nadu should follow the example of the Governments of Maharashtra and Kerala. The Government should take action against silicon sand quarrying, particularly in Vetharanyam area. The Government should form a committee to asses the situation in Tamil Nadu.
16. Even though the Gram Panchayats and Panchayat Unions have the right to monitor and issue licenses for sand mining, the members of the Gram Sabha should not be allowed to take sand from riverbeds for household purposes. The Government should ban profit motivated sand quarrying. The cases registered against Government Order 4721, 1998 WMPN 7300, 7303, 7306, 7309, 1998 Industries (MMC1) Department dated 02.01.1998 have been banned by the High Court of Chennai. This order has given Panchayat Presidents the right to fix the lease amount which was earlier fixed by the District Collector. According to the G.O. No. 3, 4, 5, sand quarry and mining, (authority) should be handed over to the Panchayats.
17. Gram Panchayat Presidents oppose handing over wastelands to MNCs and other organizations. Land belonging to the Panchayat should not be given to the private sector. All the wastelands should be shared among the farmers (coolies) along with funds for cultivation of the same (with proper documents). Through Panchayat wastelands should be distributed equally among the landless poor.
18. It was stated that the procrastination in devolving powers to Panchayats is due to the placement of subjects in the 11th Schedule. If they are placed in the IV list, power devolution will be mandatory.
19. The poramboke lands within Panchayat areas should be utilized for Panchayat activities for which a resolution should be passed in the Gram Sabha. This should be further amended by the Government. Rights should be given to Panchayats

for removal of encroachment from common property resources.

20. Village maps, profiles and other related resource documents should be handed over to Panchayats. Village map modification, land resource management, transformation of common property resources, all these activities should be decided upon in the Gram Sabha. When the resolution is passed, the activities should be undertaken by the Panchayat.
21. Authority to issue licence to industries and production centres should be given to Panchayats. The Panchayats have the power to renew these licences and to collect tax. In the case of defaulting industries, the Panchayat should be provided with the power to disconnect the EB power supply and other public resources.
22. Based on the resolutions passed by the Gram Sabha, the Government departments should take necessary steps to fulfil the demands. The State Government should instruct the Government departments to inform the Panchayats about the demand based process before the next Gram Sabha.
23. Gram Panchayats should have the authority to issue licences for installation of machines. The district administration should give free pattas only to those selected by the Gram Sabha. Only with the approval of the Gram Panchayat new pattas should be issued. The Gram Panchayat's approval should be required for the implementation of any schemes in the Gram Panchayat area.
24. The Departments of Revenue and Police should cooperate with the Gram Panchayat. According to the Kerala Panchayat Act, Article 252, the police should implement the resolution passed by the Panchayat. If police violate a resolution the Government can take action against them. This provision should be incorporated in the Tamil Nadu Panchayat Act.

The Director of Rural Development responded to all the points presented by these representatives.

The Government of Tamil Nadu ordered the Electricity Board to collect the details of unpaid electricity charges and also recommended to fix meters in every Panchayat. Further, they are going to investigate about the total un-payable amount and then allot a separate amount from the Panchayat funds. It will be handed over to the Panchayats to pay for the electricity charges.

The increase in electricity charges was decided by the Government (from Rs. 1.60 to Rs. 3.40) hence, it should be brought to the notice of the Government.

According to the Panchayat Act, Section 205 can not be removed till an alternative is found out. So instructions could be given to the District Collector to use it sparingly.

The 2003-04 quarterly funds upto the month of March would be given to the Panchayats without deduction for EB charges and this was informed to AD Panchayats also, to take necessary action.

Revival of house tax matching grant would be taken up for consideration.

The Departments of Revenue and Police would be instructed to work with the Panchayats.

It was not possible to interfere with the Forest Department, but action may be taken to insist on their for getting permission from the Panchayats to cut down the trees in the Panchayat area.

For handing over the sand quarrying and mining, the appropriate G.O. copy should be sent to the particular departments.

Technical installations can not be handed over to the Panchayats but necessary steps would be taken to prevent malpractices.

The Director assured that many of the demands would be considered.

The EWRs stressed the importance of monthly periodical meetings with the District Collector. The Director suggested that month-wise meetings might interrupt the busy schedule of the District Collector and that organizing meetings with the District Collector once in three months be desirable. Already orders have been passed in this regard. The DRD advised the EWRs to highlight their issues specifically, so that action can be taken immediately. After the meet, the EWRs met Thiru. G.K. Vasan, President, Congress Party, Tamil Nadu, Chennai and the Secretary and the Treasurer of the DMK Party, Chennai and placed their demands before them. They assured them to include some of their issues in their party manifestoes.

Meanwhile, the EWRs discussed their demands with the Panchayati Raj Institutions supportive personnel like Ms. Kalpana and Mr. M.C. Das and sought their suggestions. Both of them asked them to highlight the following issues:

- Reduction of EB charges,
- Retrieval of common property resources from encroachers,
- Direct fund for Panchayats,
- Co-operation of several Government departments,
- Revenue for Panchayats from mines and minerals,
- Proper fund allocation and scheme details should be given to Panchayats by the district administration,
- Formation of a district committee along with Union Council Chairpersons for rural development,
- Seeking the effective implementation of Namathu Gramam Scheme and more importance to be given to Panchayats instead of voluntary agencies.

They drafted a format for getting the details of electricity consumption units and charges for Panchayats from the Electricity Board. They decided to ask the ADRDs, regarding the reduction of EB charges, for proper arrangements for notifying the consumption of units, fixation of tariff as per the rate fixed for Government buildings, urging the Government to pay the EB charges, etc. They discussed the following resolution passed in their Federation meeting with ADRD:

Resolution

1. The State Government should hand over the subsidy for the SC cremation rituals, for the years 2001-2002, 2002-2003 and 2003-2004, which has been spent by the Panchayats.
2. The unpaid SFC grant for the period 30.9.2001 to 31.3.2002 and 01.09.2003 to 30.01.2004 should be given to Panchayats.
3. The Local Cess for the year 2003-2004 should be given to Village Panchayats.
4. The House Tax matching grant should be given under 1:3 ratio.
5. The Federation requests the Government to hand over the above said funds (1, 2, 3, 4) which would help the Panchayats

to relieve them from electricity debts (e.g. Tiruvarur District Village Panchayat has to pay 5 crores and 11 lakhs as Electricity Charges).

6. According to the Government Order, birth and death records should be handed over to Village Panchayats.
7. The Association requests the Government to pay Rs. 5000 per month as honorarium to the Village Panchayat Presidents.
8. The Government should allow the Panchayats to collect cable TV charges/tax and should allow the right to cut the electricity supply to households for unpaid cable TV charges.
9. The water resources belonging to Panchayats (like ponds) have been encroached upon by individuals, traditional Panchayat leaders and local associations. The Government should cancel the rights and should send a separate order to the district administration. The district administration should announce a public auction and this auction amount should be credited to the Panchayat account.
10. The Panchayat resources like threshing poramboke, grazing poramboke, cremation ground, ponds, grove poramboke, natham poramboke should be measured and demarcation should be erected stones and for the people's sake, the maps for the same should be displayed on boards. The Government should order the Revenue Department to remove the encroachments and hand over these resources to Panchayats.
11. The Government insisted that the Panchayats should provide mandatory cheques to SHGs for the maintenance of sanitary complex under the Central Government grant through the second account. This should be avoided. The Government should motivate and urge the Panchayats towards tree plantation.
12. Under the IAY scheme, houses of 200 sq.ft. were constructed at a cost of Rs. 36500. The houses constructed under this estimate are under repair throughout the State. The Government should take necessary action to raise the estimate upto Rs. 70,000 for the construction of these houses.
13. Individual household latrines are constructed for Rs. 500 under the Central Government Total Sanitation Programme. This might not be utilized by most of the people. Hence the

Federation requests the Government to raise the amount upto Rs. 6000. To make the Total Sanitation Programme effective under the Central and the State Governments allocation for the year 2005-06, the subsidies allocated for the construction of latrines, free sarees and *dhotis* and women sanitary complex might be temporarily transferred to the construction of individual toilets throughout Tamil Nadu and necessary steps may be taken by the Government regarding total sanitation.

14. There was a Government Order that the Panchayat can implement some development works at a cost of less than Rs. 1 lakh from the Panchayat A/c. No.1 by supervising the measurements with the help of engineering diploma holders registered at the block level. But the District Collectors have cancelled this Government Order by a circular. The Government should cancel this circular.
15. The jurisdiction of the Village Panchayats should be changed keeping a minimum of 5000 population per Panchayat. If this is done there could be only 6000 Panchayats resulting in reduced administrative expenses.
16. At present electricity connections to new and old houses and other buildings are provided without certification by the Village Panchayat Presidents. So the people do not get the house building approval and they do not fell the trees disturbing the electricity lines. Because of this the Panchayats loses finance also, as the electricity lines go through the trees, there are accidents as well as loses of revenue to the E.B. So, the Federation requests that the Electricity Board should provide electric connection only after the Panchayat Presidents certify.
17. The part time Panchayat Clerks should be made full time employees.
18. Under the SSA scheme, the Government insist that the Panchayats construct 2 classrooms and one room for the headmaster along with latrines under 1200 sq.ft. and allows to spent Rs. 3 lakhs for the same. For the construction of good quality buildings, the amount for each sq.ft. should be calculated at Rs. 350. The Federation insists that Government

prepare a plan estimate for the construction of *pucca* school buildings.

19. For the maintenance of street lights an amount of Rs. 250 is allowed per year. The Government should provide Rs. 500 as maintenance charges because it should consider the increase of material cost and labour charges.
20. Under the previous Government, the electricity charges per unit was Rs. 1.60. But at present it has been raised to Rs. 3.40 per unit. Considering this, the State Government should raise the SFC grant to 20 per cent instead of 8 per cent.
21. The Federation requests the Central Government to allocate funds on the basis of the 2001 census.
22. The development activities like drought relief, flood relief and other social development activities undertaken in Panchayat areas should be implemented through Panchayats.
23. The Panchayat related departments like Police and Revenue should take necessary steps regarding the resolutions passed by the Gram Sabha. The Panchayats should be given rights over these departments by the Central Government.
24. The Revenue Department, the Forest Department and the Public Welfare Department receive auction amount and fines for the Panchayat trees. According to the Government Order the share from these should be duly handed over to the Panchayats by these Departments.
25. The activities undertaken by several departments in the Panchayat areas should be carried out through the Panchayats. The officials appointed for maintenance work should be withdrawn by the Government.
26. The State Government has taken away the auctioning rights for sand quarries. The Panchayats' share from this auction should be handed over to the Panchayats. The Federation condemns the Revenue Department for denying the Panchayats' right to take sand from the Panchayat ponds for Panchayat activities.

The ADRDs responded to the above resolutions and suggested ways and means to meet each demand. He had called the respective officials for discussing several issues put forth by the EWRs during the previous interface held with the DRD.

The EWRs gave more importance to electricity charges, because most of the Panchayats are not able to pay the charges and the funds allocated to the Panchayats are taken away by the Electricity Board. Hence, at first they wanted to clarify their doubts regarding the electricity charges.

The ADRDs responded that they have decided to form a Committee in the middle of April 2005. The Committee will prepare a detailed report on the consumption of electricity and the amount spent on the electricity charges. They stated that the State Government has also recommended the reduction of the EB tariff and suggested to fix a rate which is equivalent to that charged for Government buildings. They added that several small and poor Panchayats are not able to pay the EB charges and are caught up in debts ranging into lakhs. They also stated that the Director of Rural Development has decided to organise a seminar for discussing the financial crises in Panchayats. They wanted to find out the strategies for raising the income of Panchayats with available local resources, and the ways for reducing the expenses through available non-conventional resources like solar lamps, bio-gas plants, etc. The ADRDs revealed that they would consider the severe EB issue and ask the Electricity Board to meet each Panchayats once a month and to replace the old electricity meters and to allow a responsible person from the Panchayat to note down the readings.

Regarding the subsidy allocation for cremation rituals, they said that the amount has already been allotted and DRDAs have been directed disburse the same for the past 3 years. The concerned official was asked to issue the fund allotment details. The allotment details were circulated to all EWRs and they were asked to verify the same with the block office.

For the house tax matching grant they stated that many Panchayats are unaware of the method of getting the matching grant and are not able to collect cent percent tax from the people. Hence, the amount was reduced to 1.25 per cent. Regarding the collection of cable TV charges, the ADRDs accepted that the amount may be handed over to Panchayats and offered to consult on this issue with the DRD and take necessary steps.

For the retrieval of encroachments from the traditional leaders, especially for the retrieval of Panchayat ponds, the ADRD agreed to take proper action. He assured that proper land details will be collected from the Village Administration Officers and the Tehshildar and severe action would be taken by insisting that the Revenue and Police Departments support the Panchayats during such crises. But it is a slow process, because most of the landlords are traditional Panchayat leaders and they have threatened the people residing in the Panchayat areas and causing trouble with the help of local mafias. They have even threatened Government officials and interfered in their official processes. This has dreadfully affected the *Dalit* community leaders. Hence, necessary action should be taken on this complicated issue and the common properties should be retrieved from the individuals. But it should be approached through the district authorities like the Tehshildar, the VAO and the Collector.

Ms. Juliet Susila, the President of Sriparangusanallore Panchayat, Srivaikundam Union of Tuticorin District, narrated an incident in her Panchayat. Her Panchayat had passed a resolution in the Gram Sabha for the construction of a water tank. Even though she submitted the appropriate references regarding the water tank there was no follow up action taken by the district administration. Whenever she approached them for getting the work order, the officials asked her to wait and convinced her that the papers were pending. For the past nine months this has been taking place. The ADRD keenly noted down this incident and asked her about for classification. He assured her that he would consult the concerned department officials and would take necessary steps after consulting this issue with the DRD.

Regarding the appointment of a full-time clerk, the ADRD suggested that the salary for the clerk may be increased but there was no chance for their promotion from part time to full time assistants.

The officials agreed with the EWRs regarding the sand theft in the Panchayat areas and the drastic fall on the ground water level. The sand taken from the old damaged traditional ponds would increase the ground water level and the income from these sources should reach the Panchayat regularly.

The Forest and the Public Welfare Departments would be urged to take several steps for the prevention of expensive tree theft and the renovation of old buildings which are situated in Panchayat areas. They stated that they would try to bring tree auctioning rights to Panchayats.

They referred to the availability of innumerable schemes implemented by the Forest Department and they asked the EWRs to get tree saplings from the Department and suggested that every Panchayat can create orchards, gardens and parks and can enrich the environment.

The subsidy for the local cess was cancelled by the Government. Hence, the amount was not given to the Panchayats. The unpaid SFC for the past 9 months would be taken up for consideration and necessary action would be taken regarding this issue.

Instead of giving power over 29 subjects, the Government has decided to hand over three departments namely, Education, Health and Nutrition to the Panchayats. They have decided to create a good rapport between these department officials and the Panchayats. They want to implement this through Village Development Committees, which was in the records.

Regarding the Tiruvallur incident, they suggested that proper investigation would be made and they assured that the Government would take action against misbehaving leaders and provide security to honest leaders, who would not be punished. The ADRD appreciated the demand regarding the formation of District Level Village Development Committees along with the members of Union Councils and their requisition regarding the publication of a journal by the district administration for learning about the Panchayat i.e., information regarding new schemes, updated Government Orders and other district issues related to Panchayat administration etc.

For the entire demands, the ADRDs stated that he would bring them to the knowledge of the DRD and surely take steps through several departments. They insisted that the EWRs approach the district administration with proper records and try to solve them. The unsolved major problems should be immediately brought to the knowledge of the DRD with several records and solved through the proper channel, they stated. They appreciated the Federation for its continuous action for the sustainability of the entire Village Panchayats.

Then the EWRs met the political party leaders and again urged them to raise their issues during the Legislative Assembly sessions. They also met the print media for wider dissemination.

Follow-up

The Federation has tirelessly highlighted the demands before several higher officials, political party leaders and other Panchayat supportive institutions. They decided to urge the Government continuously specifically on the reduction of EB charges, direct funds for Panchayats, income sources from local resources and retrieval of common properties. They did not seek more funds but asked for their rights to get the sources which are available in their Panchayat areas and expected the cooperation of Government officials during crises.

11

Interface with Media

The mass-media have been reporting the functionings of the new Panchayati Raj Institutions for the past 10 years. However, this reporting has been one sided. It has been found that the media choose to report and make public only the failures and mistakes of these institutions. The need for a positive approach by the media in disseminating information on Panchayati Raj is greatly felt. The media must take into consideration two points while reporting on Panchayati Raj Institutions. They are economic development and social justice. These are the basis for the functioning of the Panchayati Raj Institutions which need to be focused in the media. Besides this, basic human right is one of the key issues in Panchayati Raj Institutions which has to be focused in the media. With the right information management, effective decentralization can be achieved. The media should highlight certain sections of the 73rd Constitutional Amendment like Article 243G which states that socio-economic development is a compulsory duty of the new Panchayati Raj Institutions. There are two important factors which influence this process, one is globalization and the other is decentralization. Unless there is a constructive relationship between these two factors, powers of the Panchayati Raj Institutions cannot be fully harnessed. At stake in this relationship is the fate of the people below poverty line. The question of their advancement cannot be answered by pumping in funds which do not directly address their plight. Therefore, the question of participation has to be ensured before devolution of funds. And the only via media for effective people's participation is in the development of Panchayati Raj Institutions. These institutions cannot develop on their own when the powers of decision-making lies with the State. Thus, decentralization in terms of decision-making according to the demands of the common people should be the priority.

Decentralization does not take place in a vacuum. It needs support structures. The media is a helpful tool in fulfilling this requirement. To be effective as a tool for decentralization the media should acknowledge the following:

(a) only Panchayati Raj System can effectively provide the basic amenities to the common people.
(b) the media alone can make public the debate concerning dismissal of elected leaders by the State by focusing on the provision 205 of the Panchayati Raj Act.
(c) the media must analyse and identify where the fault lies in the interaction between the Government and Panchayati Raj Institutions. The reporting of such faults should be impartial, i.e. faults of both Government as well as the local bodies should be highlighted. Even though Presidents are dismissed by using the 205 provision. It is still very small numbers when compared to the achievements of the Presidents in office. This has to pointed out by the media.
(d) One other area where media can be use is concerning the issues involving women and *Dalits* in Panchayati Raj situations. The auctioning of posts in the Local Bodies and to ensure the election of candidates unanimously and prevention of women and *Dalits* from contesting the election are certain issues which have to be highlighted by the media.
(e) Besides this the problem of socio-economic deprivation of the weaker section of the society like inadequate child care and exploitation of children have to be reported in order to make the Local Bodies more responsive to these issues. Media should realize that social issues are local specific and so they need local activities and initiatives. This could be achieved only by Panchayati Raj Institutions. The media might take cognizance of the fact that 94 per cent of the State exchequer is used up for salaries and pensions. The media must understand that in the west, powers were devolved on demand from the people unlike India. This is mainly because the concept of self respect is present in higher degree in the west than in India. This phenomenon can be provoked by tracing the history of Indian polity where functions,

> functionaries and fund were given by order not by law. This has now become a way of doing things and the society has come to accept such a governance. Therefore, the new Panchayati Raj Institutions came into existence. The general opinion was that they are there merely to carry out some executive orders and supervise Governmental works. In reality, Panchayati Raj System has assured power to the people. It is precisely because of Panchayati Raj Institutions being made to execute orders, practices like auctioning of posts and prevention of weaker sections from contesting are curbed. However, after ten years of new Panchayati Raj Institutions in Tamil Nadu, one can see great improvements. It is noticeable that, there are more number of contestants in the second and third Panchayati Raj elections conducted, based on 1994 Tamil Nadu Panchayati Act than the previous ones. Secondly, the participation in Gram Sabha meetings have increased. Inspite of this one must take notice whether there is an increase in participation of women and *Dalits*. The deprived sections in the western society were effectively prepared by the Government itself for their participation. This resulted in the supply-driven phenomenon changing into a demand-driven phenomenon. The former phenomenon is still prevalent in India. This is mainly because just approximately 4700 persons are representing one million people. In such a scenario, it is impossible to ascertain the demands and expectations of the masses. In this light, decentralization becomes important. As some of the studies conducted by the Rajiv Gandhi Chair for Panchayati Raj Studies show that many Panchayat leaders have themselves assumed certain powers to discharge their responsibilities. It gives ample scope to the media to highlight such activities and initiatives.

Information dissemination is important for the success of any programme. In establishing a sound grassroots governing institutions information dissemination plays a vital role. It has to create a din and a complex socio-political-economic context. Unfortunately, the system of governance that has been in vogue for the past five decades in India had not created a positive climate to provide the needed information to the stakeholders. The Government and the official are always strong and they act on information. But people don't have the information as do the officials. As long as information is kept with Government. It is logical that the officials will be empowered and people are rendered powerless. But, in a decentralized democratic institution people and the representatives need to have the information relating to governance and people's participation in governance. System, at the lower level are created as per the design and desire of the Central and Local Governments. This information has not been disseminated to the people. The leaders have to equip themselves on information relating to power and responsibilities entrusted to the newly created Panchayat bodies. The Panchayat leaders and people always complaint that the Government at the State level does not provide the needed information. When the Government gives information it is fragmented and not integrated. Sometimes, it provides information in the negative light to the Panchayat system. Information which is needed by the representatives of the people in Local Bodies and members of the Gram Sabha is available in the Government offices, but it is not distributed among the different stakeholders. On the whole the picture emerging from the press is not positive towards decentralization. On the contrary, the higher level officials bring to light some interesting and valuable achievements of the Panchayats which they had gathered during the field visits. Even in reporting the success stories of the Panchayat leaders, particularly *Dalit* and women in the media, their actual struggle is not projected. The process of achievement is more interesting than the outcome. On most of the occasions the media have missed the hidden issues and underlying principles.

The Rajiv Gandhi Chair for Panchayati Raj Studies brought up above discussed issues with some of the leading media persons and scholars. They approached these issues with an open mind and suggest that the media representatives should be oriented and sensitized on the issues of decentralized governance and empowering people. Mr. N. Raam, Editor in-Chief of '*The Hindu*', Mr. Maalan then editor of *SUN NEWS*, and Mr. T.G. Nallamuthu Chief Information Officer, Press Information Bureau helped in this process. The Media workshop was organized in Chennai by the Rajiv Gandhi Chair for Panchayati Raj Studies and the EWRs with the financial support from The Hunger

Project. It drew the attention of all. Based on this experiment, the Rajiv Gandhi Chair for Panchayati Raj Studies developed the information package to the media. The experts on decentralized governance were identified and they were sensitized on decentralization and governance. The sensitized media representatives expressed their willingness to focus on the women in Panchayati Raj provided regular information is available. It was brought to every one's notice that Rajiv Gandhi Chair for Panchayati Raj Studies regularly brings out the required information which can be used by the media. In the meantime, Rajiv Gandhi Chair for Panchayati Raj Studies conducted the media workshops in different centres. During the media workshop, members of the EWRs association were invited and they themselves discussed their problems with the media representatives. These media workshop was an eye opener for the media representatives. Sensitized media representatives provided needed space in their magazines and started focusing on the Panchayat issues. The magazines which are worth mentioning, *The Hindu, The New Indian Express, Financial Express, Frontline, Dinamalar, Dinamani, Daily Thanthi and Kumutham.* The electronic media also joined in the process. SUN TV played a major role in this endeavour as Mr. Maalan took the lead. In the panel discussion held on SUN TV experts and Panchayat leaders were drawn and major issues affecting the Panchayats were discussed. The issues like providing fiscal independence to Local Bodies and sensitizing the community that the Local Bodies indeed provide space for an alternative governance.

The disturbing trends in Local Bodies in Tamil Nadu where *Dalits* are prevented from filing nominations and their problems are covered up. The anlaysis of Tamil Nadu Panchayats Act and the changes to be made in the Tamil Nadu Panchayats Act were discussed in a few dailies. Many newspapers also covered the activities of the EWRs Association particularly their Annual Meet.

The newspapers focused the problems of the women leaders in governance. They brought articles under the caption "Bureaucrats Treat women Panchayat Presidents as Servants". In that, a study report was discussed. The study has revealed that most of the EWRs were conscious of the problems of women such as environmental pollution, alcoholism and other evils such as problems of drinking water, sanitation, violence against women and they were afraid to discuss these issues either at Panchayat meetings or Gram Sabha meetings. These EWRs also bear the brunt of the threats posed by anti-social and criminal elements and were compelled to maintain a low profile. When the Government of Tamil Nadu introduced cheap liquor, the association of EWRs, threatened the Government through media. Newspapers widely covered this issue and one of a major national leading dailies published the issue under caption "Women Feel let by a Woman".

The media also covered the positive aspects on women in governance. The media stated that the EWRs are more keen on development. They invariably take up development issues and address them more than the others do. Inspite of their limited literacy skills they have demonstrated that they can manage finances of the Panchayats efficiently.

The steps taken by Rajiv Gandhi Chair for Panchayati Raj Studies and EWRs Association have yielded fruitful results. The media have increased their reporting and coverage on women in Local Bodies. They have highlighted their demands and issues. After reading the success stories from different districts, many Panchayat leaders have asked their respective district administration to extend such support to the innovative schemes undertaken in their Panchayats. The media are acting as a powerful instruments in empowering women and Panchayats.

12

Are They Withdrawing from Public Space?

Fourth Annual Mela

"We have experienced power for eight years to carry out activities for the benefit of people as seats have been reserved for women in local bodies for two consecutive terms and now the principle of rotation has to be operated and as a result the women who have come to local bodies in the past two terms from the same constituency either to contest in the General Constituency or withdraw from the public space or take another lower or higher level position in the same Panchayat system" observed by Ms. Susila one of the office bearers who assembled in Gandhigram on 11th and 12th of August 2005. The discussion was around the space which they have occupied now.

Struggle to Come Out from Their Cocoons

Reservation of seats for women in local bodies pulled and pushed them from the house to the pubic space. Working as MLA or MP or in any office by women would not bring this much of pressure to the women as the elected women representatives at the lowest level who confront with plethora of obstacles and problems. Till date many of the elected women representatives are struggling to come out from their cocoons to office when they have to discharge their responsibilities. They claim that coming out from their houses to office itself as victory as many of them are not able to come out from their house on the day of election. Such a kind of repressive husbands co-opted their wives to retain power with them and for which they have used the women. Elected women representatives association is working for the release of the house bound elected women representative through Government orders. The dominant discourse in many of the places was that as soon as the seats were reserved for women, the men who prepared themselves to context in the election adopted a strategy of preparing a women candidate from the respective families or social group and saw such women elected to the positions. Behind all women, men were working with high enthusiasm before the election with the belief that if they were elected, positions would handled by men of the respective families. After the election, scenario was different and many players started acting in local bodies to build up the capacity and skill of the leaders, passing orders prohibiting men in attending official meetings on behalf of the women leaders. Yet, a segment of bureaucracy is not sensitive towards the issues of women and hence, the officials preferred to discuss official matters with the male members of the elected women representatives with an argument that the uneducated family women do not know anything about the administrative system. Under this pretext, they neglected the elected women representatives and sometimes the EWRs were sidelined.

Capacity-Building

Many of the EWRs are not attending training programmes not because they are not interested but they are not allowed by their male family members to attend the programme. They put a condition to the EWRs that they would attend the training programme alongwith EWRs. When this demand is unmet, the EWRs are not permitted to attend the training. Trainings are of two types. One is official and government-oriented. The other one is semi-official and real leadership preparation. In all Government training programmes, EWRs are threatened that unless they obey the officials, they can not run the Panchayats. They have been asked to carry out the Panchayat administration as per the direction of the officials. In a sense, it is a preparation of slaves to the Government dictates. There is yet another aspect, where negotiating skill is built up in the leader. A detailed analysis of devolution and where the Panchayats are now, what is to be done in Panchayat for the people and what should be done to strengthen Panchayat are being discussed in a participatory way.

In a residential training, a book consisting of the original Act, Government Orders, details of rural development schemes and rules are given and training is given to EWRs about how to make use of all those documents for Panchayat administration. The training is not an one time affair. It is a continuous process. The role of the training institution is not only to offer training but also to guide the Panchayat Presidents while they are on the job. It is almost a support structure. EWRs are attending the programmes without fail in Gandhigram as it is a support structure and it works and helps EWRs when they are in trouble. Whenever EWRs face problem, EWRs use the three phone numbers 0451-2451063, 0451-2451775, 044-22235659. When EWRs are harassed by the officials, even letters are being drafted in Gandhigram and send to the concerned officials and such a kind of intervention is being extended to the Presidents in Gandhigram.

Struggle to Succeed

A sizeable section of women leaders had been drawn out of their houses and had been made to attend the meetings and interact with officials and the elected women representatives have been made to realize their worth and they have started functioning as leaders in managing the Panchayats. Their vision is broadened and their understanding of the society has been widened. When they start functioning intensively, they have to face a volley of problems and yet the joy that they have enjoyed is immeasurable. They feel that the stigma attached with them as incompetent women has gone. The continuous crisis management in Panchayat, and crowd management in Gram Sabha have made them courageous. But the process is painful. Just like a student they learn every day about the society, Panchayat and Government. Further, small progress made by them in the Panchayat enables them to have confidence in themselves and in the system.

The advancement made by EWRs are captured through the media. Even the sagas of struggle encountered by the EWRs are also captured and they are being published, telecast and broadcast because of the efforts of the Hunger Project. When media brought to light the achievements, of the EWRs the other Panchayat Presidents developed aspirations to follow the models. The continuous sensitization programmes conducted for media helped a lot to capture the successes and struggles faced by the EWRs.

Learning to Struggle

The elected women representatives by their performance, by their struggles, and by their achievements, got recognition in the society and this recognition made the other women folk to develop aspiration to become Panchayat Presidents. For the past eight years, the elected women representatives have learnt the art of mobilising the people to conduct Gram Sabha, and developing partnership with officials and other social bigwigs to perform their role and discharge their responsibilities. Further, the elected women representatives have become conscious of the women issues because of the continuous capacity-building exercise and periodical interaction with activists. Working on the issues of women need specific strategy and before that people have to be conscientised and unless people are conscientised on the issues of women, the problems of women cannot be addressed. It is also realised by the elected women representatives that the problems in the society and specifically the problems of women, children, *Dalit* and other marginalized groups could be attacked through collectives. Thus, they have realised the potentials of the collective action. They have deeper understanding of the issues of the marginalized. This is because of the continuous training. The thought processes and mindset of the women leaders in the beginning are no way different from the men leaders. But in the course of training and regular interaction with gender specialists, the attitude, perception, views and understanding of the women leaders on the issues of women have changed.

Women to Women

Yet another serious issue, namely, conscientising women on their own problems. They need four literacies, namely word literacy, money literacy, body literacy and civil literacy. It is to use task to be carried out. Since the advent of Self-Help Groups women are visible and they have become a force to reckon with. They can be used for this purpose. To some extent they are now liberated. It has been realised by the elected women representatives that with the alliance of SHG members, women leaders in Panchayats can perform several functions especially for children and women. Women leaders have come to the stage of developing vision for their Panchayats, for the children of their villages. They have realised the importance of social development. Now it is easy for the Government to push through social development agenda through the elected women representatives. To that level, elected women representatives are sensitized and oriented. Environmental protection, health governance, governance of education, vulnerability reduction and internal resource mobilization are the major subjects on which the women leaders are trained. At the Panchayat level, they are able to manage the issues effectively. But these models have to be spread to other areas. The models are limited in number. Elected women representatives have come to the level of working on the millennium development goals. There are leaders who have developed leadership to get the attention of the political parties. Now political parties have started luring the elected women representatives who have commanded great amount respect among the people by their excellent performance.

The elected women leaders who have legitimately occupied their space and manage the institutions are concerned about the confinement of the elected women leaders by their male family members. The EWRs through their associations and federations persuaded the officials not to allow the male members in any of the official meetings in the place of EWRs. In many of the places, even higher officials allow the male members to run and carryout the activities on behalf of the EWRs in the name of achieving targets. If this malaise is not cheeked, the formation of critical mass will be weakened.

EWR and CPR

Common properties are the lifeline of the poor and also another source of income to the Panchayats. Removing the encroachment of the common properties is not an easy task and yet, elected women representatives have taken steps to remove the encroachments. In this process they have to undergo ordeals. There is a fitting case that Urapakkam Gram Panchayat President Ms. Menaka had to sacrifice her life when she took steps to remove encroachments in her Panchayat area. Vanduvanchery Gram Panchayat President Ms. Rani Muniyakannu moved the protect the silicon soil. Appipalayam Gram Panchayat President Ms. Easwari has fought against industrial pollution in her Panchayat area. Now the elected women representatives have learnt the art of fighting for justice. A large number of elected women representatives have taken innovative steps to augment resources from the assets and natural resources of the Panchayats. Many of the Panchayats have regained their common properties. Series of steps have been taken to improve the conditions of the commons. The elected women representatives have changed the conflict between Panchayats and SHGs and now both of them are playing complementary role to each other for the benefit of the people in the rural areas. Elected women representatives have realised the importance of governance and poverty reduction and development at the grassroots. They have internalized the practice of supervision to be done by the Panchayats on the service delivery institutions. They have given the utmost importance to health governance, environment governance and educational governance.

Obstacles

It is a truth that the so called beneficiaries of the Government (really they are not eligible to become beneficiaries but they got their names included by wielding political influence, never allow Gram Sabha to speak truth and hence, they have a strategy of disturbing the Gram Sabha by using several strategies which include the use of unparliamentary words and indulging in character assassination. In the absence of a strong support base many of the women leaders are in a perturbed mental state.

The officials always exhibit their non-cooperative attitude towards the elected women representatives and more over, they want to dominate the women leaders. Many times women leaders whenever they go to office, they go with the statistics and Government orders to convince the officials. Many of the occasions, the officials are exposed as the elected women representatives bring issues and speak with authority, especially when the officials do not have such authentic documents. This negotiating capacity has been injected into the blood of the EWRs in Gandhigram through etc. training programmes. The Act, Government Orders, Rules, Scheme details are provided in the form of a book to every one of the trainees and they are being oriented as to how to use the data and how to use the book. Every Panchayat leader should negotiate with the officials with self-respect and self-dignity and this has been taught to them by the Gandhigram training team. The officials encourage only the male members of the elected women representatives as it is easy for the officials to negotiate with the husbands and the other family members. The corrupt system wants to coopt the women also. But the EWRs do not succumb.

The administrative structure is complicated in our society. Government officials are finding it very difficult to bring convergence or synergy among the officials working in different departments. Likewise, the departments are acting on the basis of direction from their higher officials in the line department not on the basis of the orders of the Government. A Government order passed by the Rural Development Department is not respected by health department. All departments are sectorally divided and they do not have a perspective for serving the people but they have a perspective of keeping the department activities in tact in achieving their target and satisfying their officials.

This is a case in Pudukkottai district. When K.Rayawaram Gram Panchayat President, Ms. Rani Sathappan approached the District Collector for financial sanction to desilt the tank managed by PWD the sensitive Collector passed orders immediately and sanctioned money. But to carry out the work, the President had to get a no objection certificate from the Public Works Department (PWD) office. To get such a letter she has to visit the office fifteen times. On the fifteenth day, the officials took only two minutes to prepare such a letter and she got it. From this, one can imagine how Government offices are responding to the Panchayat leader's demands.

As the Panchayat leaders work with the near people, they are always responsive and accountable and they perform their duties perfectly, but the officials are not having that mentality and people do not have hold over the officials. Excepting the politicians, no body can control the officials. It is an irony that the leaders who are responsible and responsive do not have the power, on the other hand the officials, who do not respond and responsive to the people, have power. Panchayat leaders submit petitions to the Government offices and for which there is no response. Thus, the leaders who are having enough influence are respected in the offices and others are fighting against the bureaucracy. There is yet another serious issue, the namely managerial perspective which is so essential for the administration of the Panchayats. Neither the State Government nor the Panchayat leaders have managerial perspective to look at the functioning of the Panchayats. It is unfortunate that many of the Panchayats from the perspective of management, are unviable. Such Panchayats have to be merged with the neighbouring Panchayats to make it administratively and managerially viable. As a result, Panchayat leaders find it difficult to run the administration and people are also suffer.

Our system is always favourable only to the rich not to the poor. Here is a case where the Panchayat has been asked to carry out the work and the amount can be claimed later and for which Panchayat President has to invest money from her own purse and then only they get each money from the Departments. Where will a poor women representative go for money? So she has to rely on the moneylenders. Since the system is so complicated and corrupt this kind of practice will lead to deterioration. For the elected women representatives, capacity building is the only salvation. Periodical interface with other leaders and officials would help them a lot. Refresher courses have to be conducted. Visiting other States and interacting with the leaders of other States would help them a lot. Here also one has to recognize the role of Gandhigram Rural Institute. Gandhigram Rural Institute arranges for the EWRs to visit other Panchayats within the District, within the State and other States. It is a powerful learning instrument. Elected women representatives had already visited Kerala, West Bengal, Karnataka and New Delhi.

There are different strategies to be adopted by both organisations working for women empowerment and devolution of powers and by women leaders to achieve what they ought to achieve in the space created for the elected women representatives. The strategy adopted by Gandhigram Rural Institute is appreciated by many of the elected women representatives as the strategy envisages a smooth transition for EWRs from their houses to public space without making much ado. It always aims at building alliances with all stakeholders in the process. The assertion of the EWRs are not through oral dialogue but through performance. They are exposed to the building capacity, skill and capability and alliance and they perform their roles and responsibilities to carry out them efficiently.

In the political and administrative arena, one has to understand the level of corruption, otherwise, it is very difficult to manage the Panchayat. Many of the EWRs have noted the corrupt practices and they fall a prey to this. But the same women leaders do not understand the whole process. The reason why officials do not like to interact with women representative is that they are not in a position to understand the nuances of corruption. They do not even understand the language as corruption has a language and its won vocabulary. As a result, many of them are in a quandary. In many places, male family members of the elected women representatives move in the fast track by co-opting themselves with the officials and as a result there was no problem for those women leaders. In the world of reform through technology, the administrative procedures have to be made simple instead they are made cumbersome. Now an ordinary person cannot understand the administrative procedures and as a result the Panchayat leaders face problems. The women leaders time and again discuss the methods by which they can emerge as role models for others. In this context one has to recognize the struggles of the EWRs. On many of the occasions the EWRs are badly projected by the media. Of course the media can highlight negative issues of the Panchayats. There are remarkable achievements made by the women leaders and they are to be captured by the media. But it is not happening. Of course, the scenario is changing as Gandhigram Rural Institute is taking earnest efforts to sensitise the media through its media workshop. In the media workshops, outstanding women representatives are invited to share their experiences with the media. But this kind of efforts have to be taken massively throughout the nation.

It is a pity that training programmes are not seriously thought of and conducted by the Government. Major part of the women leaders are not trained fully. The elected women representatives who are in the federation of women are well trained as they are trained by The Hunger Project in Gandhigram. Some of the experts who are taking class for the women leaders are the retired Additional Directors of

Rural Development, Government of Tamil Nadu. They are thorough with the Acts, Rules, Procedures, Government Orders and Schemes. They have commitment also. Whenever the women leaders express doubts, the resource persons clear them. They give directions and advise. Gandhigram Rural Institute is acting as a supporting resource centre providing the wherewithal to stand on their own. Of course, the Government is also conducting training programmes. Resource persons are the Extension Officers and Block Development Officers and they teach the dictum, "Follow the officials" otherwise you will be booked under Section 205. They teach what not to do in Panchayat instead what to do in the local people's instead what to do the constitutional courts Panchayats?

Section 205 is a provision in Tamil Nadu Panchayat Act, 1994 which gives arbitrary powers to District Collector to remove the elected Gram Panchayat leaders. This provision has been used by all the officials in the State to threaten the elected representatives. By using this provision the Government officials for the EWRs to dance according to their tunes. If we take a list of the elected representatives who have been sacked by using Section 205, most of them are either women or *Dalit.* Women leaders who are not strong being easily handled by the officials through the Panchayat Clerk. There are wise women leaders who carefully managed to elect another women as Vice-President and both of them select a women as a clerk. The others without knowing this strategy, end up having men as Vice-Presidents who tend to dominate the EWRs. In that context, the elected women representatives' Federation has demanded that the State Government should reserve the Vice-Presidents post along with President posts for women. Whenever the Panchayat leaders are not cooperating with the officials for their misdeeds, the officials use to threaten the Panchayat leaders by asking them to bring the account for verification in the Block Development Office. The women leaders who are strong, knowledgeable with needed support are able to face the challenges and they won't budge. Others succumb to this tactics adopted to by the officials.

There are Panchayat Presidents who did commendable work in the Panchayats who were not recommended for the awards and incentive which are being given by the Government. But instead, ruling party oriented Panchayat Presidents have been selected for such awards and incentives. This kind of practice developed by the officials has demoralized the really straight forward EWRs.

A good number of Panchayats draw the attention of the media and outsiders by their commendable performance. They are being appreciated by the higher officials. But the same higher officials never helped those Panchayat leaders who were in deep trouble because of the lower level officials who indulge in corruption. It is obvious from the experience of the Panchayat leaders that the lower level officials are not really under the control of the higher officials. Unless the officials at the lower level are properly oriented and controlled by the higher officials, the lower level officials will continue to harass the EWRs and destabilize the Panchayats.

There are women representatives who are in need of counselling as they are undergoing torture in the family due to the harassment of their husbands. There are umpteen number of cases and they have several stories to tell. These women leaders are neither in a position to reveal the problems openly or in a position to solve them amicably with in the family. Some of the women leaders had been asked to sign the documents as per the direction of their husbands and all the husbands are totally corrupt and the EWRs have to face corruption charges. They in fact bow their heads in shame in front of others and the officials. There are several reports of wife-beating by the husbands because the women leaders refuse to accept the directions of the husbands. Compared to SHG, the local body institutions are not getting due attention from the State Government. In our State there is no secretary for the Panchayats, there is no director for the Panchayats. As a result, all the officials at all levels pay attention to the progress of the schemes and programmes not really for the progress of Panchayats. They find fault with the Panchayats if they are not carrying out their schemes and programmes. They do not have perspective to look at the Panchayats as institutions of governance. The officials look at the Panchayat with contempt and treat them as their rivals.

For the Panchayat activities, the Panchayat leaders do not get the needed support from the sectoral departments. Panchayats put forward certain demands based on the needs of the people but the officials do not care for these demands. The occasions, the officials in their own way select their pet projects. They give money only to a few Panchayats whose Presidents say "yes, sir!" to the officials. This kind of patronage has demoralized the other Panchayat Presidents. It is the experience of the leaders that the officials want only "yes" from the Panchayat leaders. They do not want leaders and they need only subordinates. At every level, officials feel that they are the superiors. This culture has to be changed. The women leaders are fighting against this culture. Yet, it is a painful struggle. Corrupt PRI leaders are perfectly having alliances with the corrupt officials and nobody bothers about it. Poor women leaders and *Dalit* leaders who are the victims of these procedures because they refuse to form alliances with the corrupt officials.

MLAs and MPs are having constituency development funds and they spend the funds without having any consultation with the Gram Panchayat leaders. People project their demands in the Gram Sabha and they are being consolidated by the Presidents and they are presented to the MLAs and MPs. But the MLAs and MPs allocate the money to some other works which are not the felt needs of the people. They are the priority work of the party men and the same party men get that benefits and not the villagers. When such a kind of privilege is given to MLAs and MPs what is wrong in demanding such funds to the Panchayat Presidents as the Panchayat Area Development Fund.

Every one knows that money is being wasted by the MPs and MLAs. It is a simple calculation, that an MP will get 10 crore rupees during the five year period. If he or she gets 10 per cent of the total amount from the contractors through them all activities are carried out by the MP and MLA, one can manage one crore rupee for the next election. Likewise, the one MLA can manage 50 lakh rupees. It is a known fact that MP LAD and MLA Constituency fund are meant for development but they are wasting peoples money. Even for small facilities, the Panchayats are starving for money but MLAs and MPs are spending their money on sand, brick, and mortar. It is sad to note that these MPs and MLAs are deciding the fate of the Panchayats.

MLAs and MPs are looking at Panchayat, as rivals bodies. A good Panchayat leader by his/her performance gets the whole-hearted support of the people and the local Panchayat leader becomes powerful. Some of the wise Panchayat leaders corner the MPs and MLAs with the support of the community. The elected women representatives adopted a strategy by which a resolution was passed in the Gram Sabha and by which for a specific work, they sought the funds from their MLA and MP. For the MPs and MLAs, there is no other option but to accept it as it is the decision of Gram Sabha. If the demands are not met, they cannot go to the village again for votes. A simple devise which made every one accountable and reasonable.

Whenever capacity-building training is devised only the elected local body leaders are targeted but officials from top to bottom and MLAs and MPs are left out conveniently. For a smooth functioning of the local bodies, cooperation of the officials and support of MLAs and MPs are essential. But these officials and leaders are not sensitive either in decentralized governance or in the crisis of social development. It is necessary to train the officials and MLAs and MPs. MPs and MLAs are having their own agenda of activities. But it is unfortunate that they are compete with the local body leaders in carrying out the activities. Proper training is needed for all not only for the Panchayat leaders. The political parties are also doing a lip-service to the Panchayats. They are doing a number of dharnas and struggles but they are not taking the devolution of powers to the local bodies it is a serious issue. Their stand on devolution has to be vindicated.

It is unequivocally stressed that the elected women representatives should have negotiating skills to negotiate with the officials and other representatives to get things done for the people. While analysing many of the successful cases in Panchayats by the women leaders' it is demonstrated clearly that wherever the elected women leaders display the negotiating skill, they have succeeded in their attempts. Yet, one more skill is needed for the elected women representatives i.e., crowd management. In the Indian context the crowd management is very essential as it is demonstrated that public have developed a strategy that for getting things done, they pull the crowd and by showing the crowd they get things done. In the Panchayats, managing Gram Sabha is a tough job for the elected women leaders. Whoever has got the art of managing the crowd has won and succeeded and others are drowned in it. Hence, Panchayat leaders needs such a kind of orientation. In the Panchayats along with the President, Vice-President's position should also be reserved for women. In most of the places, the Vice-Presidents (men) have tried their level best to sideline the women Panchayat Presidents with the help of the clerk and the Ward Members. Only strong women Presidents can withstand the pressure from the men Vice-Presidents. Especially, there in the case of the elected women representative is a *Dalit* women, and the Vice-President is a caste Hindu, the Panchayat administration is in the hands of the Vice-President. It is a struggle for the elected women representative to redeem the Panchayat from the clutches of the Vice-President.

There is yet another issue preventing the elected women representatives from occupying the position for which they were elected. Officials encourage the male members of the elected women representatives to attend the official meeting, and in carrying out the Panchayat activities, and claim the cheques. The elected women representatives are not oriented in corrupt practices of the administration and hence, they want to get things done only through the male members of their family and this practice has to be curbed. The concept of community well-being is not working in the minds of the people. It is always the individual benefits that works in the minds of the people. In this context, it is very difficult to take community-oriented decisions. In many Panchayats, the elected women representatives have taken tough decisions by earning the displeasure of many families and finally after seeing the implications of such decisions, people started supporting the Panchayat President. Till people see the outcome of such tough decisions, the Panchayat Presidents are put to a lot of troubles.

There is yet another issue which is significant in the process of decentralization of the powers it is micro-level planning. Micro-level planning is so important as it would alter the existing paradigm of development activities. The supply-driven activities can be changed into demand-driven activities only through planning at the micro-level. People will look at their lives, conditions and resources only through this process. Community will take the ownership of the development only through such a plan. But it is not happening in all the Panchayats. Without the people, official plan and implement the plan. In many Panchayats, headed by women already planned did planning successfully and now they are carrying out the activities. Even in implementing the plan, they have to struggle a lot. Wherever honest officials are in position, EWRs are getting the needed support to implement the plans. In other places, officials expect money.

The elected women representatives especially, from the *Dalit* community proposed substantial plans in their villages for development. They have been facing problems and this challenging position made the *Dalit* women think whether the needed ambience has been created for the *Dalit* women to contest in the elections. Many of them are losing their faith, as they are not able to function independently. The *Dalit* women leaders who are co-opted have no problem. But they do address the problems of the marginalized or the *Dalits*.

It is also observed that in their interaction with the existing corrupt system of administration, women are finding it very difficult to manage the Panchayats. There are several category of leaders among women. One group solid achievers. They have demonstrated their capability and by which they manage the Panchayat, people and the officials. They are forerunners. They are pathfinders. There is yet another group of leaders, struggling in the Panchayat with a little capacity and commitment to achieve. One would see a number of problems in their life. The third category always in the hands of the men folk. Both the Panchayat President and her the male members of her family jointly run the administration. The fourth category of elected women representatives have been asked to remain in the house and the entire Panchayat works are carried out by the male members of the family. The first two groups joined together to bring the other segments from the clutches of such men. They found it very difficult. That is why the elected women representatives demanded that the male members should not be encouraged to attend the official works and meetings. Women feel that they can contest only in the seats reserved for women. It is necessary to dispel this belief that women can contest in any one of the seats. Seats are limited only for men not for women. They could go beyond the 33.3 per cent of seats. For men it is only 67.7 per cent for women it is 100 per cent.

In a caste-ridden and patriarchical society, women on their own conduct transparent administration which in fact strengthened their leadership and they are strong in their dealings. They are the pioneers and pathfinders among the elected women representatives. Such women have been trained by a team of experts in Gandhigram Rural Institute and other training institutions. Yet the problems confronted by the elected women representatives are innumerable. How to overcome the obstacles and problems is a major question? In many of the consultative and training workshops, they were in search of an organizational mechanism by which EWRs will gain collective bargaining power to deal with the problems.

Working in Innovative Projects

It is interesting to note that many of the innovative concepts are being tested in the Panchayats where women are leaders. For instance, the concept of bio-village was effectively implemented in many Panchayats headed by women as women leaders have already demonstrated their potentials in making the village green, planting avenue trees, planting wood giving trees in the Panchayat lands, and planting fruit-bearing trees in poramboke lands. The vital policies and programmes of the State and Central Governments are being reviewed by the elected women representatives. Government of Tamil Nadu has issued a 15-point programme to make Tamil Nadu number one State in the country and this was reviewed and they made recommendations also. Mostly have the programme touched upon the social development issues and natural resource management issues. It was reviewed by the elected women representatives and they have suggested ways and means to improve and they have also pledged their support to this new programme.

There is yet another issue which is being discussed in many fora that is to have a separate allocation for women development. There should be a separate plan for women development. The women leaders have quoted the extensive practice of such plans in Kerala. Yet the State Government does not move forward to accept it. They are also pursuing this matter with a sense of hope. By following the foot prints of the women leaders, the *Dalit* leaders have also demanded the same for the *Dalits*. Thus women leaders are trendsetters. One can see the participation of the people in public activity in the Panchayats headed by women. They allow all individuals who want to speak and to express their views the leaders patiently listen to the people. A large number of SHG women are brought to Gram Sabha for discussion and deliberation. SHG members are taking keen interest in attending Gram Sabha meeting as they are allowed to speak freely whereas in other Panchayats they can not expect that much freedom as the Gram Sabha has been made leader-centric.

There is yet another interesting observation that many of the vital development issues which had not been discussed seriously in any of the public fora, are being forwarded to Gram Sabha by the Government for discussion. In reality, the women leaders who are already sensitized and trained on social development issues have taken up the lead and discuss with the people in the Gram Sabha meeting. In reality, progress is made in many villages on social development but in many Panchayats it does not take place as there is a lack of conscientisation process on the part of the leaders and the people. The budget and resource flow to Panchayat is still a myth to many. Internal resource mobilization is being done very actively as the Panchayat leaders are aware of the nuances of resource mobilization. But resource mobilization from the external sources also essential but they are not sure whether the Panchayats can mobilize such resources. No perspective budget analysis is being done. But the elected women Panchayat leaders are trying their level best to understand intricacies of the Panchayat finance. It is necessary that a budget analysis has to be done for the Panchayats and it is to be explained to the Panchayat Presidents.

It is the elected women representatives who have realised the potentials of the media steps to use the media to take and to project the issues which are being faced by them and the achievements made by them. A cursory analysis would reveal that a number of articles have been written on the achievements of women representatives. This media tie up has been created by the women representatives. It is noticed everywhere that in all the training programmes, the elected women representatives are serious and sincere in attending the capacity-building exercises. They used to complain that they are asked to refer to Government Orders and Notifications whenever they meet the officials. But the officials are not that much familiar will them. Thus the capacity-building exercise viewed seriously by the women leaders.

Formation of a Federation

The idea of forming a Federation emanated from a narration of a women Gram Panchayat Leader from Virudhunagar district. Initially both men and women joined together and formed a Federation. When they organised a meeting with the District Collector all were invited into the room of the Collector. All men leaders sat in the first three rows and the last row was given to the women leaders. There was a discussion between the leaders and the District Collector. But the whole discussion was between the men leaders and the District Collector. The women leaders raised their voice, but they were asked to be silent as discussion was in progress. Finally, the men leaders said that the discussion was over and all they were asked to move out. The women leaders asked them what happened to the demands given by them. The leaders said that their demands could be discussed outside the Collector's Chamber. When they came out from the room, the women leaders asked them about their demands. Men leaders said that the Collector would consider their demands in due course. On that day the women leaders felt that the women have to adopt a different strategy and hence, they formed a separate association. They got an exclusive audience with the Collector and sorted out their problems. When they narrated the experience, the idea to form a Federation emerged. Thus the Federation of elected women representatives (exclusively the Women Presidents of Gram Panchayats) was born in Tamil Nadu which was facilitated by the Gandhigram Rural Institute. Now one can see a number of Federations at different levels.

Gandhigram took the initiative to form this Federation as it organised a series of capacity-building exercises to train the Gram Panchayat Women Presidents with the active support of The Hunger Project. They were not only trained to manage the Panchayats and to administer development but also to provide leadership to the people. In our country in the sixty years of democratic governance, we have seen many rulers in the name of democracy but we could not see a leader to lead the society after Mahatma Gandhi. It was focused in all training programme, how to be with people as a leader to lead them not to rule them. To overcome this lacuna, it was decided to form an association of the EWRs. The EWR Federations periodically organise regional meetings and aggregate and consolidate the problems faced by the EWRs and conduct periodical interface with officials. Annually they conduct a Mela and in which major issues of the leaders are being highlighted for policy advocacy and they would meet higher officials, and the political party leaders. During the time of general election, they would review the election manifesto of the various political parties and check whether the issues of the local bodies and issues of women are included in the manifestos.

Over a period of six years, they have become visible and in fact they have become role model for others. By following this EWR Federation, Block Level Federation among the Block Panchayat leaders and District Level Federations among the District Panchayat leaders have been formed. Even among the Block level leaders, women leaders have formed their own Federation. SC and ST leaders have formed their own Federation. Among Gram Panchayat leaders, *Dalit* women leaders have formed their own Federation. They negotiate with the officials to settle their problems. Of all the Federations, Gram Panchayat women leaders Federation is strong and vibrant and vocal and it continues its activities. Various issues have been highlighted over a period of time. Eighty meetings had been organised in different places in Tamil Nadu and each time they focused on one or two major issues which are affecting them and the people especially women, children and *Dalits.*

The elected women representatives should strengthen their Federation at the district level. Its structure should be flexible. The Federation should have an office in every district. Once in two months the office bearers should meet and discuss their issues.

One major achievement is that the rotation of reservation has been made for each ten years which is now being quoted by many people. This is the only State, where reservation of seats for women had been made for every ten years. Yet another major break through is getting an exclusive Government Order for women to compel the Collector to convene a meeting of officials to redress the grievances of EWRs whenever they make such requests. By using this Government Order women leaders in seven districts forced the Collector to convene the meetings of the officials and got their grievances redressed. The Federation leaders also met the Prime Minister of India and handed over petitions to him and asked for direct financing of the local bodies from the Central Government.

The Federation office bearers of all the districts have met at Gandhigram and invited the Rural Development Director, Government of Tamil Nadu to participate in their meetings. From morning till evening, they raised a volley of questions to the officials and they were responded to by the Director of Rural Development.

Following the interface, they were discussing the future course of action of their Federation. Their discussion was centering around their future course of action in their Panchayats. Many of them were in power consecutively for two terms. Now they have decided to contest in the open constituency along with men. It is to be seen only during the election. They have further decided to stay in the public's arena in any of the positions in the local bodies whether it is in Gram Panchayats or in Block Panchayats. The acquired skills, capacity and capability could be effectively put to test by occupying any of the positions in the local bodies.

By creating a support structure on their own, the EWRs have highlighted the problems of the women leaders in the administration. The problems are multi-dimensional in nature and character. Further, by conducting a series of interfaces with the other State Panchayats and Panchayats within the State and with officials they have equipped themselves to tackle social developmental issues. The leaders have been conscientised on the issues of women and children. An army of elected women representatives has come to the public space and decided to stay on course. How to stay in public space is the question. Almost all have decided to stay in the public space in different forms. They have decided to contest in the general constituency. They can contest in different tiers either in Block Panchayat or District Panchayat. They informed that they would contest for ward membership of the Gram Panchayats. Being a Gram Sabha member, the experience gained by the Panchayat Presidents could be put to proper use. There are Panchayat leaders who stake claim for the MLA constituency. They are interested in seeking tickets to contest for the MLAs constituency. Even the Federation of elected women representatives could be strengthened by associating themselves with such activities.

Summing Up

The critical mass (33.3% of women elected representatives) have come to perform the critical functions (attacking the issues of hunger, poverty, gender and untouchability) despite facing a plethora of problems in the process of their governance and managing the institutions. They have their own record of achievements and stories of struggles. But they are determined to move further to occupy the public space. The journey has started and the support structure has been eroded to push forward in their onward march.

Their imprints in governance, management of the institutions, negotiating with different partners and stakeholders, attacking issues and managing the crowd are unique and different from that of men and other higher level institutions. Their expressions, perceptions, opinions and observations will provide an array of policy implications.

Way Forward

Capacity-building for elected women representatives has to be conducted within a month whenever they assume office. The training should be intensive and residential. It should not be conducted in the Block Development Offices. It should be given only in the training institutions. Training should be made mandatory and on any account the male members of their family should not be allowed to attend the training. In the training programme, Tamil Nadu Panchayati Raj Act 1994 updated version, Rules, Government Orders and Schemes of Rural Development details should be given to all the Panchayat leaders as a tool for Panchayat Management. The training package should include gender and social development components. Well-experienced Panchayat Presidents should be invited to be resource persons and share their experiences with the other participants. The same training should be given to the officials also. Periodical refresher course once in a year can be organised. Once in a month, the District Collector has to convene a meeting of the officials to redress the problems faced by the women leaders in administration of the Panchayats.

Male members of the elected women representatives families should not be allowed to occupy the chair and to participate in the official meetings. It has to be followed rigorously and religiously. They should not be permitted to sign any document on behalf of the elected women representatives. Periodically, interface has to be arranged for women leaders with the other Panchayats, preferably in other States. This opportunity has to be given a maximum number of people. Women Leaders' Federation is a registered one and hence, it has to be recognized by the Government. The support structures have to be created for women and *Dalit* leaders.

13

Integrated Analysis

Generally the elected women leaders more specifically, the Gram Panchayat Presidents wanted to go to offices at Block level and District level and for which they evolved a strategy of going together. Four or five women leaders used to form together and approached the officials for getting details regarding the schemes and programmes of the State and Central Governments. When they got success they wanted to make it as a forum for all kinds of activities. In many of the districts this was a practice wherefrom the concept of association picked up well. In Virudhunagar District, the women leaders with men leaders in the association and they experienced a discriminatory attitude of the men leaders and hence they formed a separate association for women. It appeared in the newspaper which motivated many women to come together.

For the first time in Tamil Nadu, an Association of Women Panchayat Leaders was formed at District level with the help of NGOs in Ramnad District. Then it was decided that they need a more powerful body to articulate their grievances. Women representatives have succeeded in building a visible and vocal organisation, a Federation of Women Panchayat Presidents through which policy makers in the State have begun paying attention. The role of the Rajiv Gandhi Chair for Panchayati Raj Studies has been that of a facilitator, providing support services as and when required. Rajiv Gandhi Chair for Panchayati Raj Studies is very clear that its interest and agenda should not be in the forefront of the Federation rather than it will follow the lead of the women leaders' Federation and offer such inputs as required by it. The first task undertaken by the Rajiv Gandhi Chair for Panchayati Raj Studies was to offer a series of capacity-building programmes for the leaders in social development then, the Rajiv Gandhi Chair for Panchayati Raj Studies received requests from the women that they need training programme exclusively for women. Even when they were interested in materials and processes they were unable to participate in the discussion freely because the centuries of inhibited behaviour of women in the presence of men who were not family members, in a public space did not allow them to make use of the opportunity to speak or fully engage with the issues in these workshops. Consequently, special training programmes for women were conducted. Series of training programmes were conducted and the women leaders who attended the training programme joined the Federation and got orientation separately for Federation activities and they become active member of the Federation. Thereafter, in August 2000, the Elected Women Representatives (EWRs) were invited to common a forum together with gender specialists feminists and activists to deliberate upon the transformation strategies that would be required to make them efficient and effective in their work. As a result of this meeting, the women decided that their local association of Women Panchayat Presidents needed to be federated so that they could have more cohesive presence as they tried to work for development and women issues.

The women leaders felt that remaining at Block and District levels would not provide them with sufficiently strong voice. They needed state-wide presence at the same time. There would be zonal units to address more local issues. The action framework was created. This involved many elements including capacity-building and conceintization on socio-economic issues, creation of models of micro levels and creation of movement-building at macro-level. For this reason, zonal meetings were conducted and women leaders from various zones met periodically. In the zonal meetings the gathered EWRs expressed their views, points regarding the problems and prospects of women in the administration of local bodies. At the end of the each zonal meeting the EWRs formed a zonal level association electing office bearers at the District level. There was also an awareness that the media should be sensitized to the challenges when women participate in local government and their cooperation was sought in highlighting issues, successes and challenges. EWRs also consciously developed strategies so that the number and nature of their interaction with the officialdom and State politicians could be improved for the better. When the team of EWRs met District

Collector of Virudhunagar District, the women were extremely vociferous in putting forward their demands and complaints, to the point where the Collector was almost annoyed but he was also intrigued and wondered what made this women different? They went to Bangalore to attend interface meeting at Institute of Social Sciences. In the mean time these women leaders attended several such meetings. It was the consequence of those meetings that was reflected in the transformation that so astonished the District Collector of Virudhunagar.

Rajiv Gandhi Chair for Panchayati Raj Studies recognized that there were several NGOs undertaking civil society initiatives and working to strengthen local governance. They thought an important strategic alliance would involve getting these NGOs on board. Consequently in October 2000, a meeting of NGOs working with these issues as well as women developmental issues was held. Enquiries were made about the organizations that would be willing to cooperate in this exercise of supporting the Federation of EWRs. Several NGOs agreed to be regional and nodal agencies providing resources and support. The media coverage, press release and so on associated with these meetings drew the attention of both State level and local officials further strengthening the stance of EWRs. Media attention to the EWRs for the past two years has brought the Central Minister for Rural Development, Government of India to their meeting on 20th February 2002. The Federation leaders expressed the problems that they were facing in the local bodies and requested him to intervene and help them discharge their roles and responsibilities. State level officials also participated and responded to the queries of EWRs.

On 5th August 2001, the EWRs conducted the First Annual Meet. Leaders drawn from all over the State attended the meeting. Women activists were invited to participate. They decided to highlight the problems faced by EWRs and bring them to the knowledge of the policy-makers. Further, they decided to share their experience in Panchayat administration with media for which Rajiv Gandhi Chair for Panchayati Raj Studies would take initiative. They further decided to share their successes along with their struggles. They organized the Second Annual Meet in Gandhigram on 3rd May 2002. In the second annual meeting they discussed Chief Minister's 15 point programme and made known to the Government that all the 15 point programme activities come under the purview of Panchayats. They also discussed the strategies to be followed to strengthen the Federation. They decided to form an advisory council which would include retired I.A.S. officials, academics and representatives of the media. Since the participants discussed the issues broadly, in the second annual meet, they decided to have another meeting on 9th May 2002 to make an in-depth analysis of the issues. Selected EWRs from all the districts met and analysed the problems and prepared a charter of demand to be presented to the Government.

Another important strategy that Rajiv Gandhi Chair for Panchayati Raj Studies employed was that providing EWRs in the Federation with exposure visits to Gram Panchayats in which women were playing an active transformatory role. When Rajiv Gandhi Chair for Panchayati Raj Studies shared with women leaders the good work done by women leaders in Kerala, they put forward their demand that they would actually like to see their work. Consequently, Rajiv Gandhi Chair for Panchayati Raj Studies arranged federated women leaders in teams to visit Gram Panchayats in Kerala, particularly, in Eerattupatta. The Kerala interface motivated the women leaders to work on social development issues. They decided that by carrying out activities in Tamil Nadu Panchayat should draw the attention of the entire country.

Federation leaders organized several meetings in several places. They met political party leaders and officials for presenting their charter of demand. At the end of the two years they took stock of their achievements. During the meeting with the Minister of Rural Development, Government of India, the women complained that the funds that were meant to go to Panchayats had not been released. The Director in-charge of the Department of Rural Development was present at the meeting and was called to explain. Immediately the funds were released. Again the women complained that while officials were more than enthusiastic to carry out various inspections they were less enthusiastic when they are asked to cooperate with EWRs in their developmental works.

They used to meet the press persons periodically and express their opinions on vital issues which are affecting the people especially, women and *Dalits.* Rajiv Gandhi Chair for Panchayati Raj Studies documented the problems faced by the Panchayat leaders in general and women and *Dalits* in particular. They used this document for policy advocacy. It was very difficult for EWRs to get information regarding Government orders, rules and regulations and schemes. But now they are available from Rajiv Gandhi Chair for Panchayati Raj Studies and so they regard Rajiv Gandhi Chair for Panchayati Raj Studies as a resource centre. Contacting the Minister, higher officials, MLAs and MPs is no more a problem for them. EWRs who are in this federating arrangements are highly sensitized on the issues of social development and more specifically on the issues of women and children. By following this Federation, many Federations have been formed in Tamil Nadu such as District Panchayat Presidents Association, Block Panchayat Presidents Association, Block Panchayat Women Presidents Association, Block Panchayat SC and ST Women Presidents Association and *Dalit* Presidents Association.

Though Tamil Nadu has a District Panchayat Presidents Association, a Block Panchayat Association and a Gram Panchayat Association only the Federation of Women Panchayat Leaders Association is visible and sharply reacting on many of the vital issues. Even though EWRs have a charter of demands they are more keen on getting reservation of seats for women for ten years, retrieving common property resources from encroachment and ensuring the entitlements of the poor through Public Distribution System. Active leaders in the Federation are very much sensitized on the social developmental issues after visiting the Kerala Panchayats. During the first period, the women leaders were harping on transfer of power, finance and functionaries. Now they speak about issues and problems. They have gained voice and bargaining power. One major achievement they have made through their work is getting the reservation of seats for women in local bodies extended for one more term. It is unique in the whole of the country. Another important milestone in their achievement is that the Federation had made the State Government with drop the cheap liquor. Whenever it was objects. They pleaded with the Government that in every month higher level officials at the District level should convene the meeting of the EWRs and solve their problems. The Director, Rural Development, Government of Tamil Nadu, issued an order immediately to District Collectors to convene such meetings and solve the problem of EWRs. Because of the repeated pleas and activities, the Federation of EWRs association is visible to the policy-makers and 33.3 percent of seats have been reserved for women in the cooperative societies. Likewise, an order has been issued that in all statutory committees one-third reservation should be provided for women. Some of the Women Panchayat leaders were in deep trouble. It was only the Federation which saved them. Menaka, President of Urapakkam was murdered in the Panchayat office due to her stern action against encroachments. No FIR was filed till the Federation leaders went to the Panchayat office. It was only because of the Federation that the culprits were booked. Another interesting noteworthy feature is that more number of office bearers in the Federation are now from *Dalit* community and Federation has focused its attention on *Dalit* issues.

> The Chief Minister of Tamil Nadu Selvi. J. Jayalalitha was out of power, and representatives of the Federation of EWRs had met her. The media picked up the story and presented it as support extended to her by Women Panchayat Presidents. During the meeting the women had asked Selvi. J. Jayalalitha whether she could extend the reservation of seats for women for two terms. She had promised to look into the matter if she came to power. The media attention as well as the perception of the support were not also unwelcome at a time when she was a political outcast at a point of time. When she came to power she remembered women leaders' demand and asked her legal cell to look into the matter and determine whether there was any constitutional objection to such a change in policy. Consequently, the legal cell made a liberal interpretation of the constitutional guidelines and decision to go in for a rotation only after two terms was taken.

This 10-year rotation gives women leaders the flexibility to see many of their development projects through the completion instead of having them to leave half done when the seats are rotated at the end of one term. It also gives EWRs the opportunity to build a greater support base among the people. In the long run, this will be an important factor in enabling women to compete in the general category in local politics and not merely in the reserved category.

There are many shortcomings at the end of the two years in the functioning of EWR Federation. The facilitating agencies' prime objective is to muster a movement for Panchayati Raj throughout the State of Tamil Nadu. The region was so vast that the coverage becomes difficult. The leaders' demand meeting in each and every district and majority of them ask for interface programmes. One layer of EWRs is oriented and conscientized and they have taken up social development issues but many EWRs are not well oriented. This calls for more partners in different regions. The leaders have discussed a proposal for registering the Federation. During the discussion they expressed their desire that the association should be operated from Gandhigram. To rectify the shortcomings Rajiv Gandhi Chair for Panchayati Raj Studies proposed a plan of action.

Critical Issues to be taken up by the Federation

> The President of Pillali Village Panchayat was always opposed by the traditional leaders, ex-President and defeated candidate in every one of the Panchayat activities. Under the Food for Work Scheme the rice bags were stocked in a store room. But the group that opposed her filed a case against the President that she has smuggled entire food supply. They lodged a complaint and later her family members were assaulted. The President gained strong support from the district administration and people. But the Federation support is needed in this critical situation. The Federation reserved the President from the clutches of the evil-doers.

In the coming years the Federation went for a greater consolidation of power as such more and more leaders need to be identified who are articulate able to mobilize people and who are influential among the SHGs. There was a greater drive to form more local associations and also the registration of local associations was also undertaken. To prevent the dilutions of the strength of the Federation due to the differences arising out of party ideology, women leaders should have commitment that their work in the Federation will be based on non-partisan. The space occupied by the Federation can be further widened by opening up membership to women leaders from the Block Panchayats and District Panchayats as well as SHGs and not just incorporating Gram Panchayat Presidents as is the case now. Strengthening the institutional structure of the Federation by creating a permanent secretariat will also be an important step in consolidating the support base that will result in the integration or partnership atleast with the Federation from other States. In addition to this, the current capacity-building exercise should have more inputs for the office bearers of the organization.

In Usilampatti Block of Madurai District there was an illiterate *Dalit* women President and a male Caste Hindu Vice-President who happened to be a lawyer. Whenever developmental works were undertaken, the Vice-President wanted a share. The honest women President refused and was harassed. She took up the issue to the village elders who passed a resolution throwing out the Vice-President. He challenged the decision at the Collectorate terming it illegal. However, the Federation contacted the media and the Collector had no choice but to uphold the decision of the village to keep the corrupt Vice-President out of office.

After the consolidation of the network in the first two years EWRs in the association contacted the Rajiv Gandhi Chair for Panchayati Raj Studies by phone or letters whenever they have any information or assistance requirements. Rajiv Gandhi Chair for Panchayati Raj Studies has been responding to them promptly. Rajiv Gandhi Chair for Panchayati Raj Studies provides this service routinely through formal and informal methods.

A women Panchayat President from Pudukkottai District sat on the Pillion of a bike driven by a man who belonged to her Panchayat. After seeing. this some miscreants printed posters about this incident and pasted them throughout the Panchayat. The posters indulged in character assassination. She informed immediately the police but the police tried to arrest her instead of the miscreants. She immediately contacted the Rajiv Gandhi Chair for Panchayati Raj Studies to take steps save her. Rajiv Gandhi Chair for Panchayati Raj Studies directed her to meet the District Collector. In the mean time Rajiv Gandhi Chair for Panchayati Raj Studies explained the situation to the District Collector and with the help of District Collector and Superintendent of Police she handled the situation.

In addition, consultation meetings were held in which the Federation members brought up issues that concerned them and the Rajiv Gandhi Chair for Panchayati Raj Studies offered technical advice. For instance, the Rajiv Gandhi Chair for Panchayati Raj Studies organized consultation meeting in the Federation, to discuss the problems involved in strengthening the Federation for empowering the women to take up issues of social development and gender; to suggest strategies for strengthening the Federation with the involvement of feminist, gender specialist and academics. At the same time, regional workshops of EWRs were organized at Gandhigram,

Thiruvarur, Tanjore, Salem, Tirunelveli, Thoothukudi, Virudhunagar, Rmanad, Sivagangai, Madurai, Dindigul, Theni, Namakkal, Salem, Trichy, Pudukkottai, Karur, Thiruvarur and Tanjore. The objective of this meeting was to strengthen the Federation at Union and District level; to expand the activities of the association; to bring all the issues of the women leaders to the media for wide publicity.

Several interface meetings were held between the members of the Federation and the Director Rural Development, ADRD, District Collector, Project Officers of the DRDA and Secretary of the Rural Development of Tamil Nadu. These meetings have helped EWRs to obtain quick solutions to the problems faced by their communities. Apart from that they discussed the steps to be taken by the State Government for releasing SFC grant, house tax matching grant, roles and responsibilities to be delegated the Panchayats like issuing birth and death records, issuing no due certificate for obtaining household electricity connection etc.

The Rajiv Gandhi Chair for Panchayati Raj Studies also provided EWRs in the Federation with the exposure visit to Gram Panchayats when the Panchayat leaders play a transformatory role in Tamil Nadu. EWRs of Federation members were taken Oddanthurai and Semmipalayam of Coimbatore District, Michealpattinam, Devipattinam, Thamaraikulam and Sakkarakottai of Ramnad District. They were also taken to West Bengal and Bangalore.

EWRs from 14 southern districts attended five-day residential training programme in Rajiv Gandhi Chair for Panchayati Raj Studies to develop leadership skills in Federation members. The outcome has been good. The Rajiv Gandhi Chair for Panchayati Raj Studies has also regularly documented not only the problems but also the strategies and success stories related to the issues regarding empowering the Federation members for effective local governance. The Federation has been registered now as the Tamil Nadu Association of Women Presidents of Panchayat Government, Registration No.9/2002-2003. In Tamil Nadu, only EWRs at the Village Panchayat level currently about 800 EWRs have been federated within this group. An association of *Dalit* Women Panchayat Presidents has also been consultated.

The elected women representatives consider the space which they occupy as a space for development. However, illiterate they are, however backward they are, they want to achieve something in life when an opportunity is given. They tend to seek a support base for their activities, especially for increasing their efficiency and capability. They improve their skills constantly and their skill is used for managing the Panchayats. Issues of women and development are brought to the public for debate. They are open to learning and patient to listen. They convert challenges into opportunities. They assume responsibilities and attempt innovations. By their actions, they create new contours of decentralization of powers. They build alliances to get support for their activities and to spread their innovations and achievements. They run the administration transparently and reduce corruption. They develop alternative governance to achieve development with the participation of the people. A new culture is being evolved and a new value profile is being evolved at the grassroots by the women leaders through their activities. They are emerging models to be emulated. They have registered a striking difference in governing the grassroots institutions. Now, the women Federation leaders are voicing a demand that all Gram Panchayats should be reserved for women since, in Tamil Nadu, the Gram Panchayat is free from political contest. All these observations are based on the study conducted in the fifty two Gram Panchayats headed by women in Tamil Nadu spread over 28 districts.

14

Conclusion

The EWRs have come to the grassroots institutions with varying socio-economic backgrounds. Their educational background varies to neo-literate to retired college teachers. There are leaders drawn from SHGs and various political parties. Leaders who are drawn from SHGs and political groups are oriented in social development and politics respectively. These women leaders enter the power structures with all drawbacks and barriers due to existing socio-economic structure in the society. How they perform their roles and responsibilities, how they conscientize on the basic issues of women, what are all the problems they face while performing their duties and responsibilities and the role of institutional intervention to enable women leaders to discharge their functions are discussed in this book. The EWRs who have occupied positions in Panchayati Raj System perceive that the Panchayati Raj Institutions are to provide services to the people to the level of the satisfaction of the communities. Their entry into the political domain was sudden and their activities were drawn by many in the background as they could not do any thing on their own. They never dreamt of such positions in their whole life. The EWRs were controlled by the male family members when discharging their duties and responsibilities. But there is a small segment of EWRs who have come from SHGs and political parties as barded candidates who have taken up the responsibilities on their own. There is an yet another section gaining the spirit to act independently after participating in the training and orientation programmes by enhancing their skills and capabilities. Hence, the EWRs have a perception that the Panchayat Institutions have to attend to the needs of the people. A small section of the EWRs have focused their attention on development more particularly on social development. Because of their regular meetings among themselves they are able to comprehend the nuances of the governance.

To retrieve the common properties of the encroachment from mafia, Menaka, a women representative has sacrificed her life. To stop the illegal brewing and sale of liquor a women representative with her family (Ponni Kailasam) had to spend several sleepless nights in the same village and faced all kinds of adversities. Despite opposition, they did all these activities simply because of their vision, social commitments and the fire in them for the cause of the people. These women got strength and power to act upon the issues because of their association. As a single candle can lit the light of others, these women have advanced the thinking of other women and made them act on all issues affecting the community as a whole and on the issues of development.

The EWRs have joined together to promote the best practices developed by them in governance and development activities and to make them successful. A variety of support structures have been created in different domains to extend support to the EWRs. They will continue their struggle, to achieve efficiency in performing their duties and responsibilities. Even though EWRs face several inherent barriers in the context of market-driven economy and right-based development, they assume several social responsibilities effectively and perform their duties/responsibilities very effectively to the satisfaction of the communities. They are always open to the learning. When the needed support structure is provided. They perform their duties and their concentration is on social development issues. To project the issues of women they have forged alliances with the SHGs and the media.

As a result of the consolidation of power of the women leaders that has taken place through their association, they are now being wooed by political parties and NGOs. As the Federation has grown sufficiently strong to tell these entities that they cannot dictate terms. In future, the Federation is going for a greater consolidation of power as such more and more leaders need to be identified who are articulate, able to mobilize people and who are influential among the SHGs. The registration of local level of associations of women leaders had largely been demand driven. But, there will and should be a greater drive to register more local associations. To prevent the dissipation of the strength of the power of the Federation because of differences arising out of the party ideology, the Federation members should be committed that their work in the Federation will be done on a non-party basis. The space occupied by the Federation can be further widened by opening up membership to women leaders from Block Panchayat and District Panchayat as well as SHGs and not just incorporating Gram Panchayat Presidents as is the case now. Strengthening the institutional structures of the Federation by creating a permanent secretariat will also be an important step in consolidating the support base as will be integration and partnership atleast with Federation from other States.

Women have started realizing the potentials of association and Federation. Political parties have started identifying the potential leaders from Gram Panchayat and are enlisting them as their party members and proclaiming their achievements as the achievements of the party. The media has been sensitized on the women issues and as a result the media has given wide coverage to the activities of the women's Federation. EWRs have learnt the art of negotiating with the bureaucracy. They have picked up communication skill, developed bargaining powers are moving with higher officials. These have become routine affairs and the fear to meet the District Collector and other higher officials has gone. A large number of new leaders have emerged from SHGs for the Panchayats. The fear syndrome and the dependency syndrome have gone. The group activities have developed a positive attitude among the women leaders to strive for positive achievements.

APPENDIX

Photo Gallery

Leadership Training for Elected Women Panchayat Presidents

Leadership Training for Elected Women Panchayat Presidents

Regional and State Level Meet

Regional and State Level Meet

Regional and State Level Meet

Regional and State Level Meet

Interface with Officials

Interface with Officials

Interface with Media

Annual Mela

TAMIL NADU COUNCIL FOR SUSTAINABLE LIVELIHOODS
THE HUNGER PROJECT
RAJIV GANDHI CHAIR FOR PANCHAYATI RAJ STUDIES

MEDIA WORKSHOP ON PANCHAYATI RAJ
RAJIV GANDHI CHAIR FOR PANCHAYATI RAJ STUDIES
Department of Political Science and Development Administration
Gandhigram Rural Institute - Deemed University, Gandhigram

Annual Mela

Annual Mela

Association Members Meeting with the Hon'ble Prime Minister

Association Members Meeting with the Hon'ble Chief Minister

Association Members Meeting with the Hon'ble Minister of Panchayati Raj

Association Members Meeting with the Hon'ble Local Body Minister

Association Members Meeting with the Party Leaders

Bibliography

Alatas, Vivi, Lant Pritchett, Anna Wetterberg, *Local Government Organisations and the Quality of Local Governance*, Washington DC: The World Bank, Environment and Social Development Sector Unit, 2003.

Antrobus, Peggy, *Global Women's Movement Origin, Issues and Strategies*, Bangalore: Books for Change, 2004.

Asian Development Bank, *Gender and Governance issues in Local Government, Regional Report of Technical Assistance in Bangladesh, Nepal, and Pakistan*, Manila: Asian Development Bank, 2004.

Athreya, V.B., K.S. Rajeswari, *Women's Participation in Panchayati Raj : A Case Study from Tamil Nadu*, Chennai: M.S. Swaminathan Research Foundation, 1998.

Bandyopadhyay, Kanti, Kanstuv, Malini Nambiar, "Promoting Grassroots Network: A Means of Reforming Governance", *Innovations in Civil Society*, Vol. 4, No. 1, July, 2004.

Batliwala, Srilatha, et al., *Status of Rural Women in Karnataka*, Bangalore: National Institute of Advanced Studies, 1998.

Behar, Amitabh, Yamini Aiyar, "Networks of Panchayat Women Civil Society Space for Political Action", *Economic and Political Weekly*, November 22, 2003.

Buch, Nirmala, "The 73rd Amendment and the Experience of Women in the New Panchayati Raj Institutions: A Critical Evaluation", in Ambrose Printo and Helmut Reifield, (eds.), *Women in Panchayati Raj*, New Delhi: Indian Social Institute, 2001.

Bysteydzienski, Jill M. (eds.), *Women Transforming Politics: Worldwide Strategies for Empowerment*, Bloomington: Indiana University Press, 1992.

Bysteydzienski, Jill M., Joti Sikhon (eds.), *Democratization and Women's Grassroots Movements*, New Delhi: Kali for Women, 2002.

Gopalan, Prema, *Developing Grassroots Women's Leadership in Governance*, Mumbai: Swayaja Shiskshan Prayog, 2000.

Kaushik, Susheela (ed.), *Women's Participation in Politics*, New Delhi: Har Anand Publishers, 1993.

Kaushik, Susheela, *Voices of Women in Panchayati Raj*, New Delhi: Friedrick-Elbertstif tung, 2004.

Krishna, Anirudh, *Partnership between Elected Local Governments and Community-Based Organisations: Exploring Scope for Synergy*, Washington DC, The World Bank, 20004.

Leijennar, Monique, *Political Participation of Women and Good Governance in Developing Countries*, The Hague: Women and Development Division of the Netherlands, Ministry of Foreign Affairs, 1999.

Mohanty, Bidyut, Shashi Narayana (eds.), *Women and Political Empowerment 2001*, New Delhi: Institute of Social Sciences, 2003.

Murthy, Ranjani K. (ed.), *Building Women's Capabilities*, New Delhi: Sage Publications, 2001.

Murthy, Ranjani K., *Gender and Development in India*, Chennai: Initiatives Women in Development, 1994.

Nandal, Santhosh, "Reflections on New Partnerships Between Women and Local Self Government in India: A Rural Revolution?", *Journal of International Women's Studies*, Vol. 5 No. 1, November, 2003.

Narasimhan, Sakuntala, *Empowering Women an Alternative Strategy from Rural India*, New Delhi: Sage Publications, 1999.

Narayana, D., "Local Governance without Capacity-Building Ten Years of Panchayati Raj", *Economic and Political Weekly*, June 25, 2005.

Narayanan, Yamini, *Women Aiding Sustainability in Local Self Governance in India*, Murdoch: Institute of Sustainability and Technology, 2000.

Omvedt, Gail, "Women in Governance in South Asia", *Economic and Political Weekly*, October 29, 2005.

Pal, Mahi, "Panchayati Raj and Rural Governance", *Economic and Political Weekly*, Vol. XXXIX, 2004.

Palanithurai, G. (ed.), *Are they Withdrawing from Public Space*, Gandhigram: Rajiv Gandhi Chair for Panchayati Raj Studies, 2005.

Palanithurai, G., "Building Alliances and Capabilities among the Elected Women Representatives of Grassroots Institutions", *Women's Link*, Vol.10, No.1, Jan-March, 2004.

Palanithurai, G., *Elected Representatives and Emerging Alternative Governance*, Gandhigram: Rajiv Gandhi Chair for Panchayati Raj Studies, 2001.

Palanithurai, G., *Empowerment of Women: Experience of the Elected Women Representatives in Grassroots Institutions*, Gandhigram: Rajiv Gandhi Chair for Panchayati Raj Studies, 2004.

Palanithurai, G., *Empowerment of Women: Problems Faced by the Elected Women Representatives in Tamil Nadu*, Gandhigram: Rajiv Gandhi Chair for Panchayati Raj Studies, 2001.

Palanithurai, G., J. Vanishree, *Governance from the Perspective of Elected Women Representatives (EWRs)*, Gandhigram: Rajiv Gandhi Chair for Panchayati Raj Studies, 2004.

Palanithurai, G., *New Panchayati Raj System as Prosperity Movement*, New Delhi: Kanishka Publishers and Distributors, 2001.

Palanithurai, G., V. Ragupathy, *Building Alliances and Capabilities among the Elected Women Representatives of Grassroots Institutions*, Gandhigram: Rajiv Gandhi Chair for Panchayati Raj Studies, 2003.

Purushothaman, Sangeetha, *The Empowerment of Women in India Grassroots Women's Networks and the State*, New Delhi: Sage Publications India Pvt. Ltd, 1998.

Rai, M. Shirin, "Political Representation, Democratic Institutions and Women's Empowerment: The Quota Debate in India", *Democratization*, Vol. 6, No. 3, Automa, 1999.

Ramesh, Asha, Bharti Ali, *33.3 per cent Reservation Towards Political Empowerment,* Bangalore: Books for Change, 2001.

Rani, A. Celine, *Emerging Pattern of Rural Women Leadership in India,* New Delhi: Kalpaz Publications, 2002.

Roy, Anupama, "Community Women Citizens and a Women's Politics", *Economic and Political Weekly*, April 28, 2001.

Sridharan, Damayanthy, Vesna Rodic (eds.), *Breaking the Political Glass Ceiling Women and Local Governance in South Asia*, New Delhi: Friedrich Ebert-Stiftung, 2004.

Stephen, F., N. Rajasekaran, *Sheep and Lambs An Empirical Study of Women in Local Self Governance in Karnataka* Bangalore: Search, 2001.

Tambiah, Yasmin (ed.), *Women and Governance in South Asia: Re-imaging the State* Colombo: International Centre for Ethnic Studies, 2002.

UNDP, *Essays on Gender and Governance*, New Delhi: Human Development Resource Centre, UNDP, 2003.

UNDP, *Women's Political Participation 21st Century Challenges*, New Delhi: UNDP, 2000.

Reports

Institute of Social Science, *A Decade of Women's Empowerment through Local Government in India Workshop Report October 20-21, 2003,* New Delhi: Institute of Social Sciences, 2003.

Karnataka Women's Information and Resource Centre, *Associating Elected Women Representatives in Local Self Governance Interim Report*, Bangalore: Karnataka Women's Information and Resource Centre, 2004.

Palanithurai, G., *Report on Annual Mela of Elected Women Representatives of Local Bodies in Tamil Nadu*, Gandhigram: Rajiv Gandhi Chair for Panchayati Raj Studies, 2005.

Palanithurai, G., *Report on Associating Elected Women Representatives in Local Self Governance*, Gandhigram: Rajiv Gandhi Chair for Panchayati Raj Studies, 2006.

Palanithurai, G., *Report on Elected Women Representatives Interface with Director of Rural Development*, Gandhigram: Rajiv Gandhi Chair for Panchayati Raj Studies, 2004.

Palanithurai, G., *Report on Elected Women Representatives Network Meeting*, Gandhigram: Rajiv Gandhi Chair for Panchayati Raj Studies, 2002.

Palanithurai, G., *Report on Formation of Women Panchayat President Association in Cuddalore District*, Gandhigram: Rajiv Gandhi Chair for Panchayati Raj Studies, 2004.

Palanithurai, G., *Report on Formation of Women Panchayat President Association in Tirunelveli District*, Gandhigram: Rajiv Gandhi Chair for Panchayati Raj Studies, 2004.

Palanithurai, G., *Report on Formation of Women Panchayat Presidents in Thiruvarur District*, Gandhigram: Rajiv Gandhi Chair for Panchayati Raj Studies, 2004.

Palanithurai, G., *Report on Formation of Women Panchayat President Association in Erode District*, Gandhigram: Rajiv Gandhi Chair for Panchayati Raj Studies, 2001.

Palanithurai, G., *Report on Inter Agency Meeting of the Partners Working on the Project Associating Women Representatives in Local Bodies*, Gandhigram: Rajiv Gandhi Chair for Panchayati Raj Studies, 2001.

Palanithurai, G., *Report on Interface between the State Level Officials and the Elected Women Representatives*, Gandhigram: Rajiv Gandhi Chair for Panchayati Raj Studies, 2003.

Palanithurai, G., *Report on Leadership Training for Panchayat Women Presidents*, Gandhigram: Rajiv Gandhi Chair for Panchayati Raj Studies, 2002.

Palanithurai, G., *Report on Networking Elected Women Representatives at the Grassroots—First Phase Annual Report*, Gandhigram: Rajiv Gandhi Chair for Panchayati Raj Studies, 2002.

Palanithurai, G., *Report on Networking Elected Women Representatives of Local Self Governance*, Gandhigram: Rajiv Gandhi Chair for Panchayati Raj Studies, 2004.

Palanithurai, G., *Report on Networking of Elected Women Representatives on Gender and Social Development Issues*, Gandhigram: Rajiv Gandhi Chair for Panchayati Raj Studies, 2003.

Palanithurai, G., *Report on Regional Level Meet on Associating Women Representatives in Local Bodies*, Gandhigram: Rajiv Gandhi Chair for Panchayati Raj Studies, 2000.

Palanithurai, G., *Report on Regional Level Meet on Associating Women Representatives in Local Bodies (North Zone)*, Gandhigram: Rajiv Gandhi Chair for Panchayati Raj Studies, 2001.

Palanithurai, G., *Report on Regional Level Meet on Associating Women Representatives in Local Bodies (Central Zone)*, Gandhigram: Rajiv Gandhi Chair for Panchayati Raj Studies, 2001.

Palanithurai, G., *Report on Regional Level NGOs Network Meet on Associating Women Representatives in Local Bodies*, Gandhigram: Rajiv Gandhi Chair for Panchayati Raj Studies, 2001.

Palanithurai, G., *Report on Second Annual Meet of Elected Women Representatives*, Gandhigram: Rajiv Gandhi Chair for Panchayati Raj Studies, 2002.

Palanithurai, G., *Report on Second Networking and Interface Programme*, Gandhigram: Rajiv Gandhi Chair for Panchayati Raj Studies, 2001.

Palanithurai, G., *Report on State Level Consultation on Feminist Perspectives in Associating Women Representatives in Local Bodies,* Gandhigram: Rajiv Gandhi Chair for Panchayati Raj Studies, 2000.

Palanithurai, G., *Report on State Level NGOs Network Meet on Associating Women Representatives in Local Bodies*, Gandhigram: Rajiv Gandhi Chair for Panchayati Raj Studies, 2000.

Palanithurai, G., *Report on State Level Workshop on Networking Elected Women Representatives*, Gandhigram: Rajiv Gandhi Chair for Panchayati Raj Studies, 2004.

Palanithurai, G., *Report on The Annual Convention of the Elected Women Representatives on Rural Local Bodies in Tamil Nadu*, Gandhigram: Rajiv Gandhi Chair for Panchayati Raj Studies, 2001.

Palanithurai, G., *Report on the Executive Committee Meeting of the Federation*, Gandhigram: Rajiv Gandhi Chair for Panchayati Raj Studies, 2002.

Ragupathy, V., *Report on Formation of SC/ST Women Block Panchayat Chairpersons Association*, Gandhigram: Rajiv Gandhi Chair for Panchayati Raj Studies, 2003.

Rajiv Gandhi Chair for Panchayati Raj Studies, *A Report of the Special Meet of the Elected Women Representatives of Local Bodies*, Gandhigram: Rajiv Gandhi Chair for Panchayati Raj Studies, 2002.

Rajiv Gandhi Chair for Panchayati Raj Studies, *Report of the Training Programme Conducted for Women Presidents of Gram Panchayats in Five Districts of Tamil Nadu*, Gandhigram: Rajiv Gandhi Chair for Panchayati Raj Studies, 1998.

Shamin, Ishrat, Ranhana Kumari, *Gender and Local Governance: A New Discourse in Development*, Report submitted to South Asia Network of Economic Research Institutes, submitted by Centre for Women and Children Studies, Dhaka Bangladesh and Centre for Social Research, New Delhi, India, Nov., 2002.

Index